Scott Bash

Microsoft Word

Also covers Word in Microsoft 365 suite

In easy steps is an imprint of In Easy Steps Limited
16 Hamilton Terrace · Holly Walk · Leamington Spa
Warwickshire · United Kingdom · CV32 4LY

www.ineasysteps.com

In Easy Steps Limited supports The Forest Stewardship Council (FSC), the leading international forest certification organization. All our titles that are printed on Greenpeace approved FSC certified paper carry the FSC logo.

Printed and bound in the United Kingdom

ISBN 978-1-84078-934-8

Contents

1 Finding your way around

This chapter quickly gets you started with Word. It shows you how to launch Word and explains all the main areas in its screen layout. You'll try some basic text editing as well as looking at the main controls and how they are organized and accessed.

Introduction

It's very important to experiment using your own examples – trying techniques a few times on test documents will give you the confidence you'll need when working for real.

Word processing was one of the first popular applications for the modern personal computer. In the early days it provided little more than the ability to enter and change text on the screen. Today, many more people have computers and tablets at home and in the office, and virtually all use a word processor regularly. As the years have passed, the capabilities of the computer and its software have dramatically increased, far beyond the expectations of the early generations of users back in the 1970s and 1980s.

Almost since the beginning, Microsoft Word has been acknowledged as a leader in its field. It is one of the best-selling software applications in any category. It grew in complexity from a program with a handful of menu commands to one with an astonishing array of features.

In updating Word, Microsoft has built logically on the foundation of the previous versions. Rather than relying on complex menus, Word works with tabbed visual controls that reconfigure themselves to suit what you're currently doing. Accordingly, this book works as a graphical teaching guide – wherever possible, pictures and illustrated examples are used to demonstrate concepts. It's not intended to replace Microsoft's documentation; instead you should view it as a way of getting up to speed quickly in a wide range of useful techniques.

If you need guidance on using the Windows operating environment, check out our Windows 10 titles: **Windows 10 in easy steps** and **Windows 10 for Seniors in easy steps**.

The full range of Word's features is covered in this and the following chapters – from creating and editing simple text-based documents to tables, graphics and research tools, as well as more advanced techniques such as viewing and editing documents on the web.

How to use this book

To gain maximum benefit from this book, make sure you're first familiar with the Windows operating environment (using the mouse, icons, menus, dialog boxes and so on). There are a number of books in the **In Easy Steps** range that can help you here.

It's a good idea to start off by going through Chapters 1 and 2 fairly thoroughly, since these introduce basic concepts that are added to later on. Once you've done this, feel free to dip into the other chapters as you like.

Starting Word

The way in which you start Word depends on whether you're using a desktop PC or a tablet, and the operating system version.

From Windows 10

1. Click the Windows **Start** button and look through the list

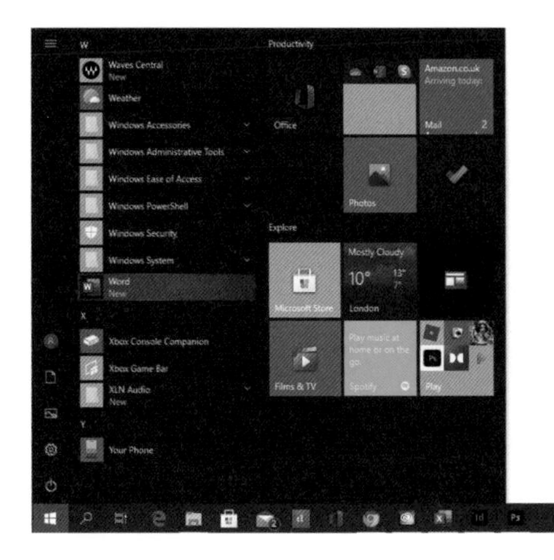

2. If Word isn't in the **Recently added** or **Most used** sections, scroll through the alphabetical list and choose Word

3. Alternatively, click on the **Office** icon in the Taskbar

4. A window opens with installed Office applications listed on the left. Click on the **Word** icon and choose **New blank document** or select a file

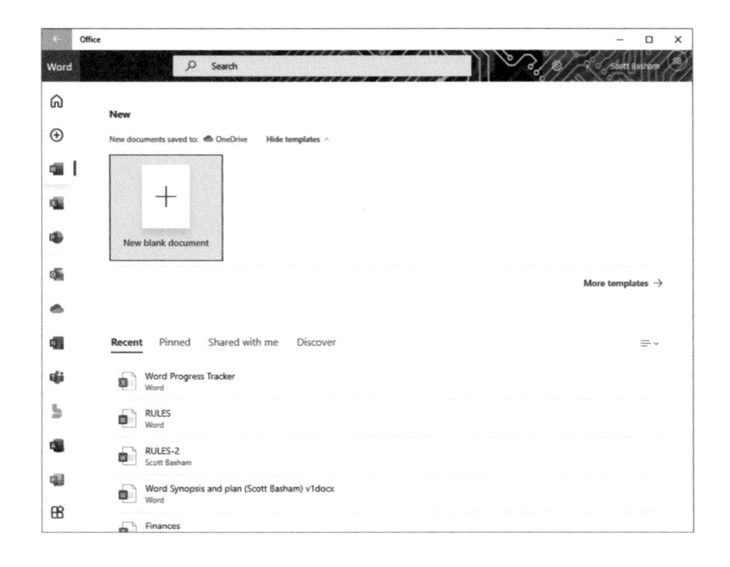

Another method is to click on the magnifying glass icon at the left of the Windows Taskbar, and type "Word". You'll see a list of matches including the Word application and any recently-used Word files.

...cont'd

Installing Word in the Taskbar

If you use Word regularly then it might be a good idea to have a quick way of launching from the Desktop.

Don't forget

For more details and help on accessing and organizing applications and documents, check the range of books in the **In Easy Steps** series. There are a number of books covering each version of the Windows operating system.

1. From the **Start** button, or via the **Search** option, locate Word. Select by right-clicking to see a pop-up menu
2. Click **Pin to taskbar** (click **More** first if necessary)

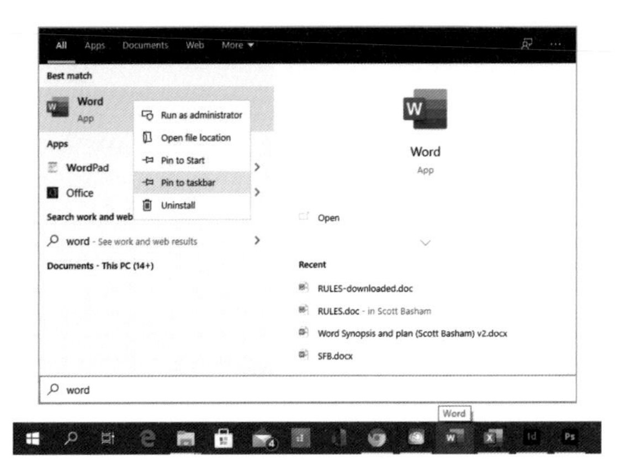

3. You can now launch Word from the Taskbar. To remove it, right-click on the icon and choose **Unpin from taskbar**

Opening a document directly from Windows File Explorer

On most PCs, Word document files will be recognized and shown with a distinctive icon as shown to the right.

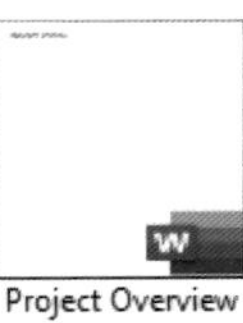
Project Overview - annotated.docx

1. Locate your Word document using Search or the Windows File Explorer
2. Clicking on a search result or double-clicking in File Explorer will launch the associated program (in this case, Word) and automatically open the file

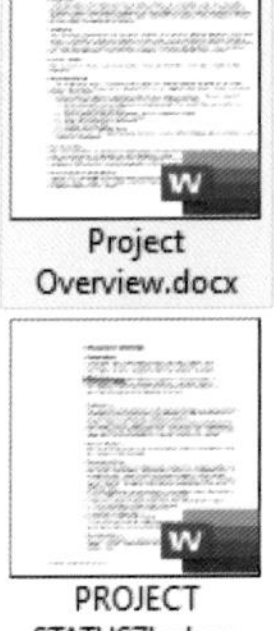
Project Overview.docx

PROJECT STATUS7b.docx

The initial screen

If you launched Word directly (not via a document) then you will see the following screen:

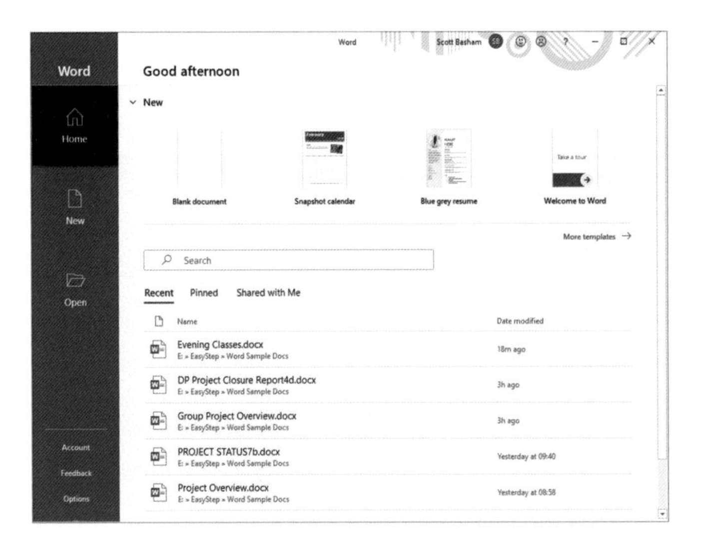

1. For a simple blank page, click **Blank document**
2. If you already have a document to view or edit, check to see if it's in the **Recent** list on the left side of the screen
3. If your document is there, click to open it. If not, click the **Open** icon on the left. At the bottom of the Open list, the **Browse** option takes you to a standard Windows file dialog

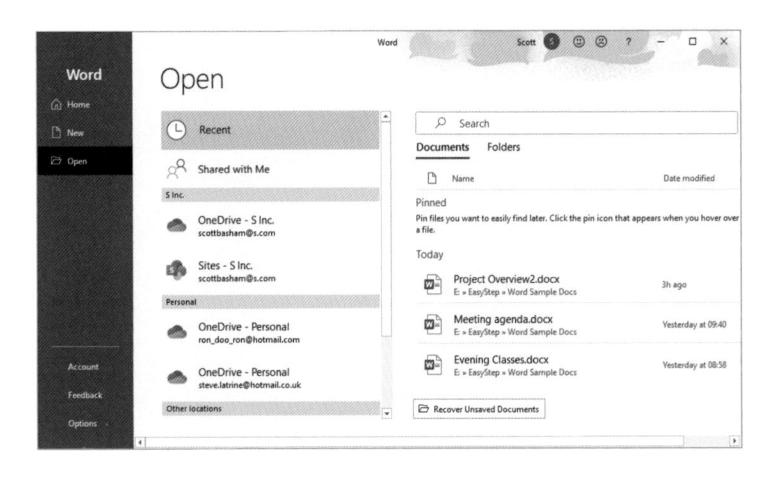

This initial screen also lets you start a new document using one of the installed templates. These are special documents with distinctive designs, which you can easily substitute with your own content. It is possible to download additional templates, or even to create your own.

The main screen

Once Word is up and running, you should see the following screen – with all the elements illustrated here:

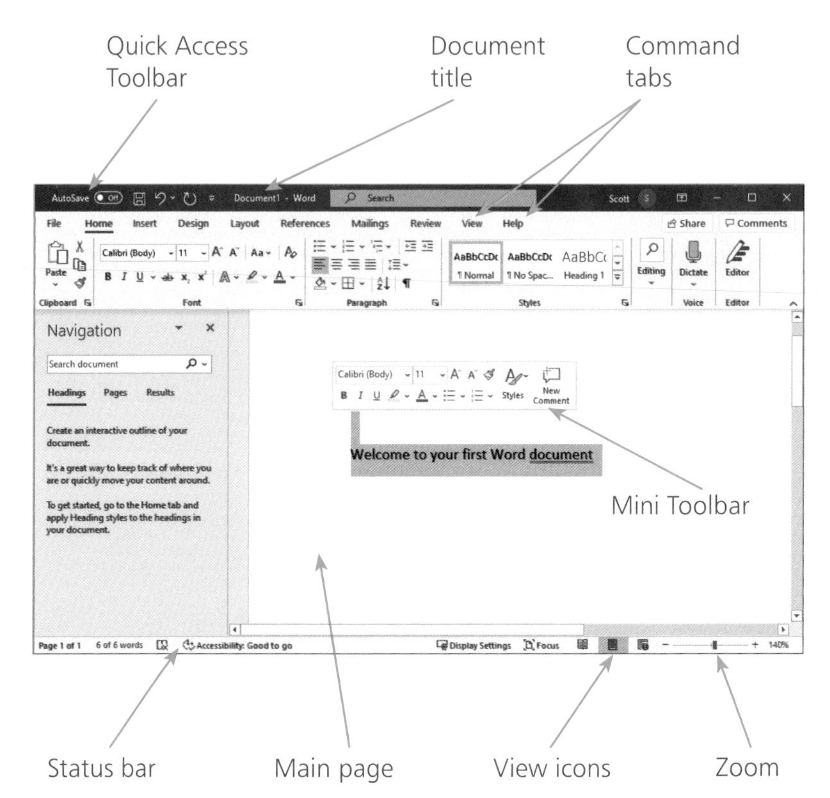

Don't worry if your screen doesn't exactly match this illustration: Word's display is highly customizable and most visual elements can be switched on or off according to your own preferences. You will find tips on how to do this throughout the book.

You can resize Word's window in the normal way by dragging on its border (if it's maximized then you'll need to click the **Restore Down** button first).

As you can see from the two illustrations on this page, Word automatically resizes and reconfigures its workspace and controls to make the best use of the space available.

If you can't see the icon or control you want, simply make the window larger or click the symbol to see what's been hidden.

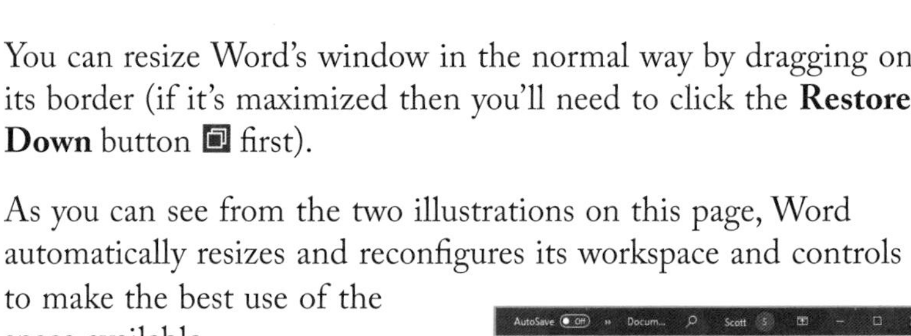

The Ribbon

Near the top of the screen is the Ribbon, which gives you access to most of Word's controls within a few mouse clicks. It's divided into a number of tabs, only one of which is active at any time. In the example below, the Home tab is showing basic text-editing and formatting features.

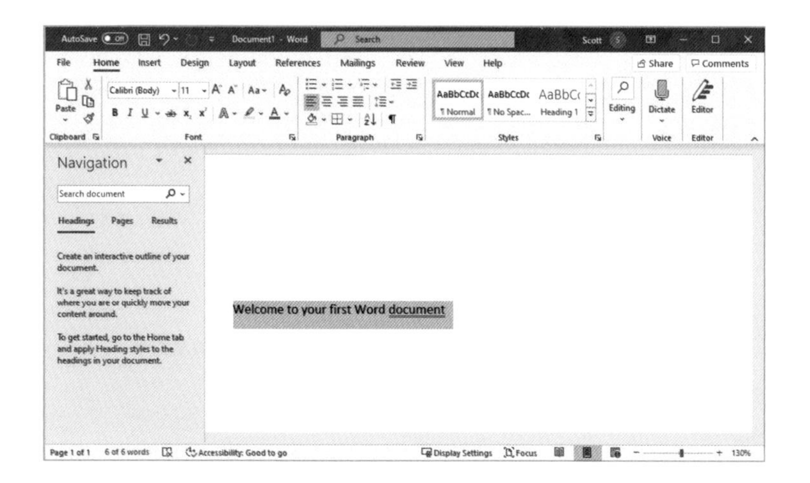

In this example, the highlighted text changes its appearance as the controls in the Ribbon are used. It is currently formatted using the **Normal** style. If the mouse hovers over the **Heading 1** style, the text temporarily changes its format to preview this style. For more about text styles, see Chapter 2.

Using different tabs in the Ribbon

1. Click on the **Insert** tab's title to activate it. You'll see it's subdivided into 11 sections

2. Each section contains groups of related controls. Let your mouse hover over one of these to see a brief explanation

...cont'd

3. Double-click on the currently-active tab to hide the Ribbon temporarily. This is useful if you want to maximize the amount of screen space available for viewing and editing your document

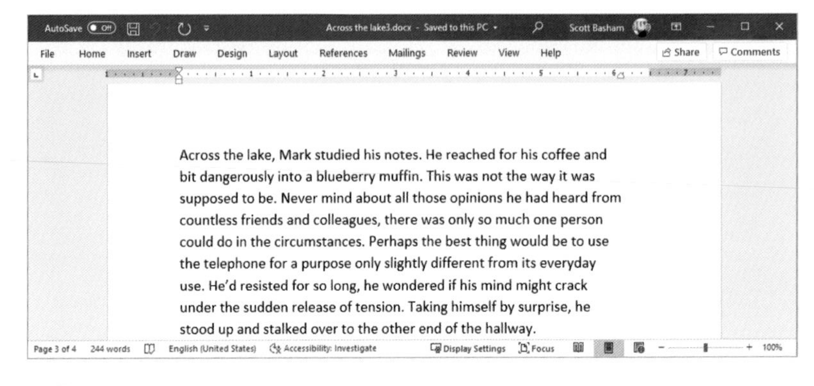

4. When the Ribbon is hidden in this way, clicking on a tab heading will temporarily reveal its contents. Double-click on a tab to restore the Ribbon permanently

5. Click on the **File** tab, then select Info to see document information, together with other options for managing documents including printing, sharing and exporting. There's also a range of global options and account tools

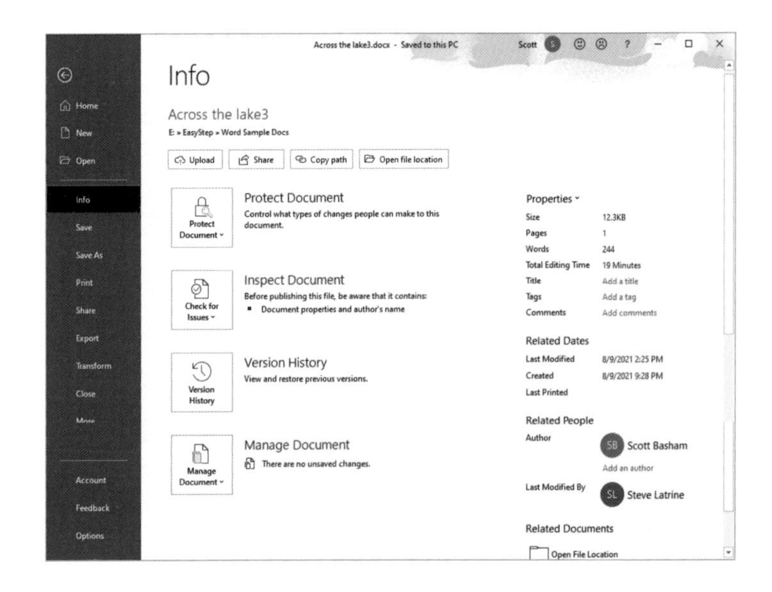

If you click on the Ribbon Display Options icon at the top right of the screen you can change how the Ribbon and tabs will display.

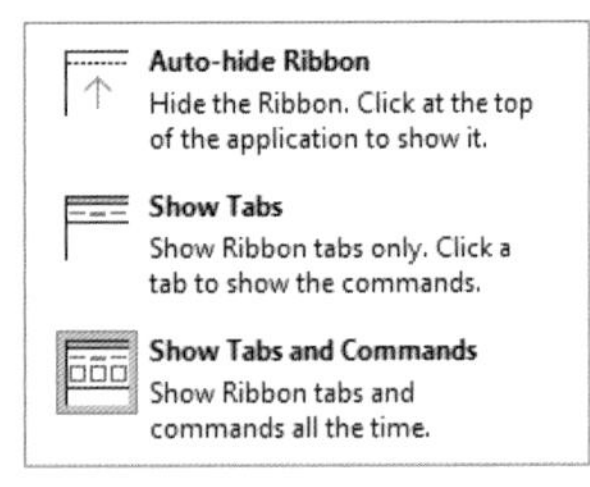

Word integrates seamlessly with a range of connected services such as OneDrive and YouTube, provided you are logged in to a valid Microsoft online account. See Chapter 8 for more on this topic.

The Mini Toolbar

Whenever you have some text selected, the **Mini Toolbar** will appear nearby. This gives you immediate access to the most commonly-used text-formatting options.

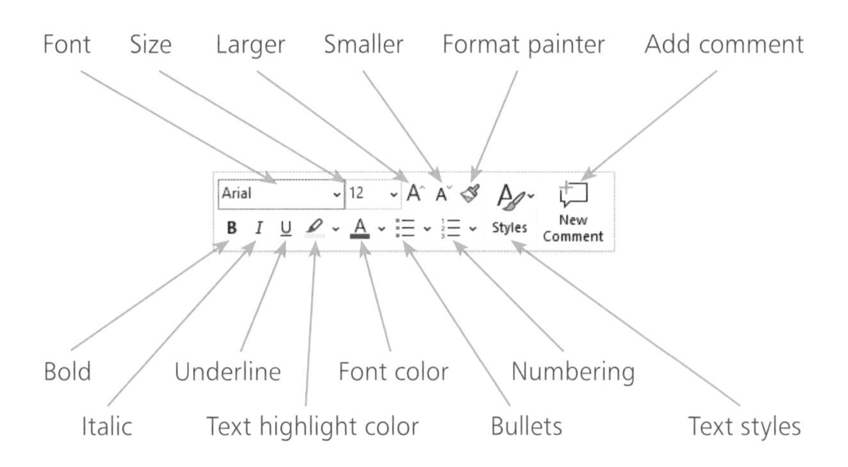

Some of the Mini Toolbar's controls have keyboard shortcuts. For example, **Bold** can be set on and off by typing **Ctrl** + **B**, and **Italic** with **Ctrl** + **I**. To find out if a control has a shortcut, simply hover over it with the mouse pointer for a few moments. There is a handy reference table of keyboard shortcuts on the inside front cover of this book.

Using the Mini Toolbar

1. Type some text and then select it by clicking and dragging across it with the mouse
2. The Mini Toolbar will appear automatically just above the text, as in the illustration below

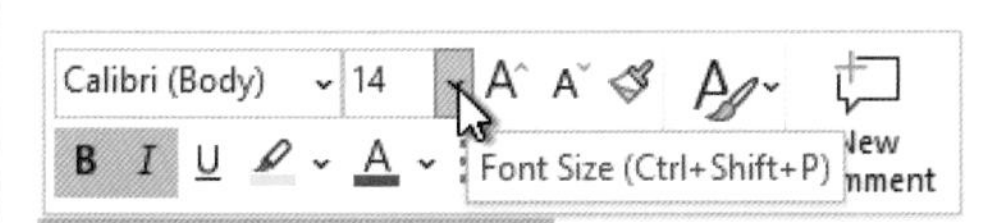

3. Click on one of the controls within the Mini Toolbar to change the appearance of your selected text
4. Repeat the process with other selected areas of text

If the Mini Toolbar fails to appear when you hover over selected text with your mouse, try right-clicking. A pop-up context menu will appear with the Mini Toolbar immediately above.

The Quick Access Toolbar

The **Quick Access Toolbar** is a small collection of tools at the top of the screen above the **File** tab.

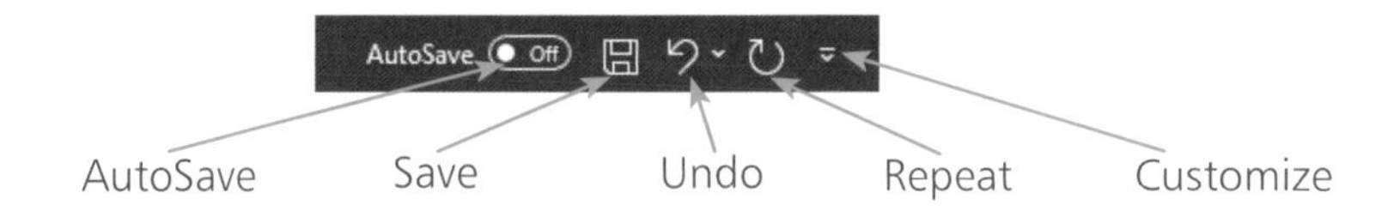

Customizing the Quick Access Toolbar

1. Click the **Customize** icon on the Quick Access Toolbar and select a command or choose **More Commands...** to see the full list. Note there is also an option to place the Toolbar below the Ribbon

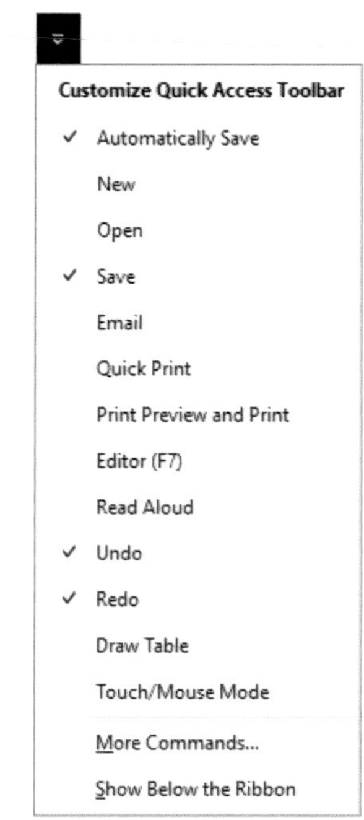

2. In the dialog, select from the **Choose commands from:** drop-down list to see a list of Word commands

3. If you want customizations to be global, make sure **For all documents (default)** is selected in the top-right corner

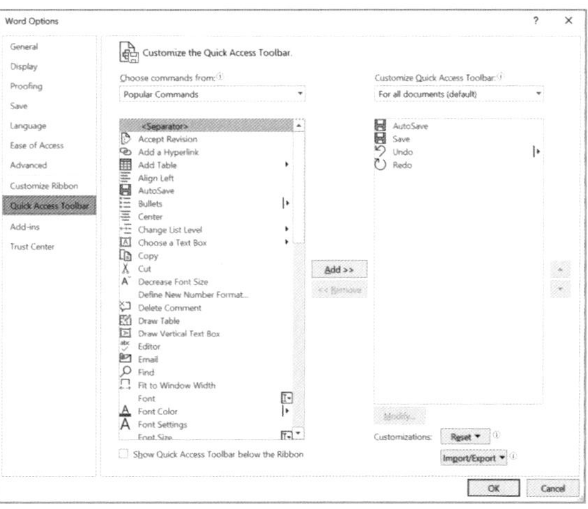

Touch/Mouse mode lets you choose between the best control layout for mouse or touch input. Touch input adds more space between commands and controls; this makes it easier to operate Word with a touchscreen device.

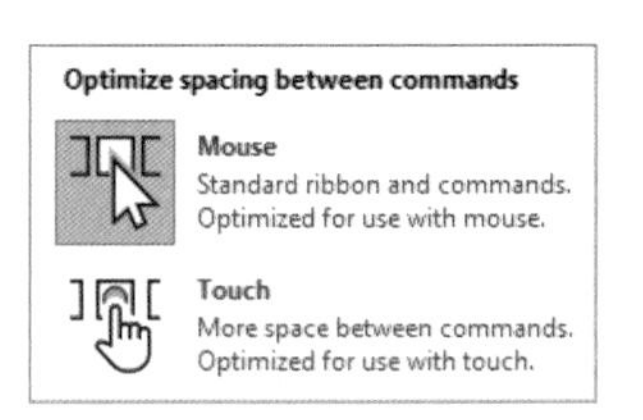

If you use the Quick Access Toolbar's **Undo** button, a **Redo** button then becomes available. **Undo** and **Redo** together allow you to step backward and forward through your actions.

4. Add icons by double-clicking in the left-hand list, or click once to select and then choose **Add>>**

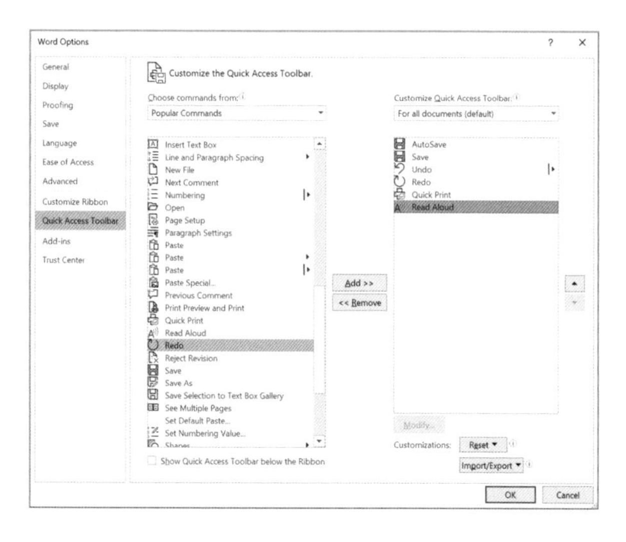

In this illustration you can see that Quick Access Toolbar is the highlighted item at the left of the dialog. If you select the **Customize Ribbon** option directly above then you will have the opportunity to completely redesign Word's layout of controls.

5. Remove icons by double-clicking in the right-hand list, or click once to select and then choose **<<Remove**

6. You can control the order in which the icons appear in the Toolbar. To do this, select a command in the right-hand list then use the **Up arrow** and **Down arrow** buttons to change its position. The top item in the list will appear as the first icon at the left of the Toolbar

In this illustration we selected the **Read Aloud** tool – this feature is covered on page 195.

7. Click **OK** when done, or **Cancel** to abandon your changes. The Quick Access Toolbar will now show the icons you've selected

From the **Customize Quick Access** Toolbar dialog you can reset the Toolbar to its initial state by clicking the **Reset** button. It's also possible to import and export your customizations to a file.

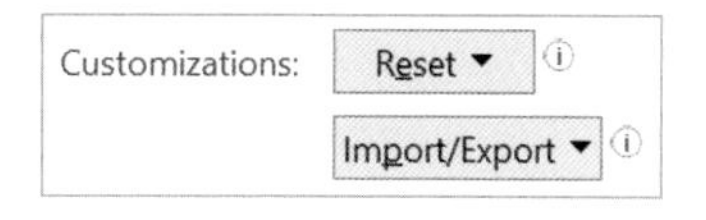

You can also access these settings by activating the **File** tab, choosing **Options**, then selecting **Quick Access Toolbar**.

The Status bar

This bar at the bottom of the screen shows settings and options.

Customizing the Status bar

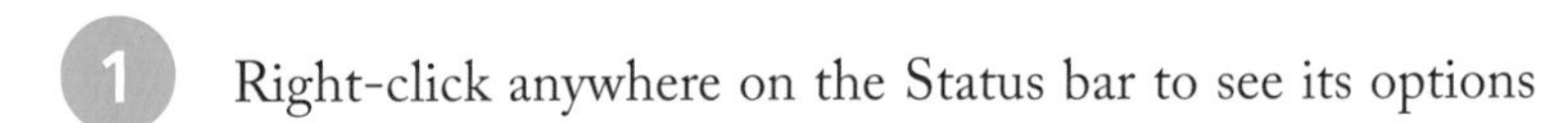

1. Right-click anywhere on the Status bar to see its options

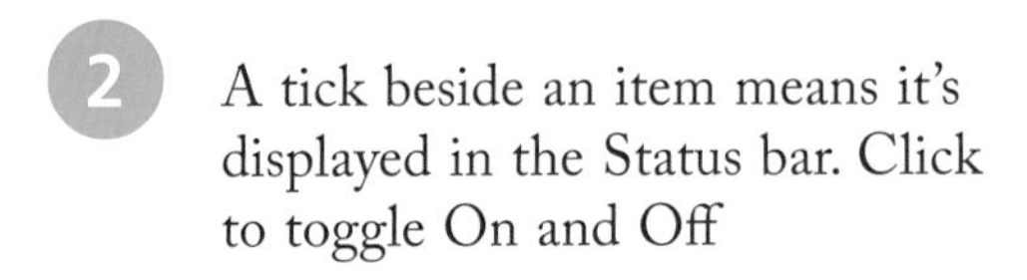

2. A tick beside an item means it's displayed in the Status bar. Click to toggle On and Off

The Status bar also shows you the current page, the number of words in a document, spelling/grammar information and zoom-level controls.

In this illustration we can see that the Vertical Page Position is 2.5 inches.

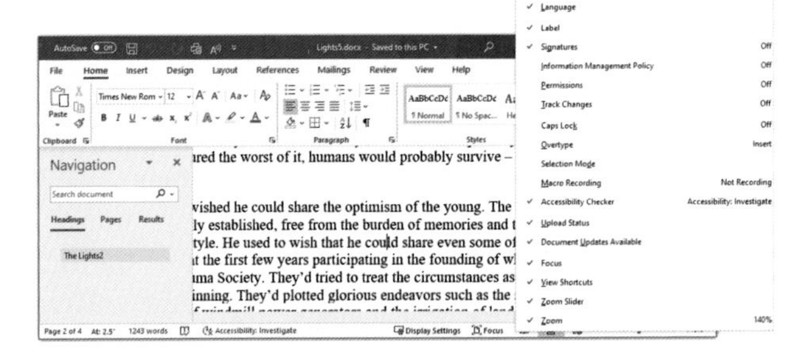

Search

1. Click on the magnifying glass icon in the Title bar

2. Type in some text. Word will show you information on related commands or options for searching Word help

Search makes use of a combination of sources including dictionaries, Wikipedia and more general web searches.

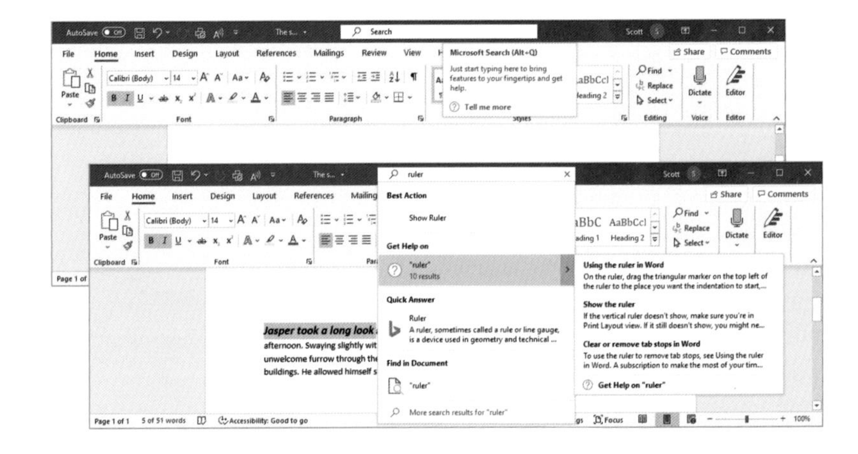

Getting help

1. Move your mouse over a command in the Ribbon. After a few moments a tooltip appears, showing you the name of the command (this is useful if it's displayed only as an icon in the Ribbon). You'll also see an explanation of its function

2. The ⧉ icon indicates that a dialog box will open if you click on it. If you hover over it you'll temporarily see a quick overview explaining the purpose of the dialog

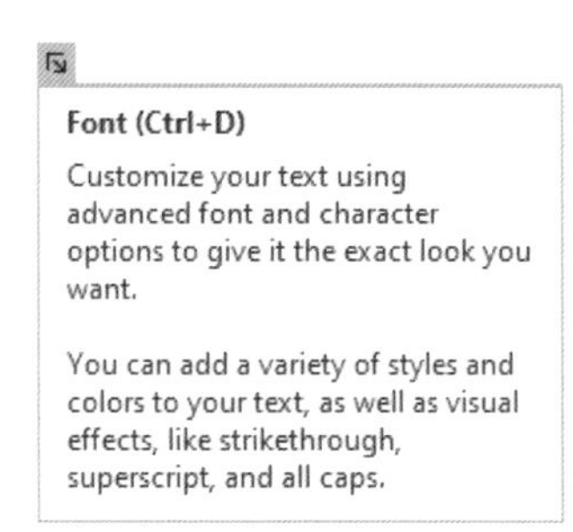

3. For more information about Word's features, press the ⓘ icon (if available) and a pop-up window will appear

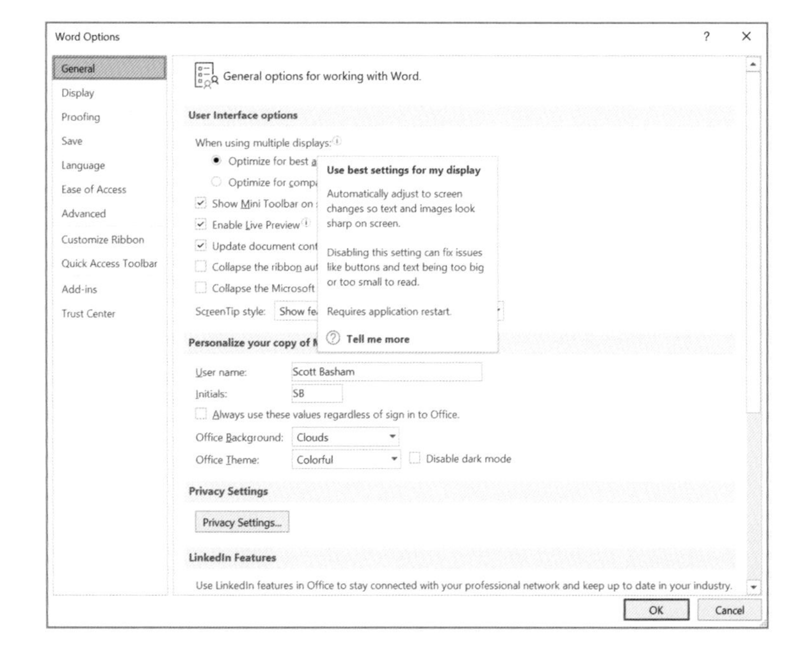

4. For more detail, click on the question mark icon in the top right-hand corner of a dialog box or press the **F1** key. If your mouse was not pointing at any controls when you pressed **F1** then a general searchable Help window appears

Help is available for most of Word's dialogs, screens and controls.

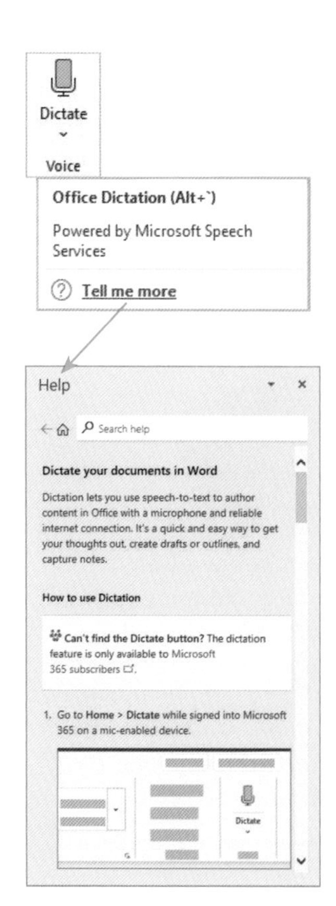

Text editing

Text editing in Word is no different from programs such as Notepad, WordPad, Outlook, or PowerPoint. If you're already familiar with these basic skills then you can skip ahead to the next section.

Getting started

The words to the right of the insertion point will automatically move along to accommodate any text you are inserting.

1. Start up Word so that you have a new blank document. If Word is already open then click on the **File** tab, then choose **New**, then **Blank document**

2. Enter some example text; enough for a line or two. Don't worry if you make mistakes as these will be easy to correct later on. Look for the flashing vertical line, known as the insertion point, which indicates where any new text will appear

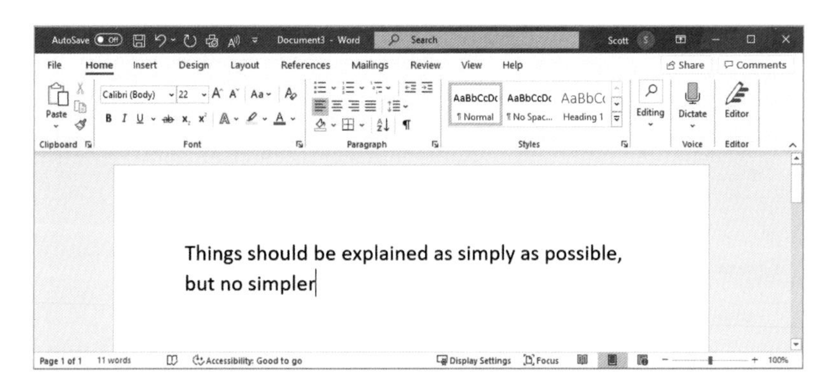

Word automatically works out when to start a new line without breaking words. If you want to force a new line – for example, to begin a new paragraph – press the **Return** key or the **Enter** key.

3. You can easily move the insertion point anywhere in your text by clicking with the mouse. The arrow keys will also let you move up, down, left and right within any existing text. Move your insertion point so that it's somewhere in the middle of your text

4. If you type more text now it will be inserted at your current position. To remove text, use the **Backspace** key to delete the character to the left of your current position, or the **Delete** key to remove the character to the right. If you hold down either of these keys for more than a moment they will "repeat" and start deleting more characters

Selecting text

Basic techniques

Selecting text is almost always the first step when formatting or editing, so it's worth knowing all the different techniques. There are quite a few methods for text selection that work consistently across many applications on your PC or Mac, such as double-clicking to select a word. As you'd expect, this works in Word, so now we'll look at this plus some more options.

Using the arrow keys, or a mouse click, or a tap on a touchscreen device allows you to reposition your insertion point anywhere within the text. If you try to move beyond the existing text you'll find that the insertion point refuses to move. One way around this is to move just to the right of the last character and then add more text.

1. Click and drag over the text you want to select. This is quick and easy for small amounts of text

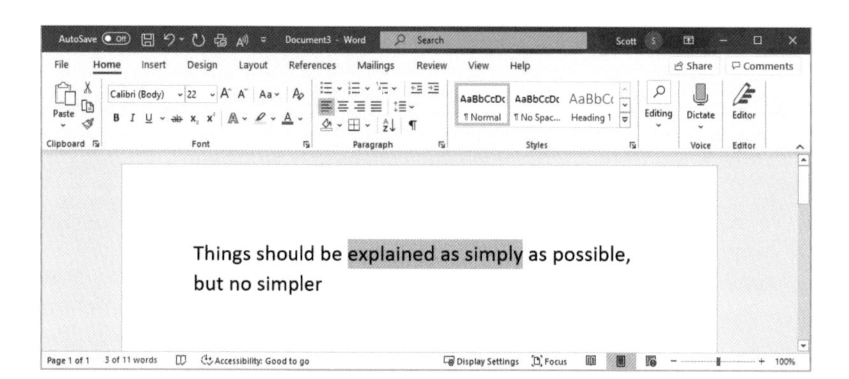

2. If the wrong text is highlighted, click anywhere in the text-editing area to cancel the selection, then try again

3. Double-click on a word to select it. Triple-click to select a paragraph. If you're using a touchscreen device, tap twice to begin selecting then drag the circular handles to adjust the start and end of the selection

Don't be tempted to add extra spacing by pressing the spacebar many times. Although this will work up to a point, it's not the most flexible way of controlling spacing. You'll learn much better techniques for this in the next two chapters.

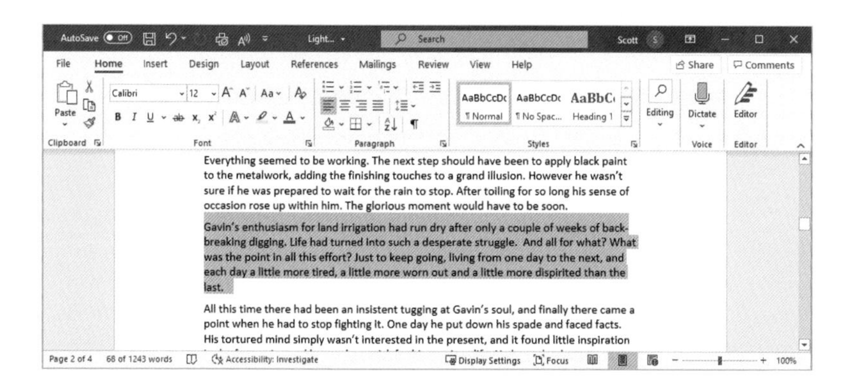

...cont'd

More advanced techniques

It's worth experimenting with selection techniques, as after a while you'll be able to choose the best method each time instinctively.

You can quickly select all the text in your document by clicking on the **Select** option in the Editing area of the **Home** tab (see page 61), and choosing **Select All**. The keyboard shortcut for this is **Ctrl** + **A**.

1. Move your mouse into the left margin area. You can tell that you are in the correct area if the cursor turns into an arrow pointing to the right instead of to the left

2. Drag vertically to select whole lines of text

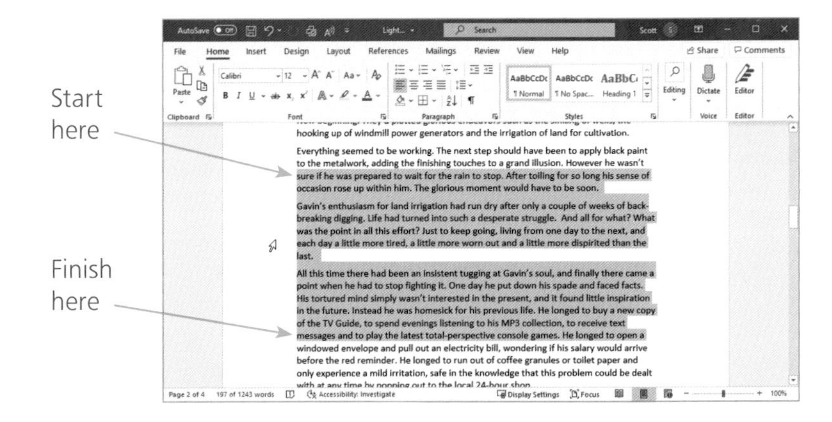

3. The easiest way to select larger amounts very precisely is to click the mouse at the start of the text

4. Locate the end of the area, scrolling if necessary

5. Hold down the **Shift** key and click. All text between the start and end will be selected. If you accidentally clicked at the wrong endpoint, simply press **Shift** and click again

If you hold down the **Shift** key when clicking in the left margin area, the current selection will be extended up to the point where you clicked.

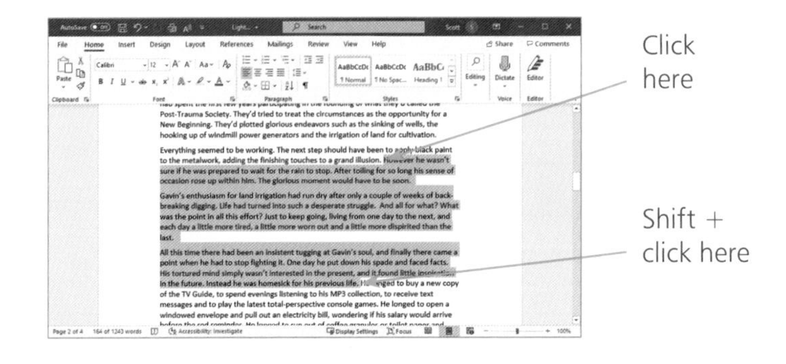

Discontinuous text selection

1. Select some text using any of the previous techniques
2. Now, holding down the **Ctrl** (**Control**) key, click and drag across some text that is separate from your original selection
3. Repeat this process to add more areas to your selection

Anything you type, even a single character, will normally replace all selected text. For example, if you have three paragraphs selected and you accidentally press the spacebar, then all that text will be replaced with the space. If this happens, simply use the **Undo** button in the Quick Access Toolbar, or type **Ctrl** + **Z**.

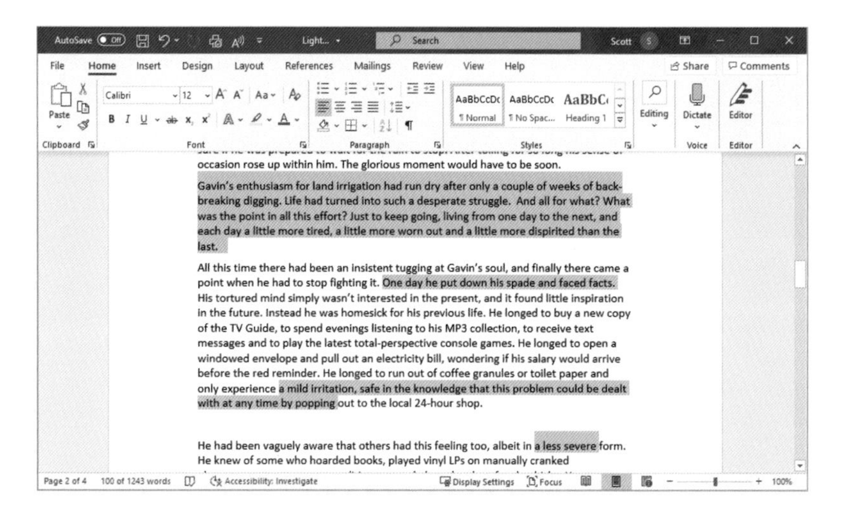

Selection with the Alt key

If you click and drag while holding the **Alt** key down, you'll select all text in a rectangular area. This is fun, although of questionable practical use.

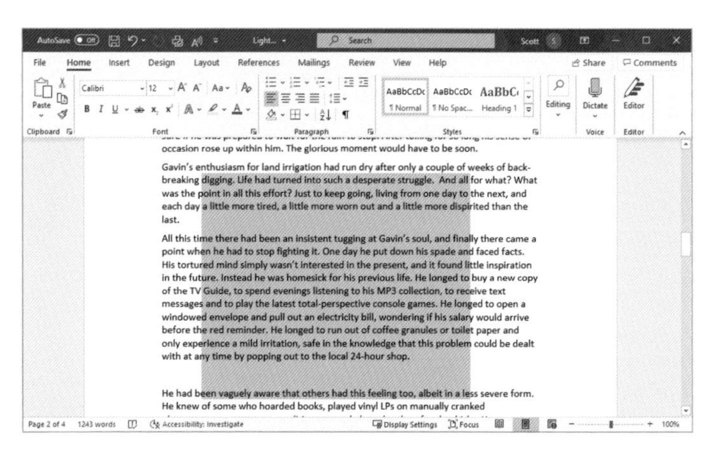

Working with files

Chapter 7 looks at file manipulation in detail, so for now we'll just concentrate on the simplest way to store and retrieve your work.

Starting a new document

When you start up Word you can click **New** on the Home screen. If you're already using Word and are ready to create another new document, select the **File** tab and click **New**

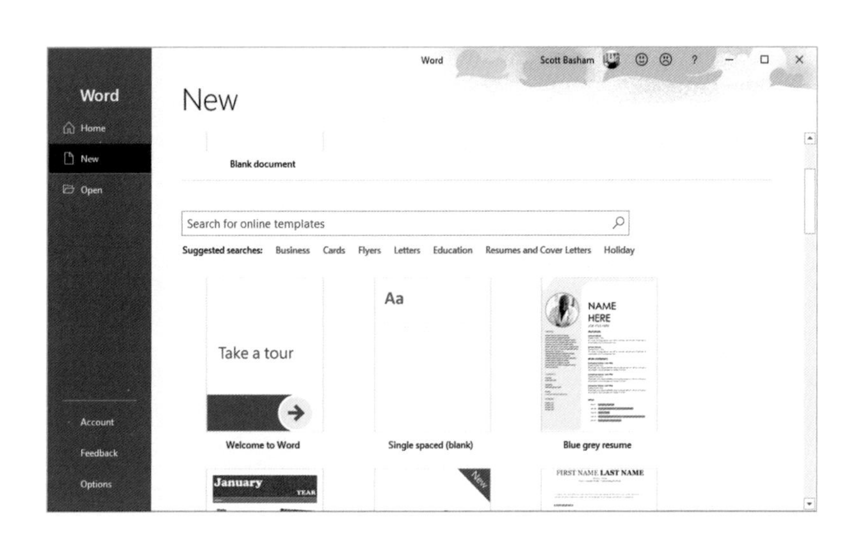

When saving a new document Word proposes a file name based on its starting text. You will probably want to edit this into a more suitable document name.

Saving your work

If you attempt to close down a new document without saving you'll see the following message. Click **Save** if you want to save your work before quitting

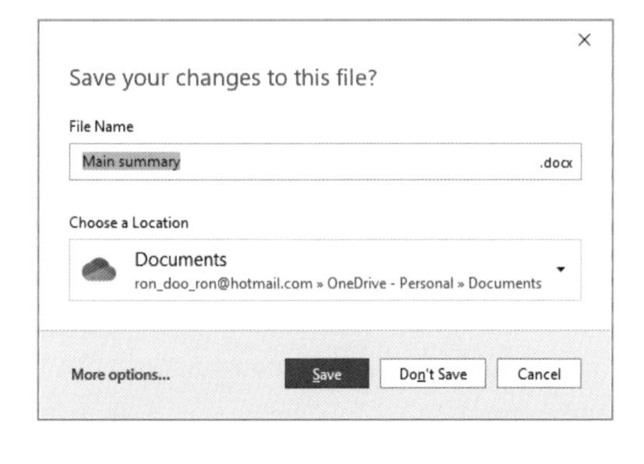

Before clicking the **Save** button check the Location field. If a suitable location is not available in the selection menu then click **More options...** to see a standard Windows file dialog box.

2. Another way to save your work is to click on the **Save** icon in the Quick Access Toolbar. If you have saved the document previously, Word simply saves using the same name and file location as before. If this is the first time the document is being saved, you'll see the following screen:

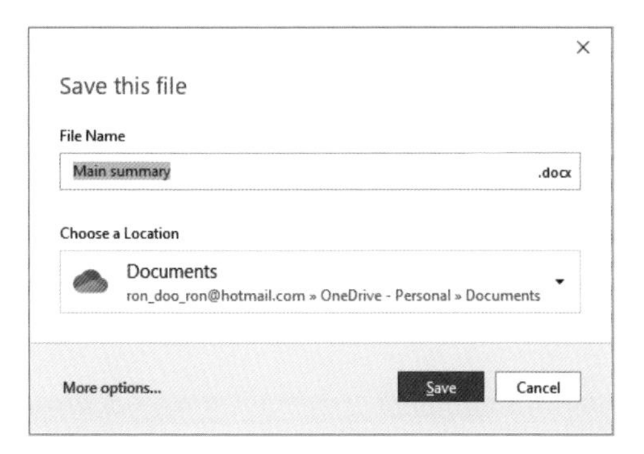

3. Choose a file name and location. If a suitable location is not one of the listed items then either choose **More locations** at the bottom of the list or **More options...**

Opening a saved document

1. Select the **File** tab then click **Open**

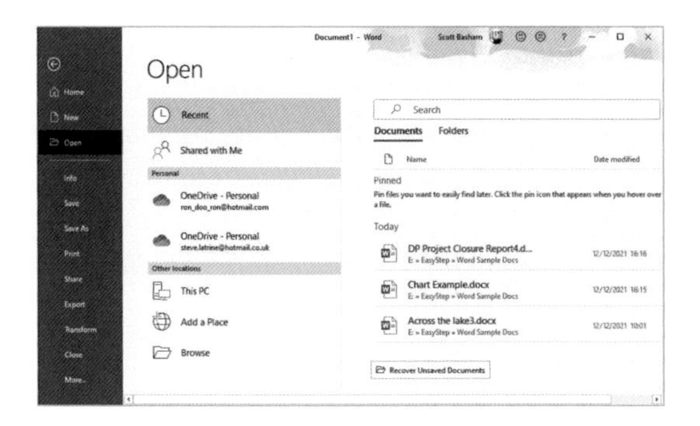

2. Under **Open**, choose from the recent files, the online storage options, This PC, or Browse to access a local file

3. If you chose **Browse** then click through the structure of folders and select a file in the standard Windows dialog

If your document has already been saved but you want to save a new copy rather than overwrite the previous version, go to the **File** tab and select **Save As** instead of Save.

If you haven't yet started up Word then you can speed things up by locating your document using your computer's file system (e.g. File Explorer or the Finder) then double-clicking on its icon. This will start up Word and open the document automatically.

Click and type

Provided you are in Word's **Print Layout** or **Web Layout** view, you can easily add text anywhere on a page.

1. First make sure that **Print Layout** view is selected from the **Page View** icons in the Status bar at the bottom of the screen

If click and type doesn't appear to work, click on the **File** tab and choose **Options**. Select **Advanced** and make sure that the **Enable click and type** option is activated.

2. Move over a blank area. The pointer icon will indicate to you whether new text will be aligned left, right or centered. The example below shows the icon for centered text. Double-click to establish a new insertion point

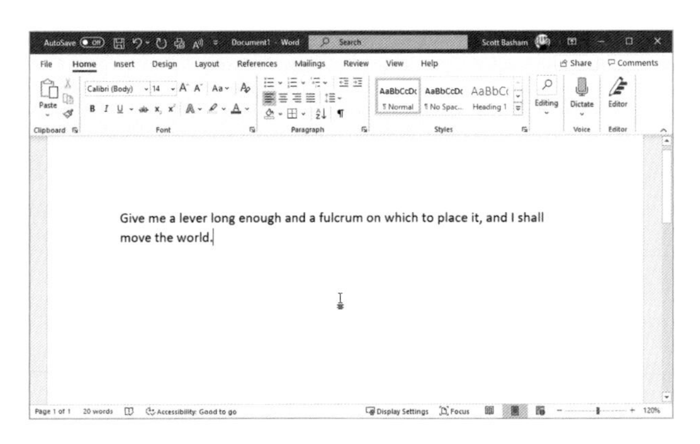

3. Type in some new text. Word will create any new blank lines necessary to allow the text to be positioned correctly. It also applies the correct form of alignment

You'll learn more about controlling left, right and centered text on page 40.

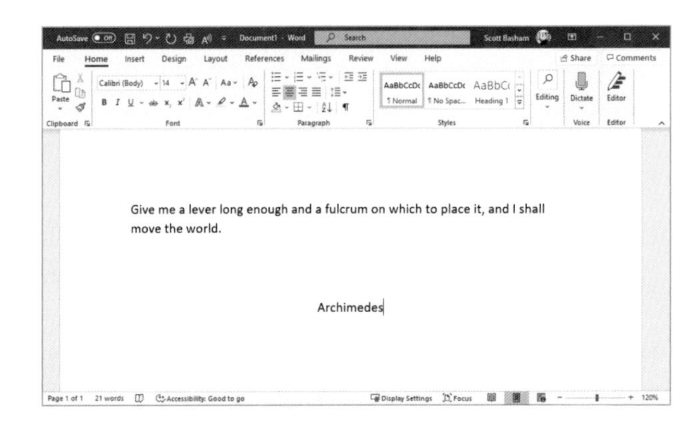

Basic navigation

When your text is too large for the document window, you'll need to use one of the following navigation methods:

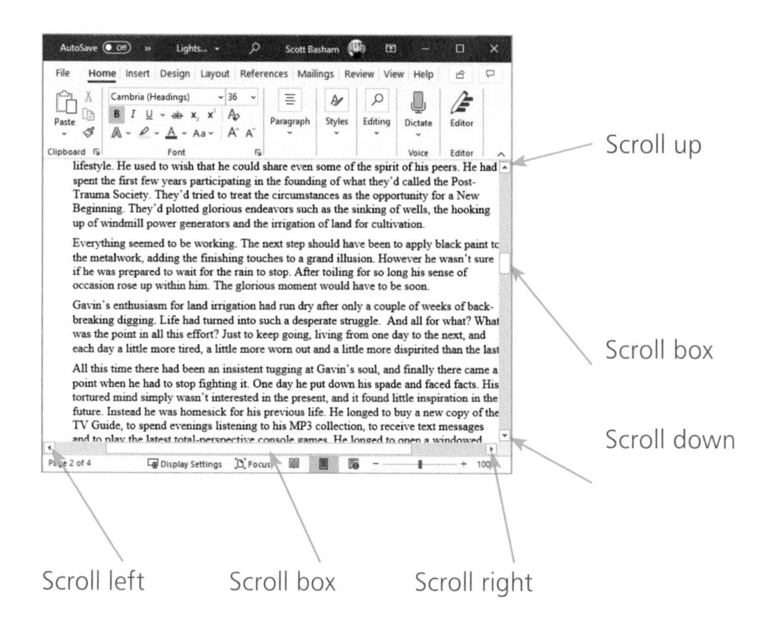

The scroll boxes' positions let you know where you are in a document. For example, when the vertical scroll box is at the top of the scroll bar, you are looking at the top (the beginning) of the document.

Quick ways to scroll

1. Drag the scroll box directly to a new position
2. Click in the scroll bar to either side of the scroll box. The document will immediately scroll in that direction one screen at a time
3. As you move your insertion point with the arrow keys on the keyboard, Word will scroll so that it can always be seen
4. If your mouse has a wheel, this can usually be used to scroll vertically through your document
5. The **PgUp** (**Page Up**) and **PgDn** (**Page Down**) keys will move you up and down one screen at a time
6. If you have a touch-enabled screen, place your finger inside the text area and swipe up or down to scroll

As you scroll down, the scroll box moves like an elevator down a shaft. The size of the box indicates how much of the document you can see (if the box occupies a third of the scroll bar, then you're viewing a third of the document).

...cont'd

Zooming

This allows you to control the level of magnification on screen. The zoom controls are in the bottom-right corner.

Remember to consider the size of Word's main window – in most cases it should be maximized. Note, however, that in this book we often use smaller windows so that we can concentrate on a particular part of the screen or set of controls.

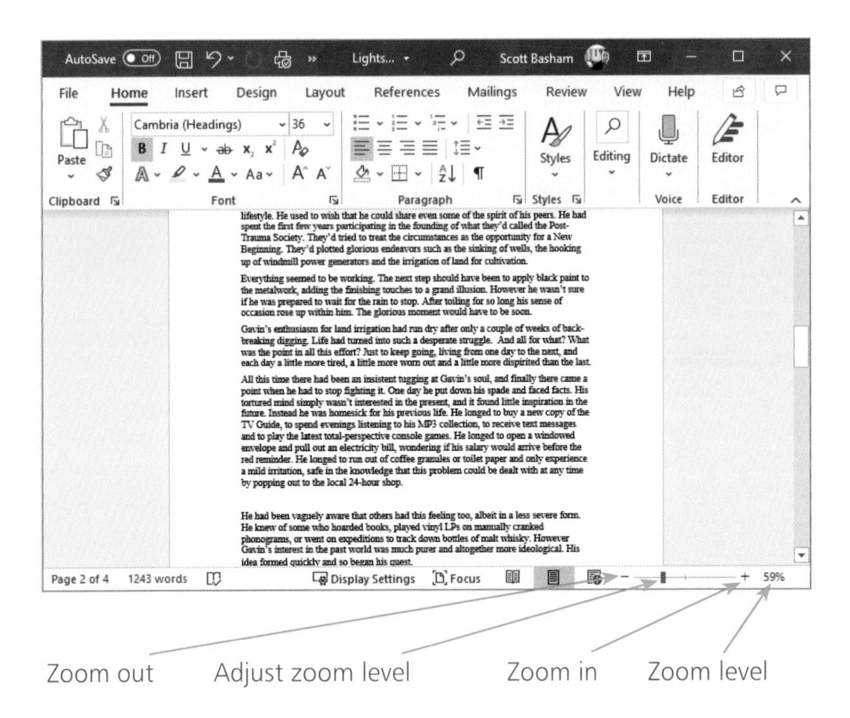

The Zoom dialog box

1. Click on the **Zoom level** icon (displayed as "59%" in the example above) to open the **Zoom** dialog box

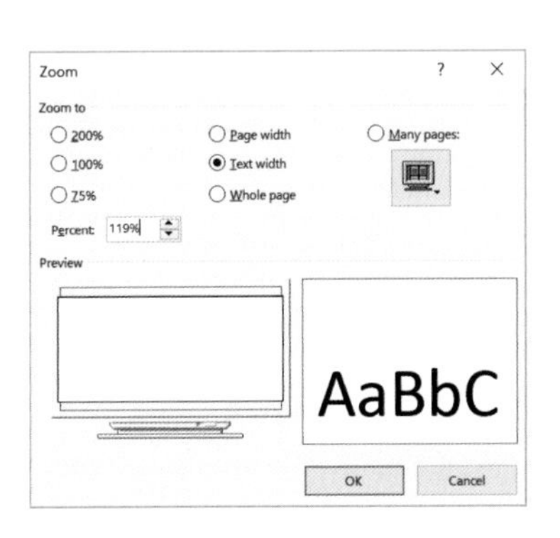

2. Choose one of the options, or enter a percentage value directly. **Text width** is a good option to use if you'd like to avoid horizontal scrolling

3. Click **OK** to apply the zoom level

2 Basic editing

Now that you know your way around, we'll look at the most common techniques for text editing and formatting.

The Clipboard

The **Clipboard** is a temporary storage area that can hold text or even other items such as graphic images. It can be used to help you move or copy text you have selected. It's also usually possible to use it to transfer text between different applications.

You can also use **Ctrl** + **X** to cut text, or right-click on your selection and choose **Cut** from the pop-up menu.

Cut and paste

1. Select the text to be moved. Choose **Cut** from the Clipboard section at the left of the **Home** tab

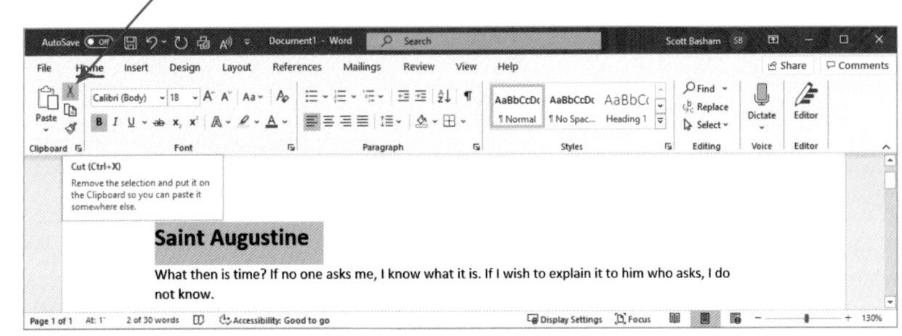

2. The text is removed and put onto the Clipboard. Now, place your insertion point at the desired destination and right-click. A pop-up menu appears offering you a choice of four paste options

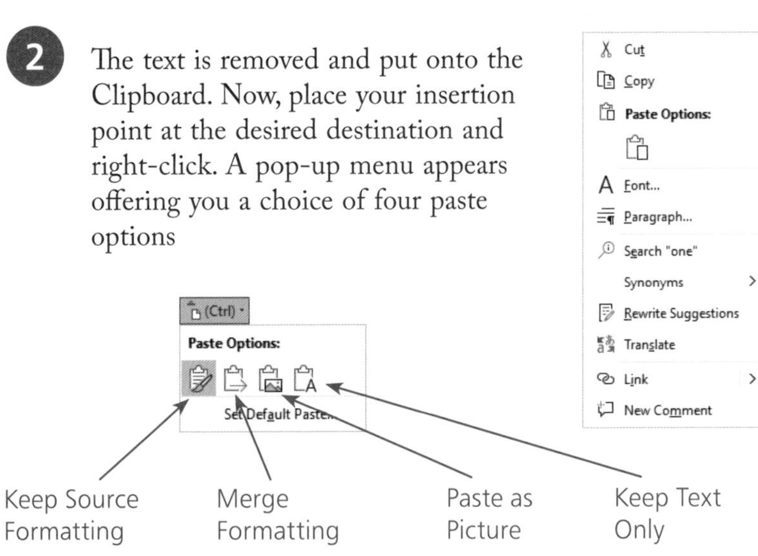

3. The source text was 18 point Calibri bold. If you want to use these attributes, click on the **Keep Source Formatting** option. If you want to use the attributes already at the destination, click on **Keep Text Only**. In the following example we right-clicked in an area of 11 point Calibri (Body) normal text and chose **Keep Text Only**

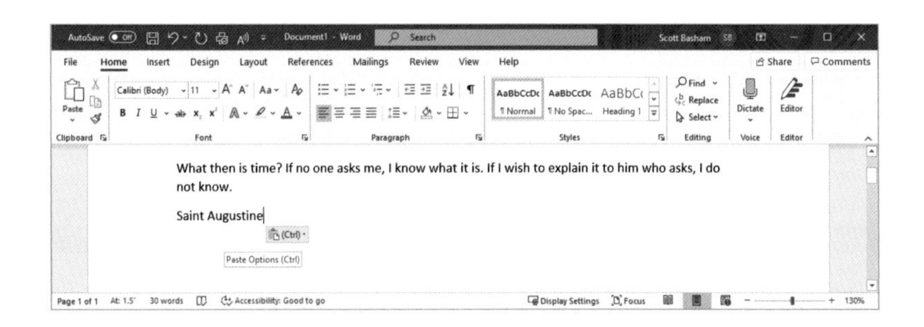

Even after you've pasted text you can still change your mind about the paste formatting options, as shown below.

Altering paste options after pasting

1. After you've pasted text you'll see the **Paste Options** icon nearby. Either click the icon or press the **Ctrl** key to review the available paste options

2. In the example below we chose the second option: **Merge Formatting**. The font and size are that of the destination, but the Bold effect has been taken from the source

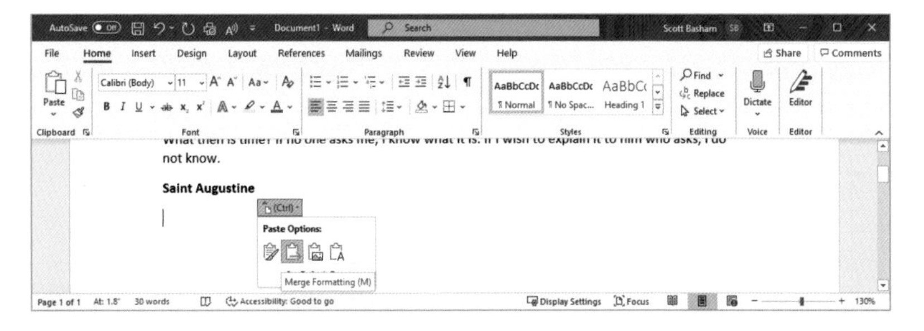

3. The paste options are available to you until you start typing, at which point the icon disappears

4. If you change your mind after this, then repeatedly click Undo until you've gone back to the point just before pasting, then paste once again. The **Paste Options** icon should appear once more

The Clipboard tools give you instant access to **Cut**, **Copy** and **Paste** in the form of icons:

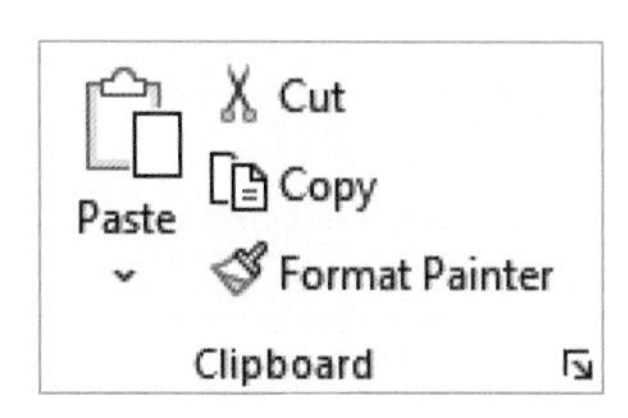

You can use **Ctrl** + **V** to paste what is in the Clipboard. **Ctrl** + **X** followed by **Ctrl** + **V** is usually the fastest way to cut and paste, particularly if your hands are already on the keyboard.

...cont'd

Copy and paste

1. Select the text you want to copy, right-click and choose **Copy** from the pop-up menu

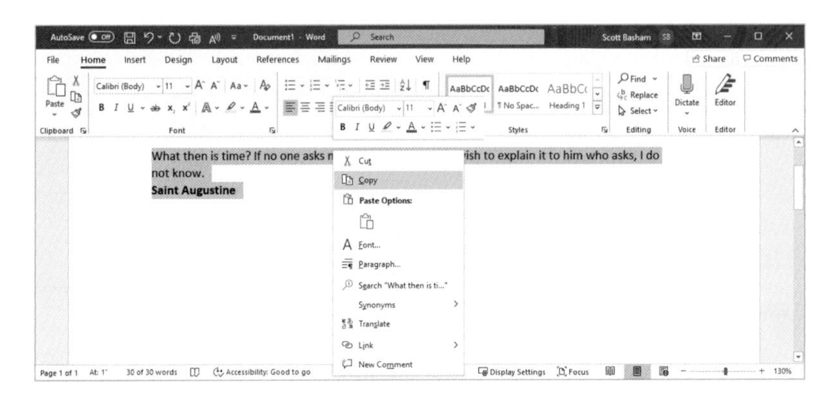

You can also click on the **Copy** and **Paste** icons in the Clipboard tools. A third way to copy and paste is to use the keyboard shortcuts **Ctrl** + **C** and **Ctrl** + **V** respectively.

2. Place the insertion point at the destination for the copied text, right-click and choose the appropriate paste option

3. Pasting text doesn't actually remove it from the Clipboard, so you can paste the same text many times

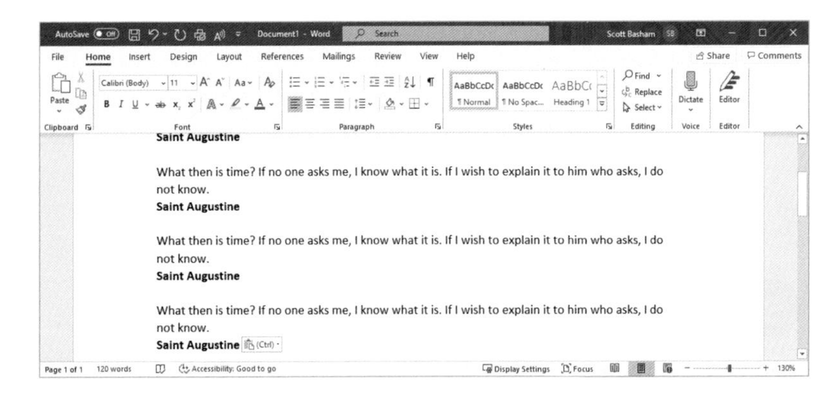

4. If you select some text before pasting, then the pasted text usually replaces what's selected. This feature can be switched On and Off from **File** > **Options** > **Advanced** (at the top of the dialog box is an option: **Typing replaces selected text**)

The Spike

The **Spike** is similar to the Clipboard in that it's a temporary storage area for text. The main difference is that you can add more and more text onto the Spike with a keyboard shortcut.

1. Select some text and type **Ctrl** + **F3**. The text disappears. It has been impaled on the Spike

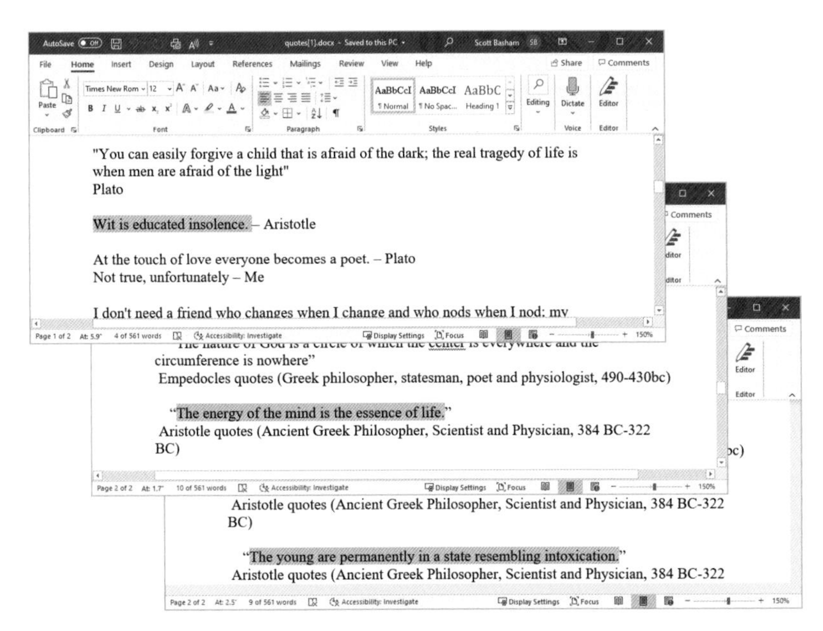

2. Move to a second piece of text and repeat the process: select then type **Ctrl** + **F3**

3. Repeat until you have collected all your text. Then, move your insertion point to your target location and type **Ctrl** + **Shift** + **F3** to paste it back into your document

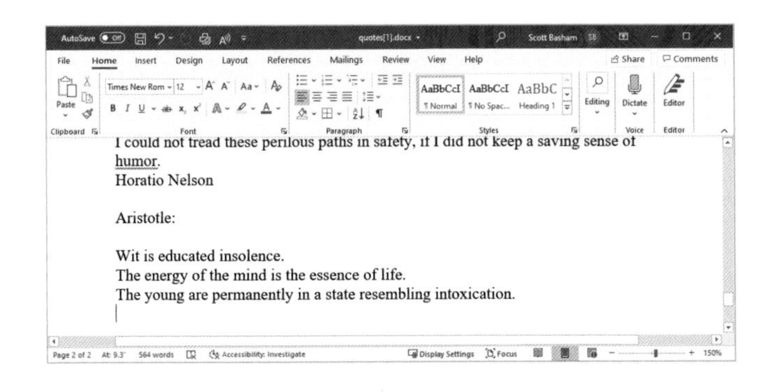

You can repeat this more times if you want to collect more pieces of text onto the Spike. Each time you press **Ctrl** + **F3**, any selected text is removed from the page and added to the Spike. Note, however, that you only press **Ctrl** + **Shift** + **F3** once – as soon as the text is back on the page it has been removed from the Spike.

The Format Painter

This is an easy way to copy attributes from one place to another.

Hot tip

To copy formatting from the current selection to more than one destination, simply double-click on the **Format Painter** icon. You can then apply the formatting to as many pieces of text as you wish. When you've finished, either click back on the icon to discharge the loaded attributes or press the **Esc** key.

1. Select a sample of text that has the desired attributes
2. Click the **Format Painter** icon in the Clipboard section of the **Home** tab. This "loads" the icon with the attributes of the selected text

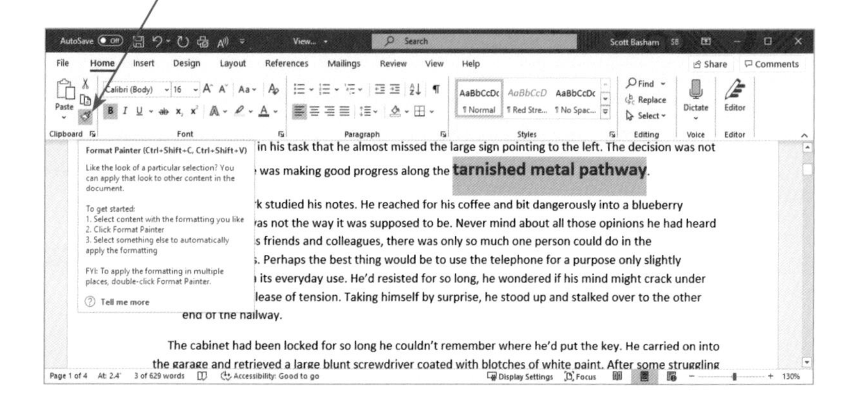

3. The pointer has changed its appearance to indicate that there are attributes loaded. Drag across your target to apply these settings

This is a very powerful feature so remember you can always click **Undo** if the results are not what you wanted.

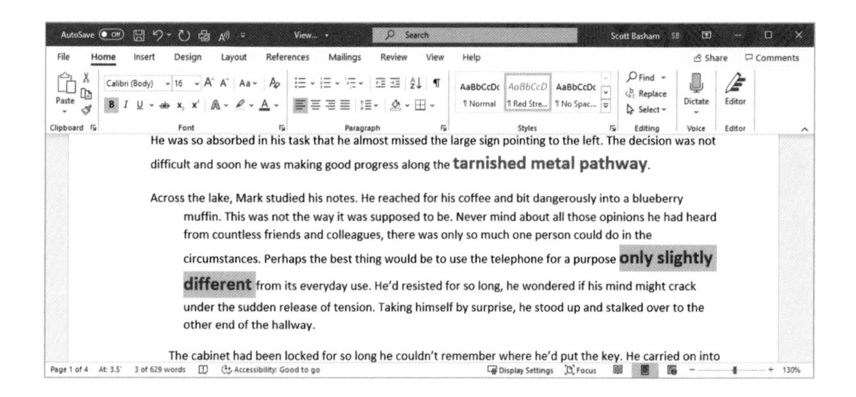

See pages 40-43 for more details on paragraph-level attributes.

This normally just copies character-level attributes. However, if you select an entire paragraph, click the **Format Painter** then select an entire destination paragraph, and all attributes (including paragraph settings such as alignment) will be copied.

Formatting characters

The **Home** tab contains the controls you'll use most often, so it's selected by default whenever you open or create a document.

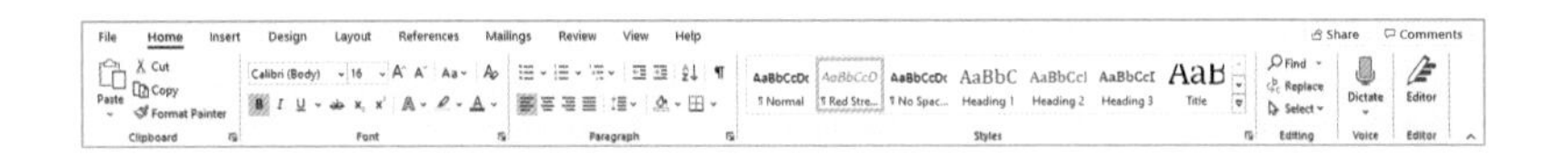

It's organized into seven areas: Clipboard, Font, Paragraph, Styles, Editing, Voice, and Editor. We'll start with the Font controls.

Choosing the font with the Mini Toolbar

The terms "font" and "typeface" come from traditional typography, and describe the visual design of letters and other symbols. Most people will be familiar with popular typefaces such as Arial or Times New Roman. Strictly speaking, a font is an instance of a typeface at a certain size and variant such as Normal, Light, Bold or Italic. These days the term "font" is often used in place of typeface, so in Word we might select a font of "Arial Black", then choose a size of 12 and perhaps apply an effect such as Italic.

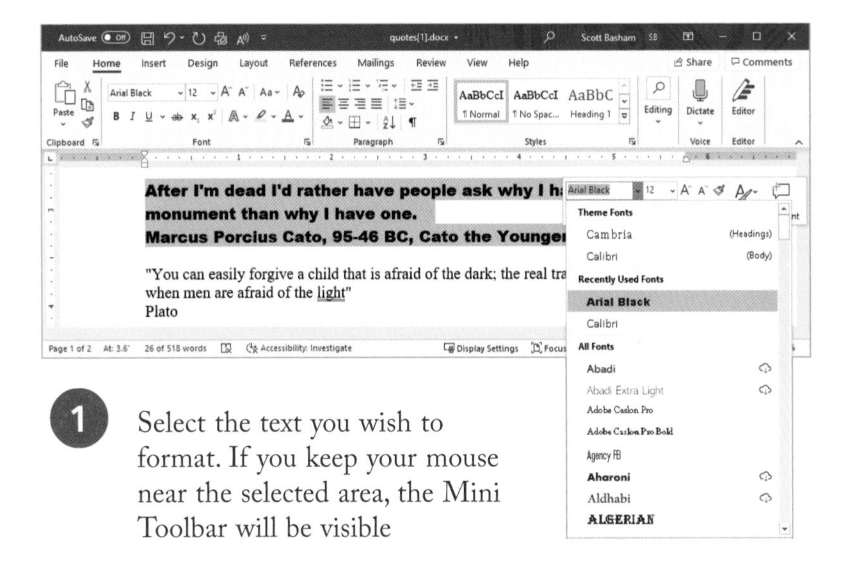

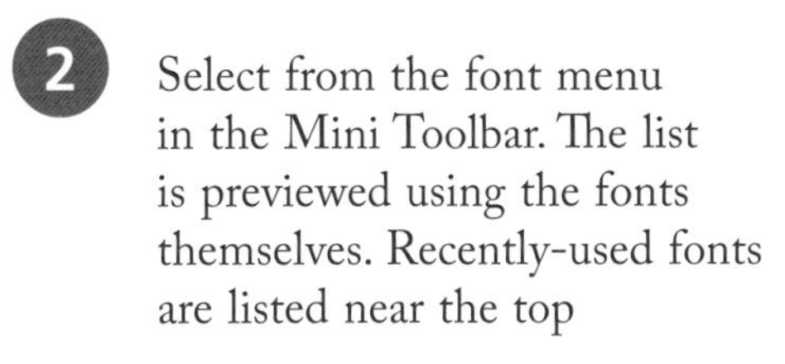

1. Select the text you wish to format. If you keep your mouse near the selected area, the Mini Toolbar will be visible

2. Select from the font menu in the Mini Toolbar. The list is previewed using the fonts themselves. Recently-used fonts are listed near the top

Font size is usually measured in points, where 72 points is equal to 1 inch when printed. Most printed body text is either 10, 11 or 12 points in size.

If the Mini Toolbar fails to appear when you hover over some text with your mouse, try right-clicking. A pop-up context menu will appear with the Mini Toolbar immediately above.

...cont'd

The keyboard shortcuts for **Bold**, **Italic** and **Underline** are **Ctrl** + **B**, **Ctrl** + **I** and **Ctrl** + **U** respectively.

Formatting with the Home tab

The **Font** section of the **Home** tab gives you access to more ways of controlling the appearance of characters.

1. Select some text. Change font, size, and other attributes by selecting from the **Font** section in the **Home** tab

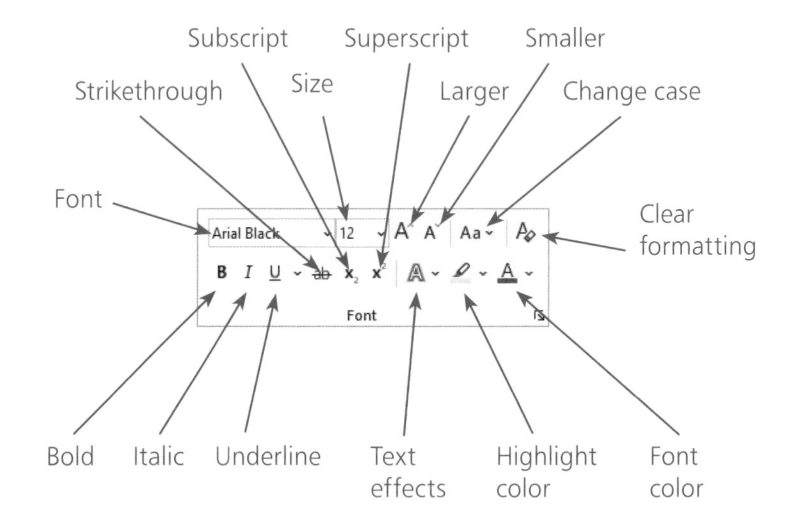

2. The Font area shows the current settings of selected text, wherever possible

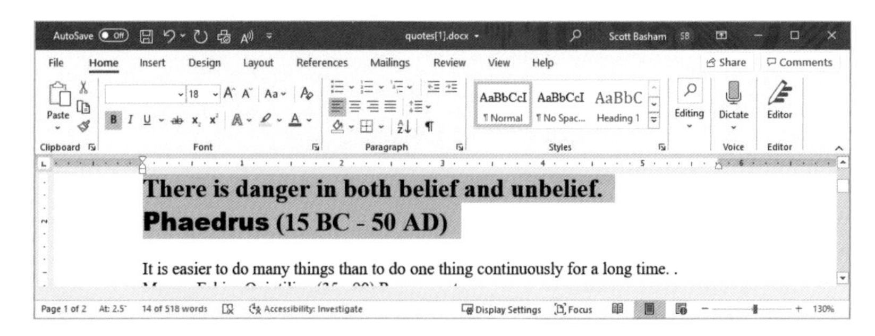

3. In this example all the selected text is 18 point in size, and Bold, so that's shown in the Font area. However, since the text uses more than one font, the area that usually displays the font name is blank. Selecting just the word "Phaedrus", or even part of that word, would cause the Font area to show "Arial Black"

The Font dialog

You can call up the Font dialog box to get full character-level control over the appearance of your selected text.

1. Select some text. Click on the dialog icon in the lower-right corner of the Font area, or press **Ctrl** + **D**

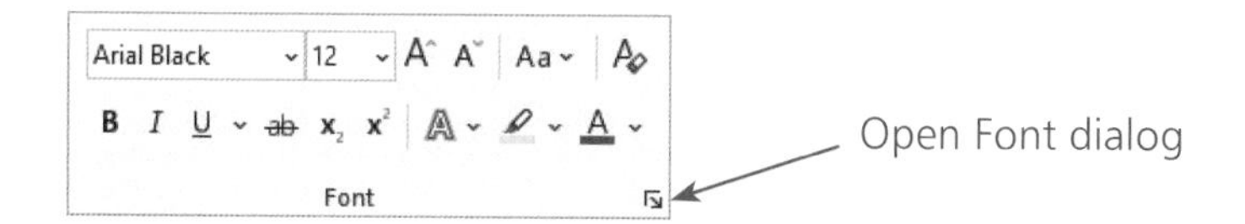

2. You now have access to additional effects, such as double strikethrough, and a variety of underline styles. The Preview box near the bottom gives you an indication of how the text would appear if you clicked **OK**

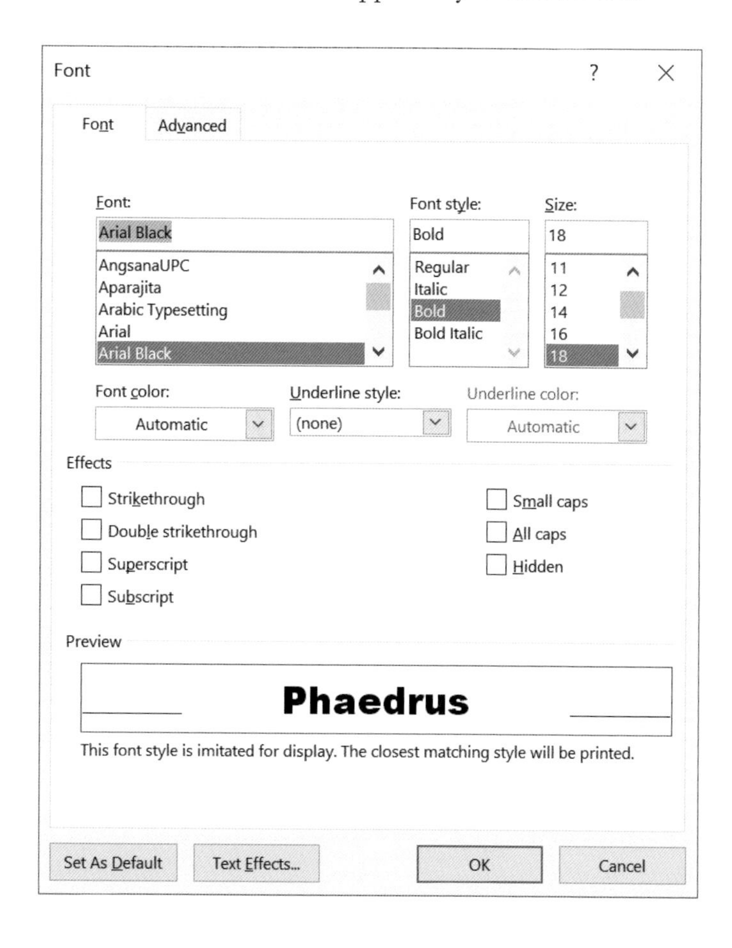

Clicking the **Text Effects...** button will take you to a dialog where you can apply a wide range of visual effects to your text. These include fills, outlines, shadows, reflections and 3D formats. You can apply some (but not all) of these directly from icons in the **Home** tab of the Ribbon, as you will see in the example on page 39.

...cont'd

Click on the **Advanced** tab to control the precise positioning and scaling of the selected characters

Beware

Scaling allows you to stretch or compress text horizontally. While this can sometimes work well for large titles, it's not recommended for use on main text as the results are often unreadable. If you need narrower or wider text then try using a different font that is already the desired shape.

Kerning

Kerning is a process used to adjust the space between certain combinations of characters. For example, when the letters "T" and "o" occur next to each other, normal spacing appears too wide. If you activate kerning then they will be brought closer together to create the illusion of normal spacing. Since kerning creates more work for your computer when drawing text on the screen, it may increase the time it takes to display. For this reason, you might want to activate it only for larger font sizes (where spacing is more noticeable).

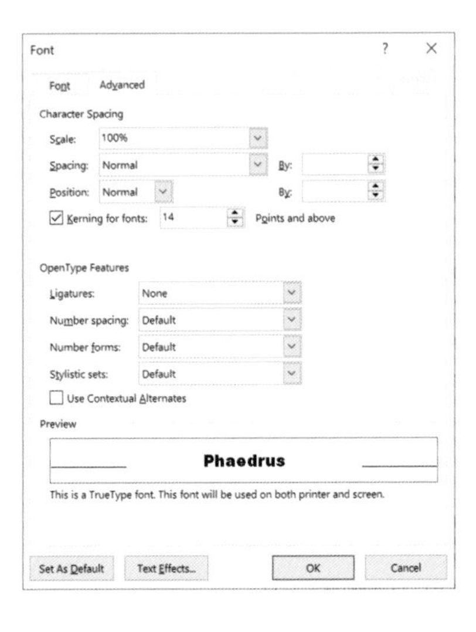

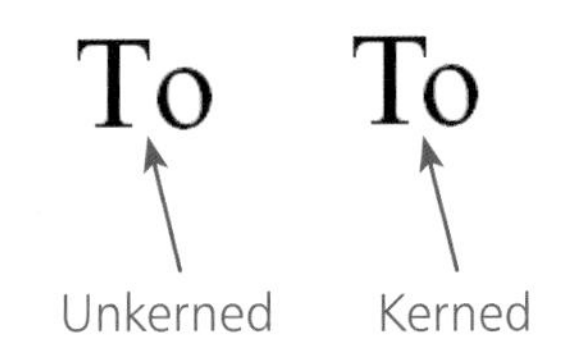

Ligatures

The Advanced dialog also has the ability to access a range of OpenType features. OpenType allows font designers to make use of features such as special small caps, ligatures, number forms and spacing. Ligatures are combinations of characters designed as a single entity. In this example you can see that applying ligatures affects the two consecutive "f" characters, which are displayed as a specially-designed single character.

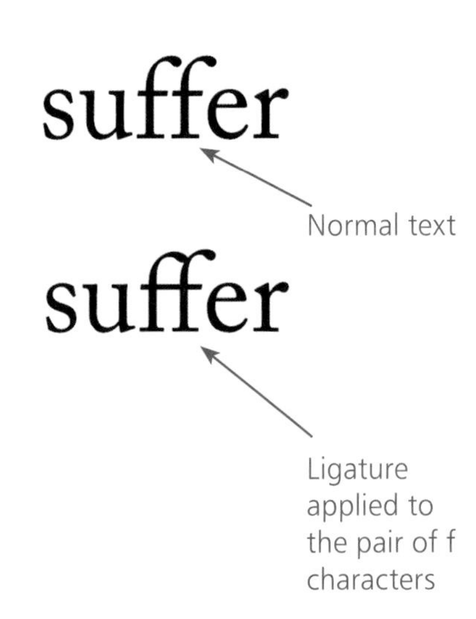

Don't forget

You might not notice any changes in the appearance of your text when you activate ligatures, as this setting will only make a difference if you are using a font that has been specially created with ligature information.

Text effects

Word gives you access to a wide range of text effects, and by using the Font area of the **Home** tab you'll get an instant preview.

1. Select some text. Click on the **Text Effects and Typography** button within the Font tools to see a menu of popular effects. As you hover over an item, your text will temporarily preview the effect. Either move to a different effect or, if you are happy with your selection, click once on the effect to apply it permanently

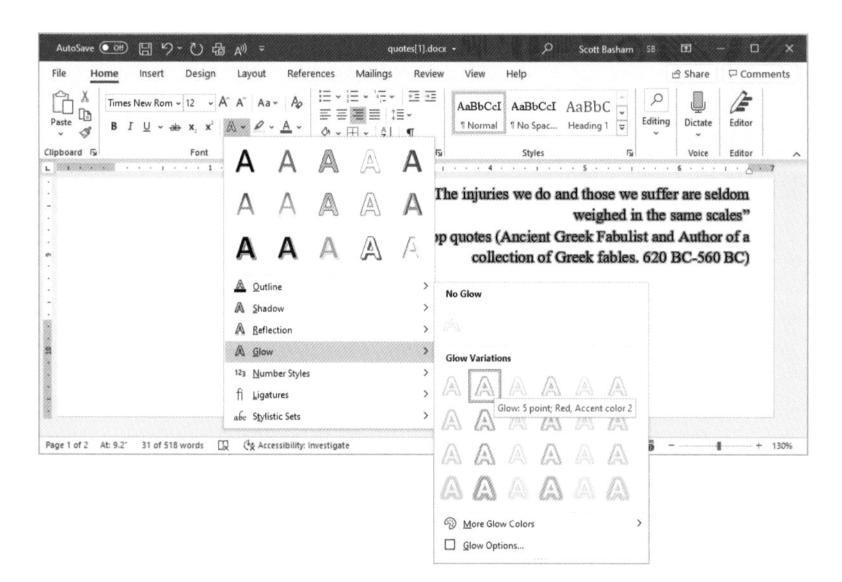

2. You can use the sub-menus to access more options within the individual effects of **Outline**, **Shadow**, **Reflection**, and **Glow**. Note that you can apply several effects at once, although just one from each category. For example, an outer shadow, a green glow and a medium reflection can all be applied to a single piece of text, as in the following example

The **Text Highlight Color** and the **Font Color** buttons also give you an instant preview of how the text will look as you hover over each color in their pop-up menus.

Formatting paragraphs

Paragraph

The Mini Toolbar gives you the ability to switch centering on and off, adjust the left indent or create a bulleted list. For most paragraph-level attributes, however, you'll use the **Paragraph** section of the **Home** tab.

Justified text has a straight edge at both the left and the right margins (apart from the final line in a paragraph). This is done by adjusting the spacing between words.

Alignment

1. If you want to change just one paragraph then simply click anywhere within it. To change multiple paragraphs, select them using any of the techniques seen earlier

2. Click on one of the alignment icons to choose left, centered, right, or justified alignment. There is an example of each type illustrated below

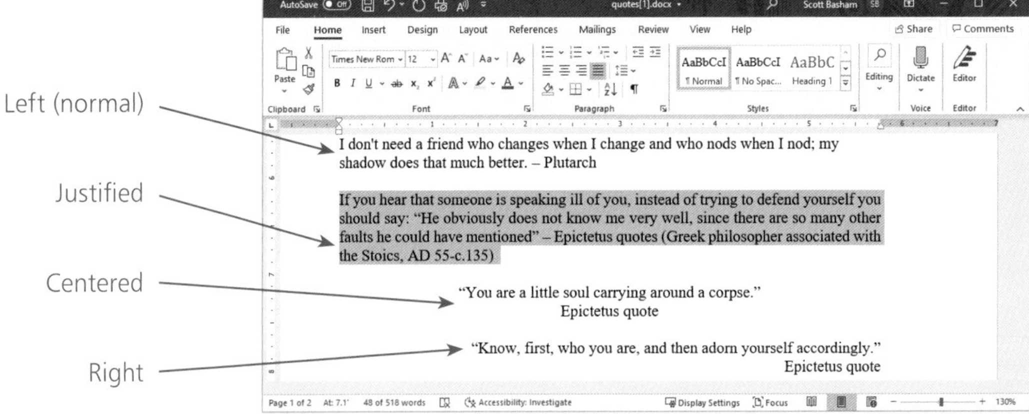

3. To see more paragraph controls, click the small open dialog icon in the lower-right corner of this section. The dialog that appears has two tabbed pages: **Indents and Spacing** and **Line and Page Breaks**. These give you accurate control over attributes such as line spacing, indentation, and hyphenation

4. Click **OK** in the dialog to view the changes to the text, or **Cancel** to discard any changes you made while in the dialog

Remember that a heading is regarded by Word as a single-line paragraph.

Bulleted lists

1. Enter the text for your list, pressing the **Return** key after each item. Select this text

2. Open the Bullets pop-up menu in the Paragraph area of the **Home** tab

A quick way to create a bulleted list is to type an asterisk at the beginning of the first line. Word will automatically change this to a bullet, and format this and all subsequent lines for you. When you have finished, leave the next line blank and just press **Return**. Word will then switch off the bulleted effect.

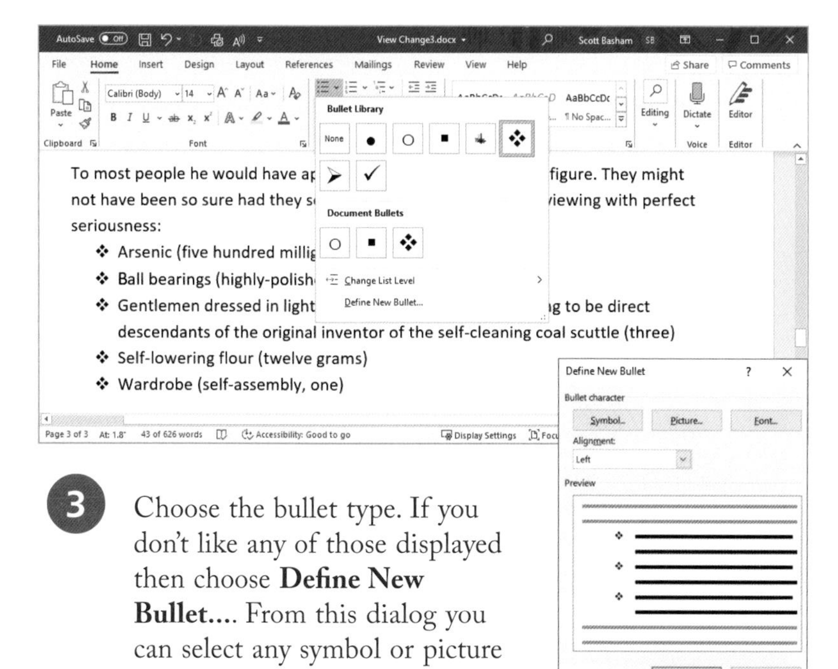

3. Choose the bullet type. If you don't like any of those displayed then choose **Define New Bullet...**. From this dialog you can select any symbol or picture

From the Define New Bullet dialog you can choose any image or character from a font for your bullet. Many fonts, such as Wingdings and Dingbats, are pictorial – this makes them a good source for bullets.

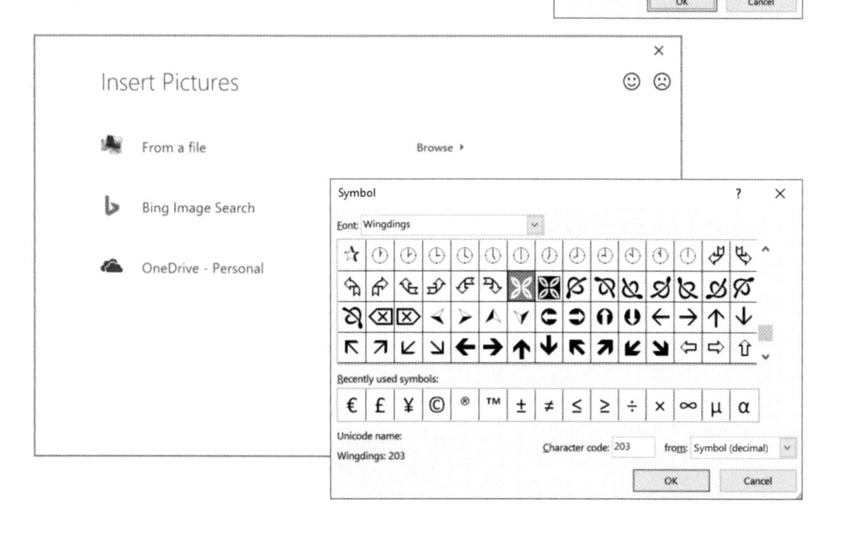

...cont'd

Numbered lists

If you choose **Control AutoFormat Options...**, you will call up a dialog with settings for this plus many other automatic features.

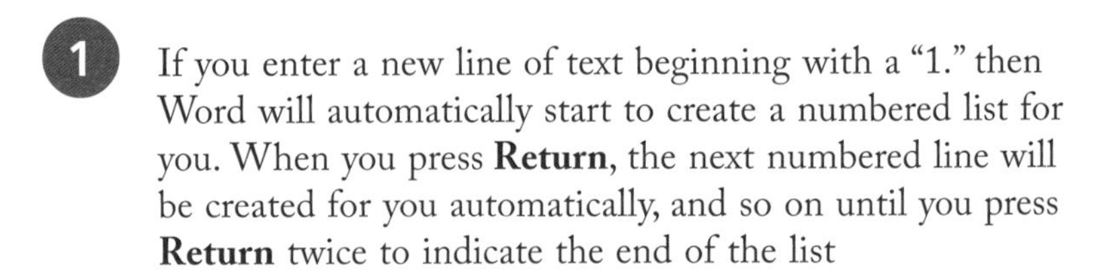

1. If you enter a new line of text beginning with a "1." then Word will automatically start to create a numbered list for you. When you press **Return**, the next numbered line will be created for you automatically, and so on until you press **Return** twice to indicate the end of the list

2. This behavior may not always be what you want. If it is not, then click on the **AutoCorrect** icon that appears by your text. You can then undo the automatic numbering just for this example, or disable the feature for future lists

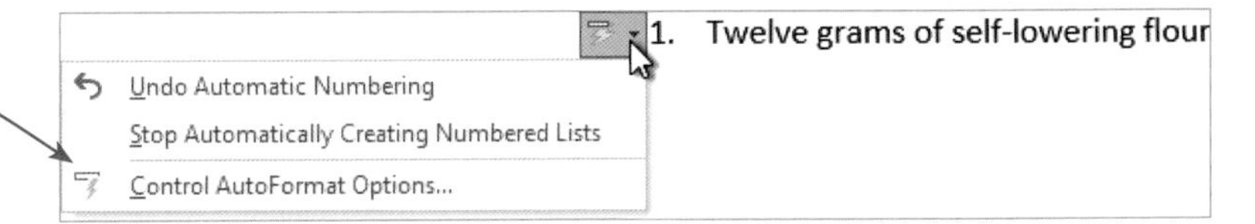

From the Numbering pop-up menu choose **Define New Number Format** to fully customize the style, format and alignment.

3. Another way to create a numbered list is to enter your text with no numbers, then select it in the normal way and open the **Numbering** pop-up menu in the Paragraph section of the **Home** tab. As you hover over the different formatting options you'll see a preview of how your text would look if you chose that option

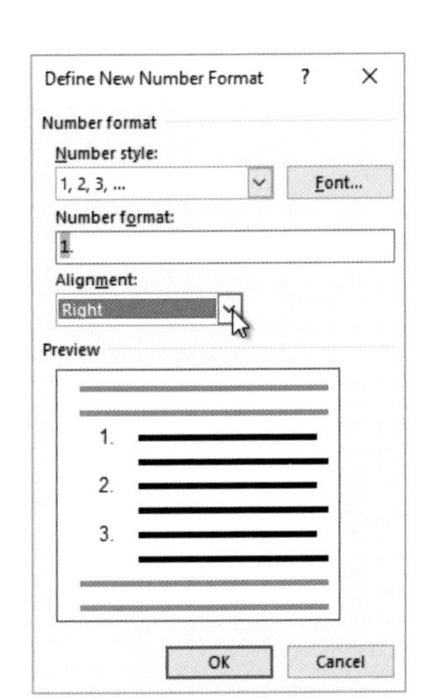

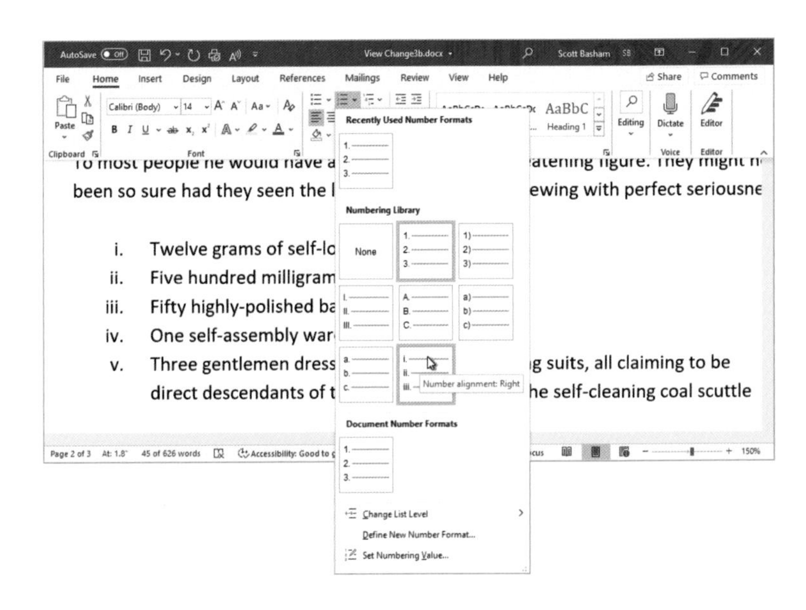

Multilevel lists

1. Create the text for your list. Press the **Tab** key at the beginning of a line once for each level of indent

2. Open the **Multilevel** pop-up menu in the Paragraph section and select the desired style

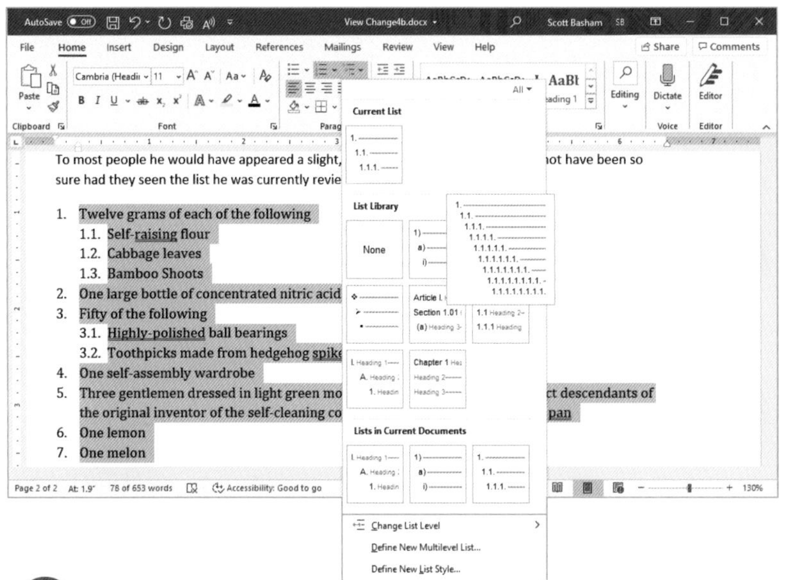

3. If you want to choose your own custom settings then select **Define New Multilevel List...**

4. By clicking the **Font** button in this dialog you can control the appearance of the number at each level of the list, separately from the main text

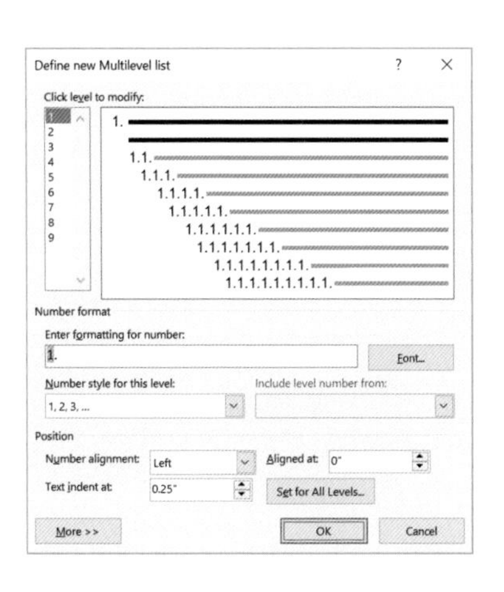

You can use the **Change List Level** option in the Multilevel pop-up menu to move an item to a higher or lower level. Alternatively, click at the beginning of a line and use **Tab** to move right or **Shift** + **Tab** to move left.

You can also sort lists as text (alphabetic), numbers or by date. To do this, first select the list then click the **Sort** icon in the Paragraph area of the **Home** tab.

Styles

Styles help you to apply a consistent set of formatting attributes to main text, headings and other elements of your document. Once you start using styles you'll be able to control your document's presentation with the minimum of tedious manual editing. Word comes with a set of styles for you to use straight away (in an area of the **Home** tab called the Styles Gallery), but it's also easy to create your own. There are two main types of style.

Don't forget

A paragraph of text can have a maximum of only one paragraph style applied to it at any time. If you select a single word and apply a paragraph style to it, then the whole of the surrounding paragraph will be affected.

Paragraph styles

These can contain information about virtually any text attribute (e.g. font, size, alignment, spacing and color). They are called paragraph styles because they are applied at the paragraph level. In the Styles area, paragraph styles are marked with a ¶ symbol.

Applying a paragraph style

1. Choose the paragraph of text you want to format by clicking anywhere within it, or multiple paragraphs using any of the techniques covered in the previous chapter

2. If you hover over a style from the Styles Gallery in the Toolbar you'll see a preview of your text using the style. Choose one of the styles marked with a ¶ symbol. To see the full list of available styles, use the scroll bars or the symbol in the bottom right of the Styles tools. Click once on the style to apply it to your text

There is a third type known as a linked style. This can contain both character- and paragraph-level attributes. See pages 52-53 for more about this.

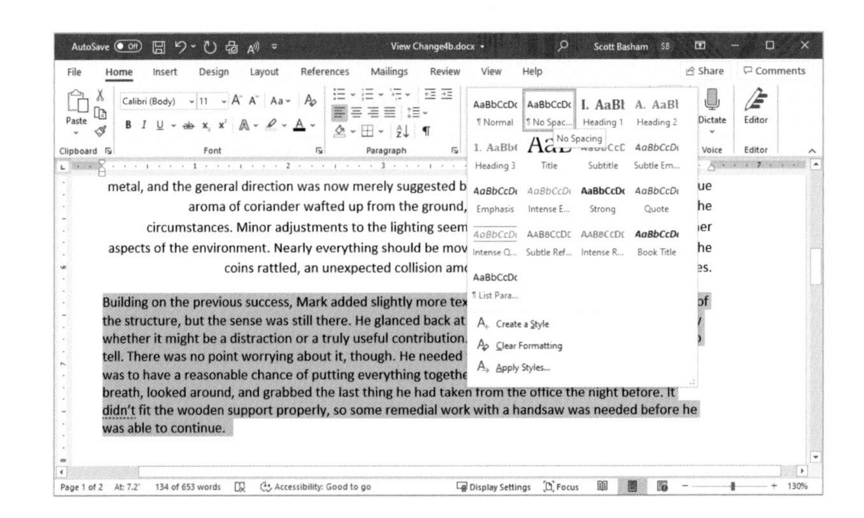

Character styles

These can contain information about character-level attributes only (e.g. font and size) but not alignment (which is a paragraph-level attribute). They can be applied to any amount of text, even individual characters or words. Character styles have no ¶ symbol.

It is very easy to accidentally override all your carefully-chosen text settings simply by clicking on a style in the Toolbar. If this happens, choose **Undo** from the Quick Access Toolbar or press **Ctrl** + **Z**.

Applying a character style

1. Select the text you want to change
2. Look for a style that doesn't have a ¶ symbol, and hover over it with the mouse. Your text will temporarily preview the selected style until you move off. Click directly on a style to apply it permanently to the selected text

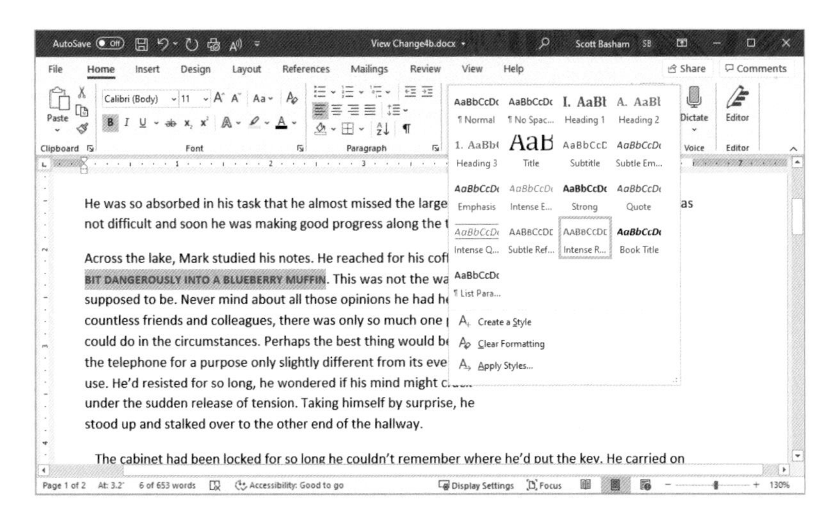

Removing a style from text

1. Select the text in question
2. Click the ⊽ symbol in the bottom right of the Styles tools to see the full list of styles plus a menu below these
3. Choose **Clear Formatting** to reset the text to a style called Normal. It's possible to redefine Normal to anything you like, as you will see in the next few pages

...cont'd

Creating a style

1. The easiest way to create a new style is to select some text that already has all, or most, of the attributes you want to use

2. Open the Styles options by clicking the icon in the lower-right corner of the Styles area

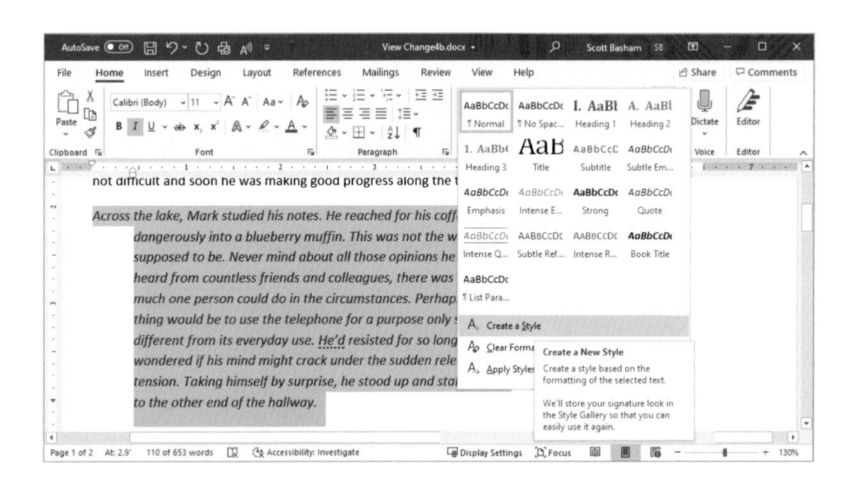

You can also create a style directly from a special Styles panel, which is described in detail on page 50.

3. Choose **Create a Style** from the menu that appears

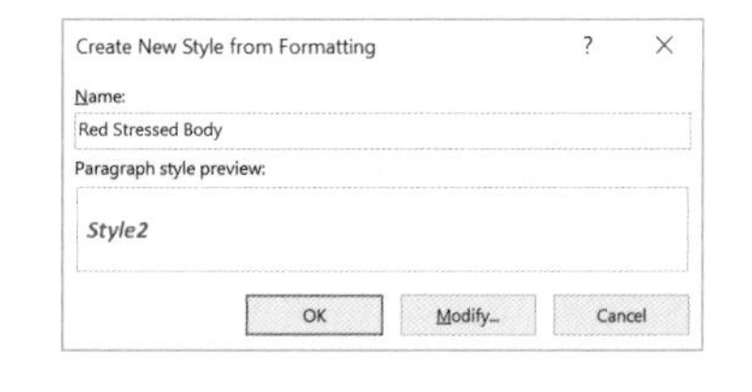

4. The dialog shows you a preview of the style you're about to create. If this doesn't look correct then click the **Cancel** button and examine the text you selected. If necessary, alter its formatting or select a different sample of text

You can apply a style to text using the keyboard shortcut **Ctrl** + **Shift** + **S**. An Apply Styles window will appear – type the first few letters of the style's name. If the desired style appears then click the **Apply** button; if not then select from the list.

5. If you're already happy with the style's attributes then click **OK**, otherwise select **Modify** to edit the settings

Modifying a style using the dialog box

1. Right-click the style in the Styles panel and select **Modify...**

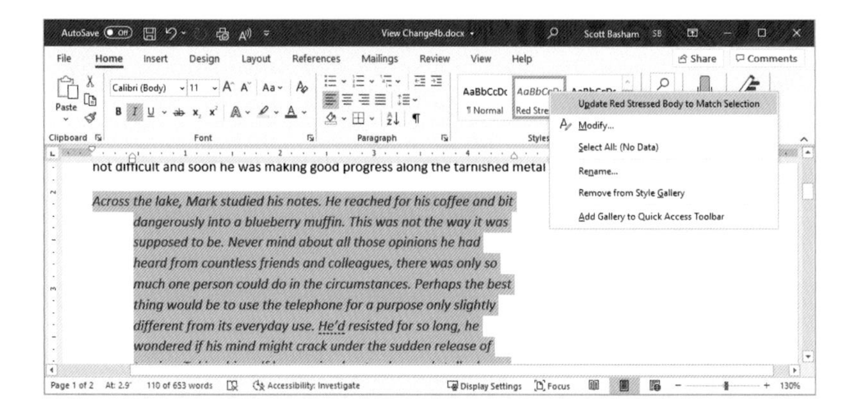

2. The following dialog appears. From here, you can rename the style or alter attributes such as font, size, or effects including Bold and Italic

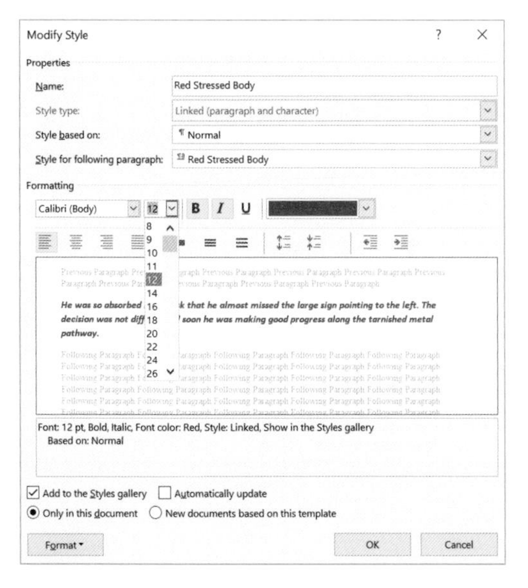

Many other useful settings can be made from this dialog. If you click the **Format** button, you can access dialogs for Font, Paragraph, Tabs and several other categories.

3. When you're happy with your settings, click **OK**. If there's any text in your document already using this style then it'll be automatically updated

Another way to modify a style is to type **Ctrl** + **Shift** + **S**. The Apply Styles window will appear – type the first few letters of the style's name. If the desired style appears then click the **Modify** button; if not then select from the list and click **Modify**.

You can also make styles available across different documents. To do this, type **Ctrl** + **Alt** + **Shift** + **S** to open the Styles panel, click the **Manage Styles** button at the bottom right, and then click the **Import/Export** button.

...cont'd

Modifying a style using document text

One problem with modifying styles via the dialog box is that you don't see the results until you return to the main document. The following method doesn't suffer from this drawback:

1. Select text that already uses the style you plan to modify, and make the desired formatting changes

2. Right-click on the name in the Styles area and choose the **Update ... to Match Selection** option

When following these steps, make sure you click the style name with the right mouse button rather than the left. Left-clicking will reset the selected text to the original style definition. If you do this accidentally then use the **Undo** button, or **Ctrl** + **Z**, and try again.

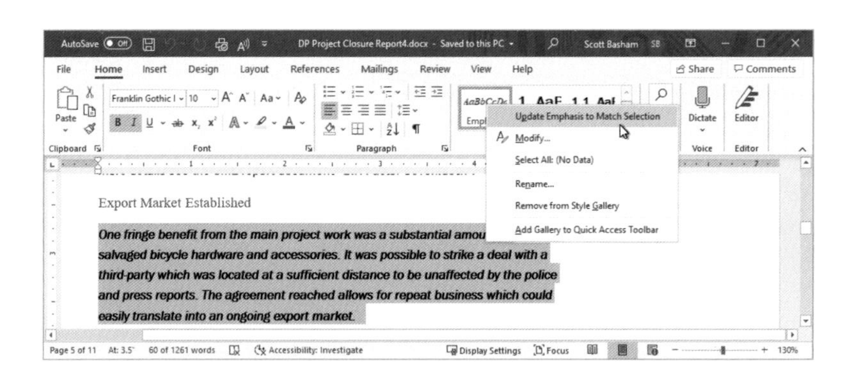

Collapsing and expanding headings

This Word feature allows you to hide or reveal text below any headings that were formatted with the built-in styles.

1. Click the small triangle ▶ to the left of a heading

2. Click again to toggle the display of the contents On/Off

If your document is structured using multiple levels of heading (Heading 1, Heading 2, Heading 3, etc.) then collapse and expand can be used at each level to hide or reveal layers of detail in your text.

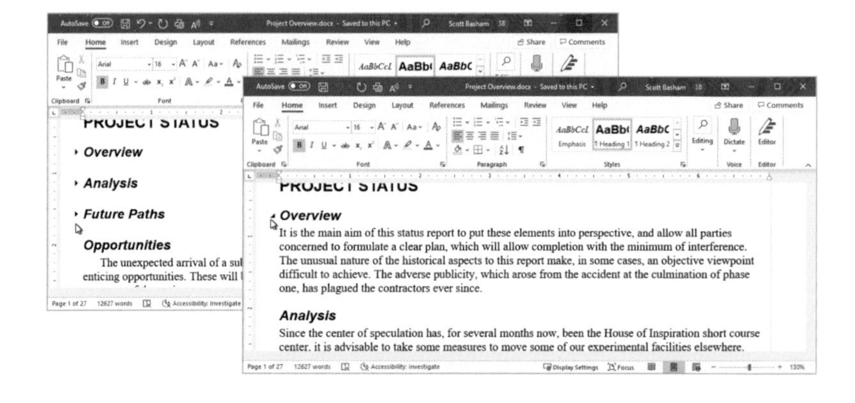

3 Editing in more depth

This chapter covers more advanced text editing including manipulation of styles, the Ruler, and using tabs to help with precision layout. It also covers some special effects, equations, and symbols.

The Styles panel

In the last chapter, you started to use styles. You can create more advanced types of style from the **Styles** panel.

1. Open the Styles panel by clicking on the icon in the bottom-right corner of the Styles area

2. You'll see a list of recommended styles

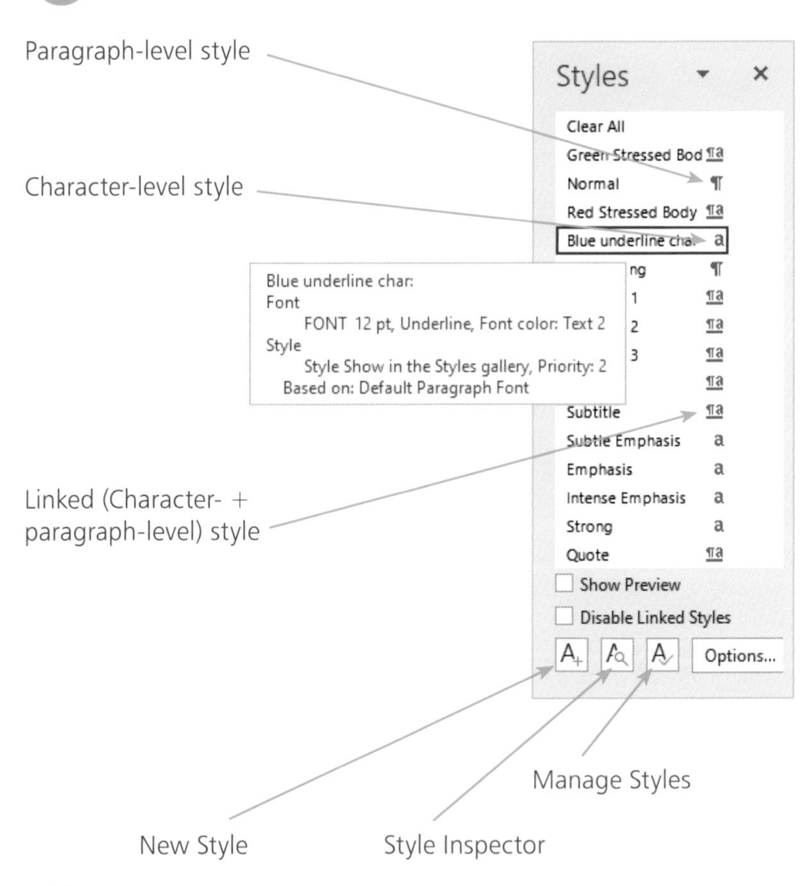

3. If you allow your mouse to hover over a particular style name, a summary box will appear. This lists the essential attributes of the style

4. Click on **Options** to select which styles should be shown in the Styles window. You can also control how they are displayed and sorted

If you activate the **Show Preview** option located at the bottom of the Styles panel, then the style names will appear using their own attributes.

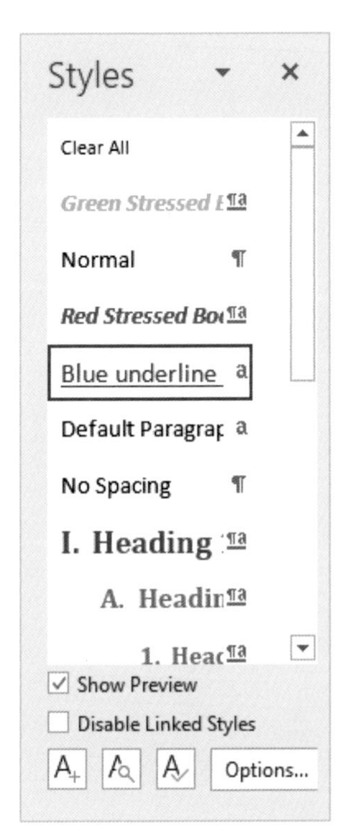

Paragraph-level styles

Creating a new paragraph-level style

1. Make sure the Styles panel is open. If it isn't, click on the icon in the bottom-right corner of the Styles area

2. Click the **New Style** icon near the bottom

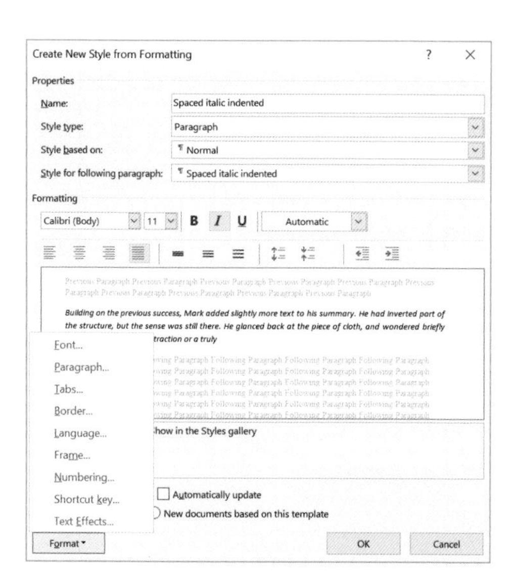

3. Enter a style name, and choose **Paragraph** from the **Style type:** drop-down

4. Select the other formatting options as appropriate. When you click **OK**, your new style becomes available in the Styles area. Note the ¶ symbol next to its name

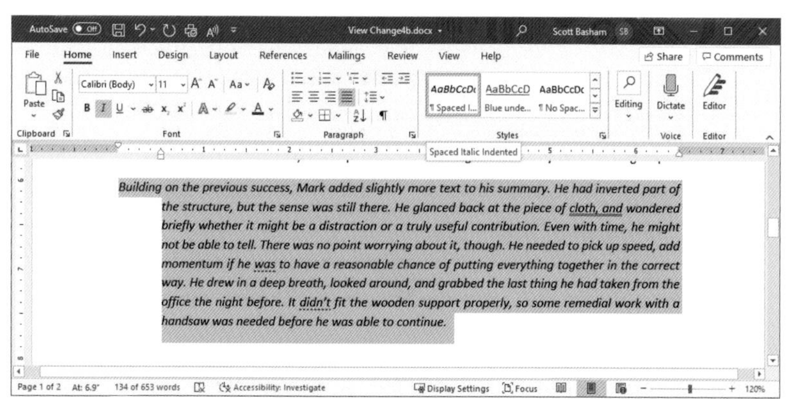

Paragraph styles are always applied to entire paragraphs. If you select just a few characters and apply a paragraph style, then the whole of the surrounding paragraph will be affected.

Linked styles

A linked style can be used at either the paragraph or the character level, depending on the amount of text selected when it's applied.

Creating a new linked style

1. Open the Styles panel by clicking the icon in the bottom right of the Styles area. Click the **New Style** icon

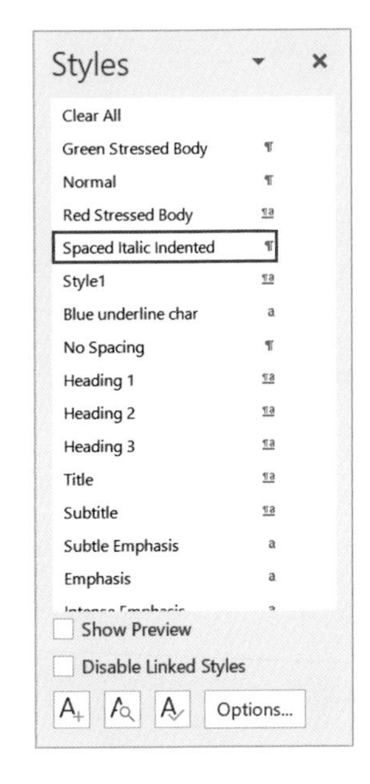

2. Give your style a name. For style type, select **Linked (paragraph and character)**

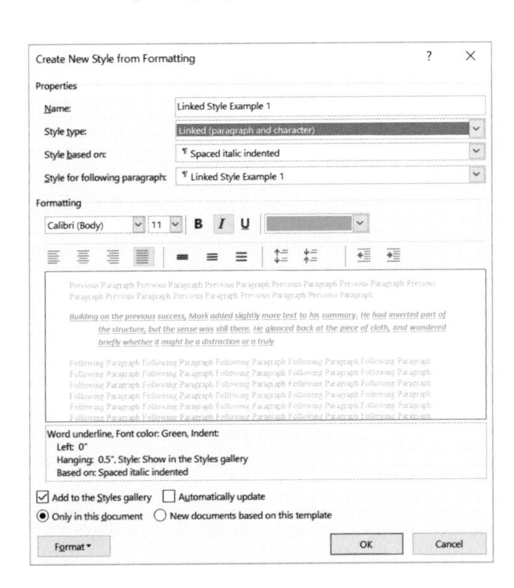

Try not to use too many effects if you have lots of small text, as they can make it unreadable.

3. Select the other formatting options as appropriate. In this example we've chosen green italic text with individual words underlined. You can set the word underline feature by clicking **Format** and choosing **Font**

4. Click **OK** when you're done. Your new style is now available. In the Styles panel, the name is followed by a ¶a symbol to indicate it's a linked style

5. Select a whole paragraph of text (the quickest way to do this is to triple-click anywhere inside the paragraph), locate your new style in the **Home** tab and apply it

6. Now, select an individual word in a different paragraph and apply the style

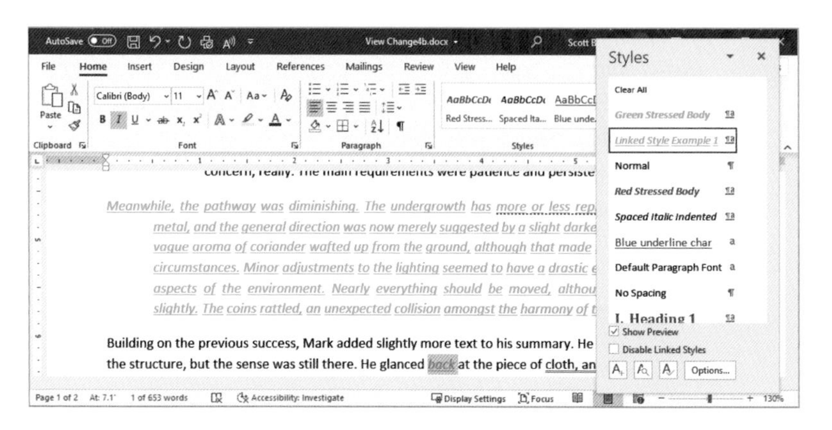

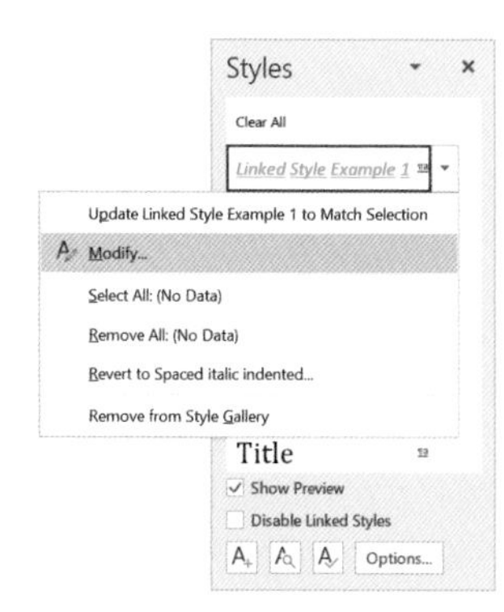

7. To modify a style, click the ▾ symbol next to the style's name in the Styles panel and select **Modify...**. Note that the style type setting is now grayed out. Once a style has been created as linked or a character, its type cannot be changed

Modify Style

Properties

Name: Linked Style Example 1

Style type: Linked (paragraph and character)

Style based on: Spaced Italic Indented

Style for following paragraph: Linked Style Example 1

Formatting

Calibri (Body) 11 B I U

Previous Paragraph Previous Paragraph Previous Paragraph Previous Paragraph Previous Paragraph Previous Paragraph Previous Paragraph Previous Paragraph Previous Paragraph Previous Paragraph

He was so absorbed in his task that he almost missed the large sign pointing to the left. The decision was not difficult and soon he was making good progress along the tarnished metal pathway.

Following Paragraph Following Paragraph

Word underline, Font color: Green, Style: Linked, Show in the Styles gallery
Based on: Spaced Italic Indented

☑ Add to the Styles gallery ☐ Automatically update

◉ Only in this document ○ New documents based on this template

Format ▾ OK Cancel

Only a paragraph-level style can have its type changed. Although you can't change the others once created, you can always create a new style based on an existing one. To do this, simply select the style in the Styles panel then click the **New Style** button. You can now set the type for the new style.

Mixing styles in a paragraph

Character-level and paragraph-level styles can be used in the same paragraph. In this case, the character-level style's attributes take precedence. The following example is a good illustration of this.

1. Select an entire paragraph and apply a paragraph-level style to it. In this example, a style called **Green Stressed Body** was used. It's Arial, 10 point, green, italic, bold text

2. Now, select a small group of words within the paragraph and apply a character-level style. Here we've used a style called **Blue underline char style**, which is 12 point, underlined and blue. The style definition has no font name built in so the font remains the same as that for **Green Stressed Body**

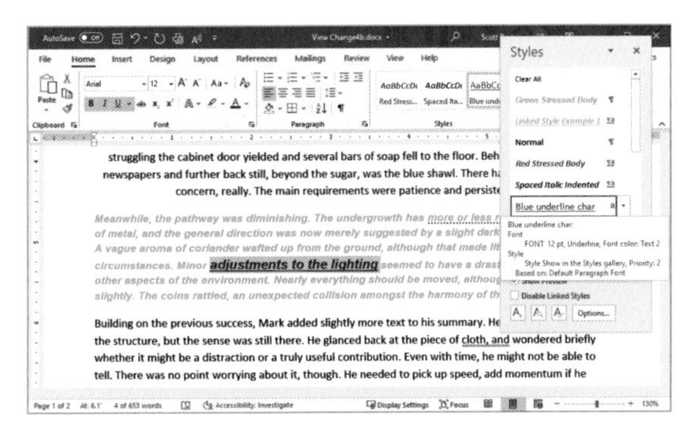

3. Note that the character-level style's attributes override those of the paragraph-level style

4. Now, with the same group of words selected, adjust the size to make it larger

5. Now, open the Styles window and click on the Style Inspector icon

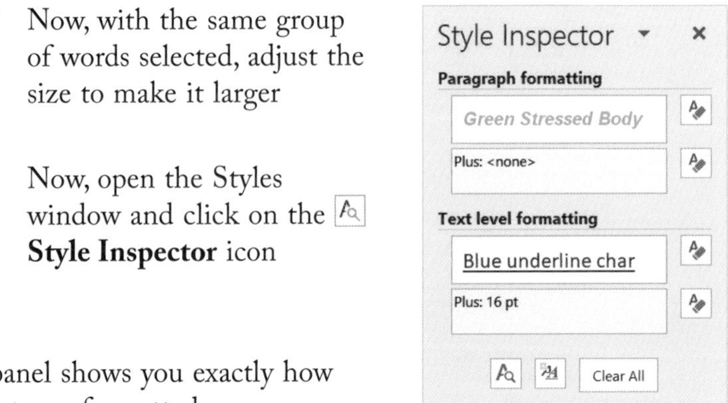

This panel shows you exactly how the text was formatted.

The selected words in this example still follow the attributes of the paragraph style, except where they have been overridden by the character-level style. So, if you edited **Green Stressed Body** to make its font Times New Roman, this would affect all the text. If, however, you made **Green Stressed Body** a darker green color, the text seen highlighted here would still be blue.

Using style sets

If you've been using Word's built-in styles, or if you've created your own by editing them and keeping the same names, then you can switch the style set to redesign your document completely.

1. Make sure the **Design** tab is active, and hover over a style set to see a preview of how your document would look

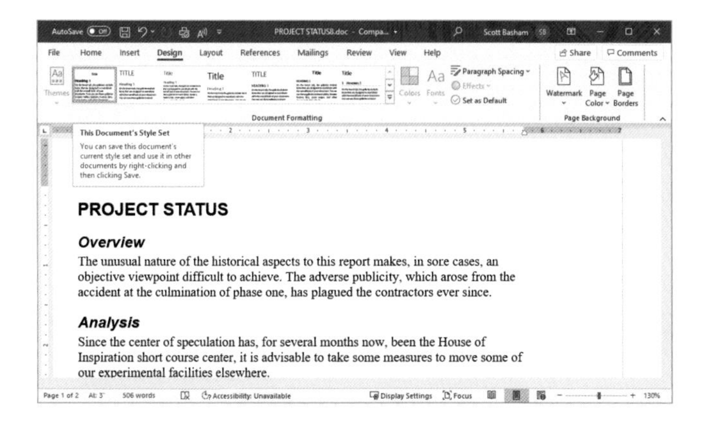

2. To see more options, click the ▿ icon in the lower-right corner of the style set area. Select an option to make the change permanent

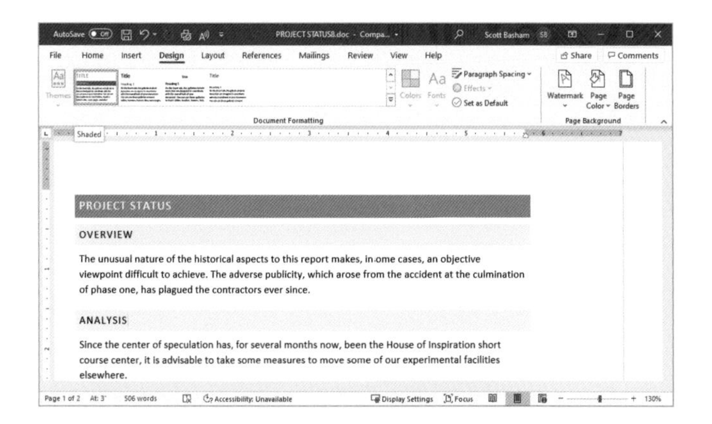

3. Each style in the style set will replace the style of the same name in your current document. Any text that uses these styles will be reformatted automatically. This allows you to give even long documents a new and consistent design with the minimum of fuss

As your documents grow, you will want to check your formatting and overall design is consistent and easy to change, so make sure you use styles rather than formatting your text directly in the page.

The Ruler

Text that is laid out neatly with accurate horizontal positioning greatly helps to give your documents a professional look. Effective use of white space, including tabulation, is the key to this.

Hot tip

The horizontal Ruler can be displayed in most page views. However, the vertical Ruler displays in Print Layout view only.

Making the Ruler visible

Make sure that you are in **Print Layout** view. Activate the **View** tab and also make sure that the **Ruler** option in the Show area is active

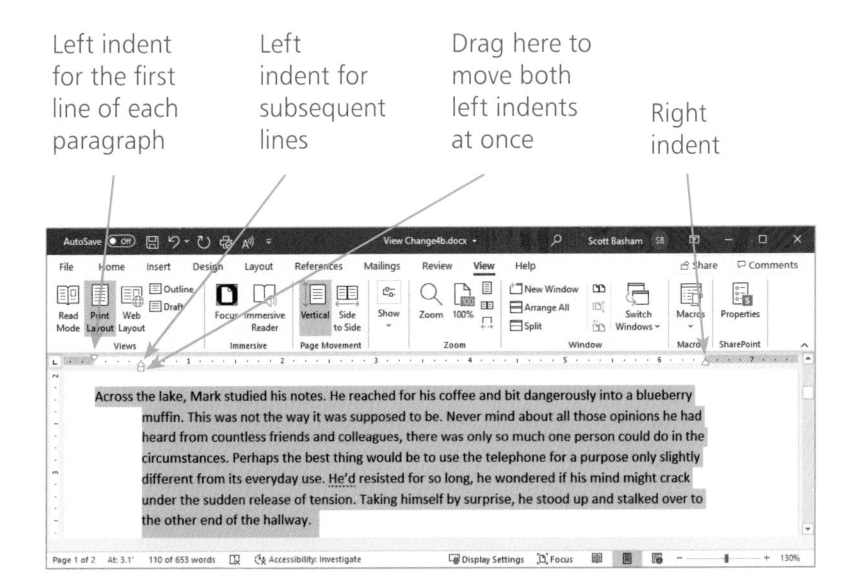

2 Experiment by moving the left and right indent markers on the Ruler and observe what happens on the page. It helps if you have several lines of text selected

Hot tip

You can change the measurements system from the File tab by choosing **Options** and then **Advanced**. In the Display section go to the option **Show measurements in units of:** and choose a different value. Points and Picas are sometimes useful as they match font sizes.

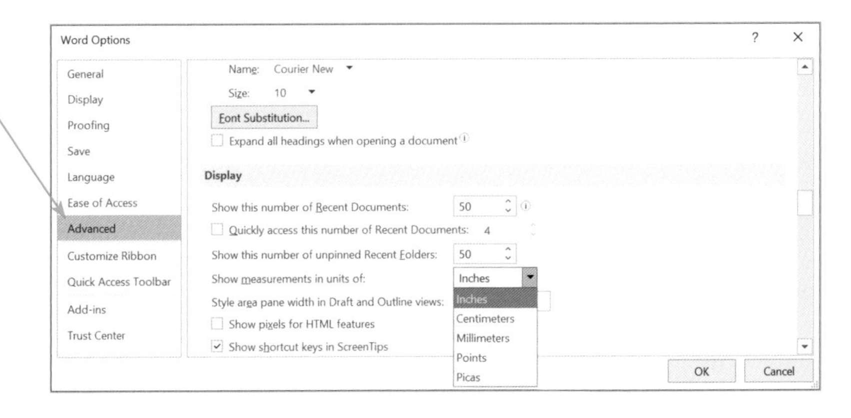

Tabulation

Tab stops are paragraph-level attributes that define what happens if the **Tab** key is pressed when entering text. If you select a paragraph and examine the Ruler, you'll see any tab stops that have been defined. If no tab stops have been defined for this paragraph then the default tabs apply. These are marked in the Ruler as small vertical lines, spaced out at regular intervals in its lower section.

Overriding default tabulation

1. Click the **Show/Hide ¶** button in the Paragraph section of the **Home** tab. This will allow you to see where you've pressed the **Tab** key – shown as a small arrow pointing to the right

2. Type in some text similar to the example below. Note that each text element is separated from the next by a tab character. Don't worry about how far across the screen the tab takes you – this will be altered soon. Make sure you only press **Tab** once between one element and the next

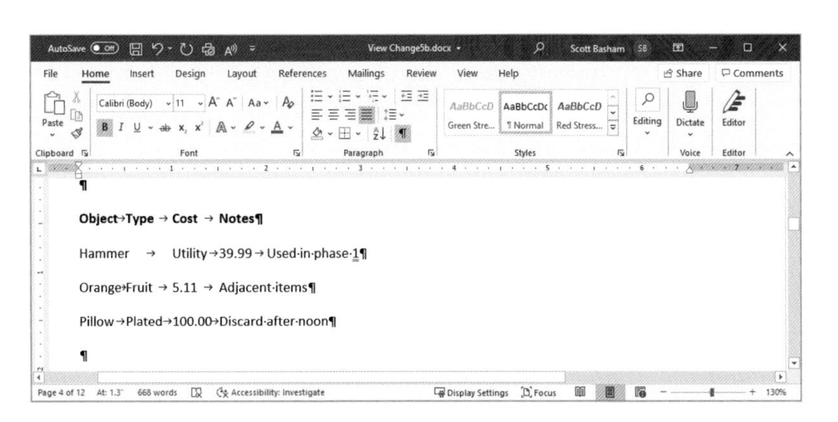

3. Also, make sure that you press **Return** once at the end of each line. This will show up as a ¶ character as in the illustration above. The tab characters you entered display as right-pointing arrows

4. Now, select all the text you just entered. With the tabs in place you are ready to control exactly what they do

When you click the **Show/Hide** ¶ button, paragraph marks also appear visibly as the ¶ character.

...cont'd

5. Make sure that the ∟ icon is visible at the left side of the Ruler. This means that when you create a tab stop it will use left alignment. If it looks different, then click on it until it changes to the correct ∟ symbol

6. Click in the Ruler around the 1-inch mark to create a new left tab. Drag it left or right to adjust its position

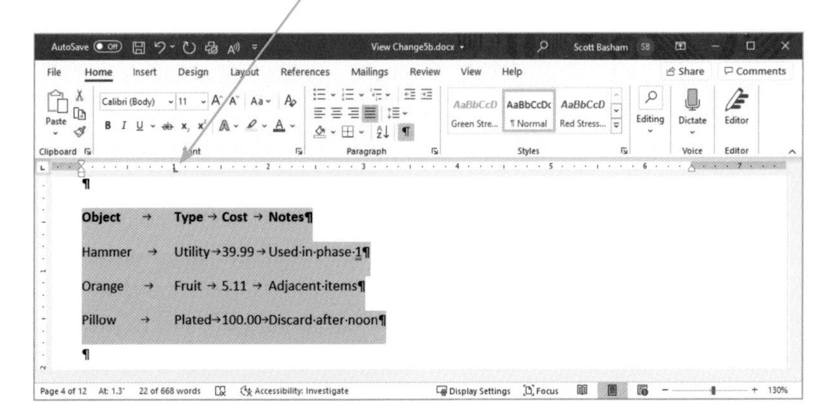

7. The characters should move so that the text following the first tab lines up vertically along its left edge. Making sure that your text is still selected, create some more tab stops. The text automatically moves to follow your new design

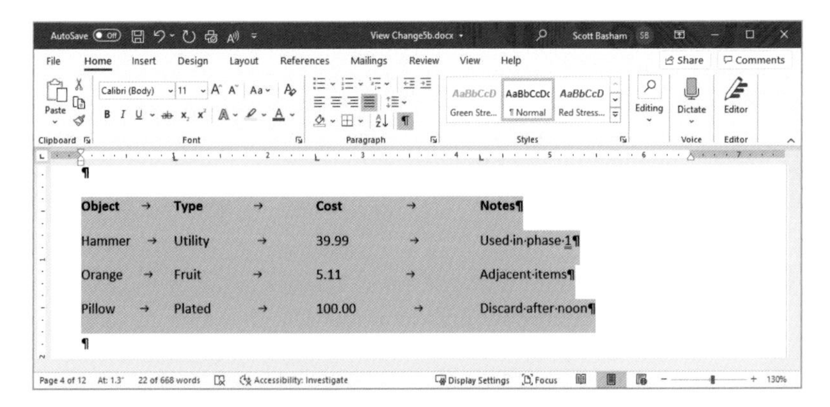

8. If you click at the end of the last line then press **Return**, you can add more lines using the same tab formatting

Hot tip

To see the distances between tab stops and the left and right indents, hold down the **Alt** key as you drag any of the Ruler icons horizontally.

Different types of tabs

1. Keeping your text selected, delete the right-most tab by dragging it downwards from the Ruler until it disappears
2. Now, click on the ⌊ symbol (at the very left edge of the Ruler) until it changes into a ⌋
3. Click in the Ruler near the right edge of the page. The text is moved so that it lines up along its right edge

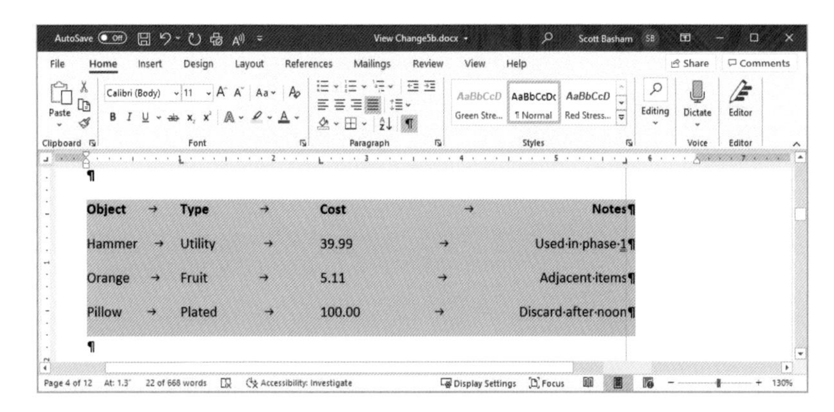

4. If the text fails to align correctly then adjust the tab positions by dragging them left or right (the screen will update automatically so you can see how things are changing). Now, call up the **Tabs** dialog by double-clicking directly on any tab

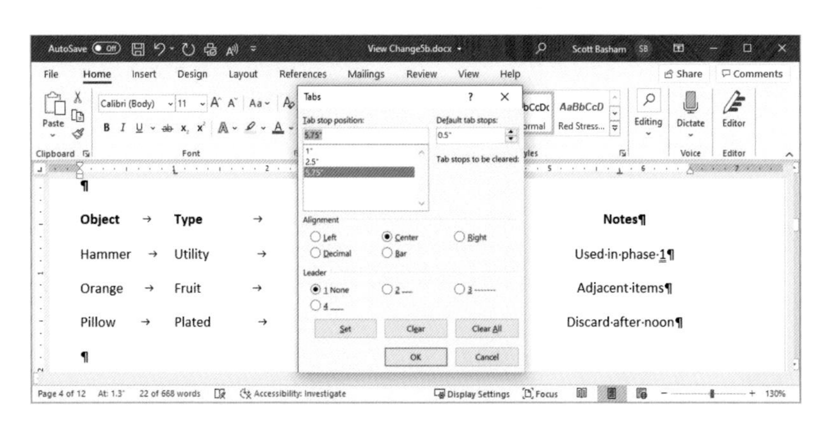

When you click on the ⌊ symbol, the icons cycle between left-, center-, right- and decimal-aligned tabs. After these there is the bar (vertical line) icon, followed by first-line indent and hanging-indent icons.

...cont'd

Tabulation can be built into a style definition, and so used consistently throughout a document.

5. Select a tab from the list. You can now change its type, add a leader (in the below example, we lead into the second tab with a line of dots), set new tabs, or clear tabs

6. Also in this example, bar tabs were created at 4 inches and 6 inches. These create vertical lines

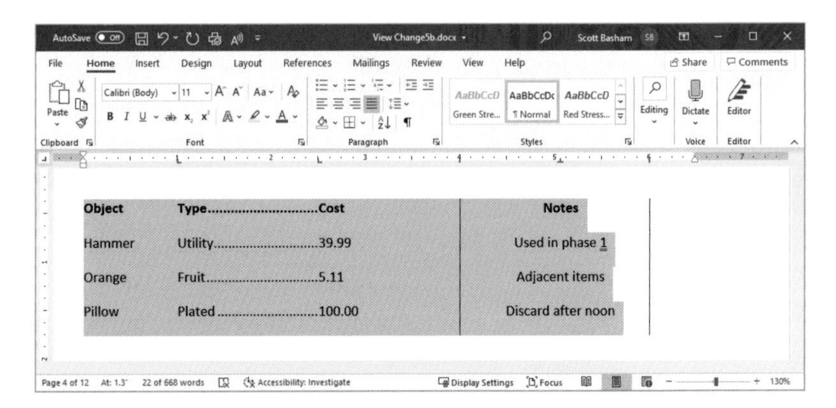

7. Sometimes the first line, since it contains headings, needs a slightly different form of alignment compared with the main text. In the above example, we might want the numbers to line up with a decimal tab, but leave the item on the first line (the heading "Cost") with a left tab and no leader of dots. Simply select the relevant lines before making the necessary changes

A decimal tab is useful for aligning numbers vertically so that their decimal point is in the same place.

8. When you're done, click the **Show/Hide ¶** button in the Paragraph section of the **Home** tab. This makes the hidden characters invisible again so that you get a better idea of the appearance of the final result

Removing all tabs

1. Make sure all the relevant text is selected, then double-click on a tab to summon the **Tabs** dialog

2. Click **Clear All**, then **OK**

Editing controls

The right-hand side of the **Home** tab contains the **Editing** area with its **Find**, **Replace** and **Select** tools. These sometimes work in conjunction with the Navigation and Selection panes that you'll see later on.

The Find button

1. Press **Ctrl** + **F** or click the **Find** button in the **Home** tab. Click on its pop-up menu rather than the main part of the icon to see three options, one of which is **Find**

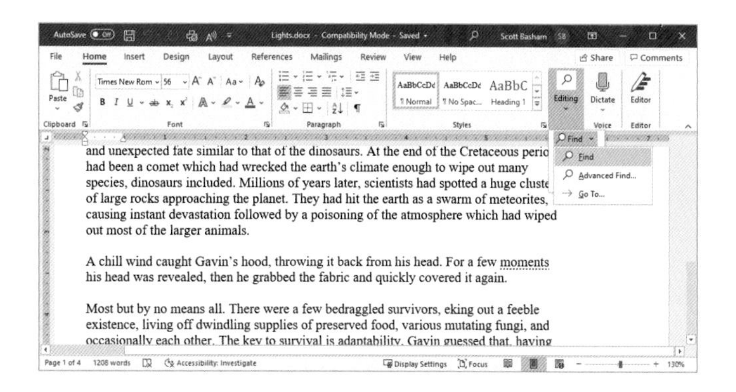

2. The Navigation pane appears along the left side of the screen. Enter your search text

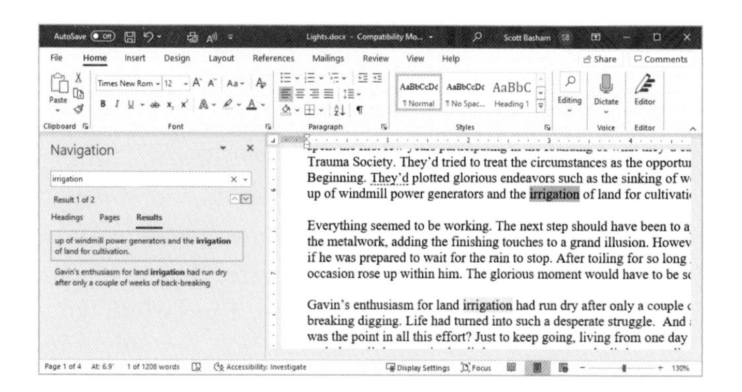

3. Word will immediately highlight all matches in the document, and also list them in the Navigation pane. If you scroll through these and click on an item in the Navigation pane, the main page will automatically move to that particular instance

If you click the pop-up menu icon (the small black triangle) next to the search text, you can ask Word to find other elements such as graphics, tables or equations. See Chapter 5 for more on pictures and graphics.

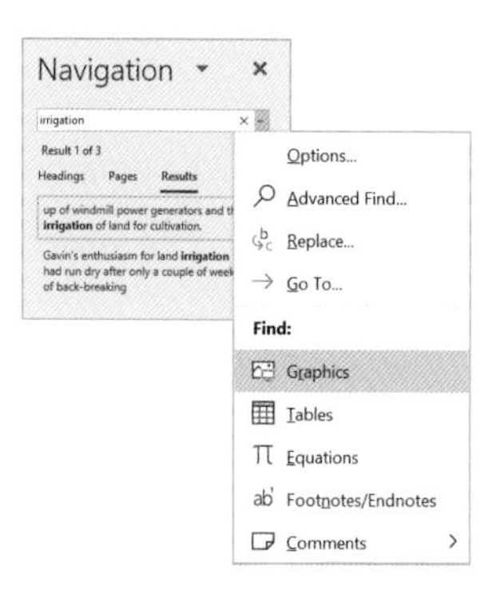

...cont'd

Advanced Find

Although the Navigation pane is useful for instant searches, you may want to use the **Advanced Find** feature to access more flexible and powerful options.

1. Open the pop-up menu next to the Find icon in the Editing area and choose **Advanced Find**

2. Click the **More >>** button to see the full set of options

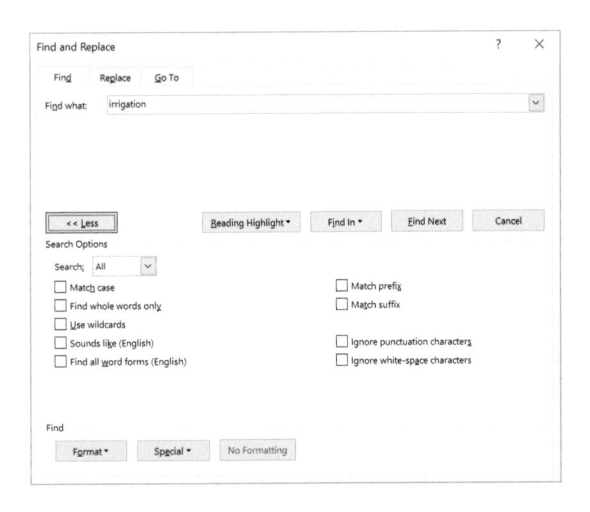

3. Enter the search text in the **Find what:** box

4. Note the option to match case – keeping this switched off means that searches are not case-sensitive

5. By clicking the **Format** button you can base your search on text attributes such as font or size. If you set some attributes and also enter text in the **Find what:** box then Word will look for that particular text, but only if its attributes match what you've specified

6. To go ahead and run the search, click the **Find In** button and choose **Main Document**. If you happen to have selected some text within your document it's also possible to search just the selection

The **Find In** button will also let you search for text within headers and footers, or inside text boxes (see Chapter 4 for more on these).

Find and Replace

Word can search through your document or selection, and substitute text, text attributes, or even a combination of the two.

1. To access the **Find and Replace** dialog you can either click directly on the **Replace** icon in the Editing area or use the keyboard shortcut **Ctrl** + **H**

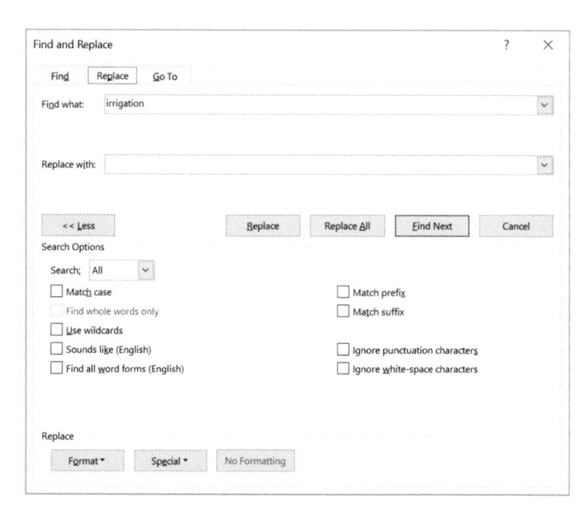

2. Enter the search text in the **Find what:** box. While the cursor is still in this field you can also, optionally, click the **Format** button to specify search attributes

3. You can specify replacement text in the **Replace with:** box. However, this example is of a formatting change rather than a text substitution. In this case, ensure the cursor is in the **Replace with:** box rather than the **Find what:** box before clicking the **Format** button

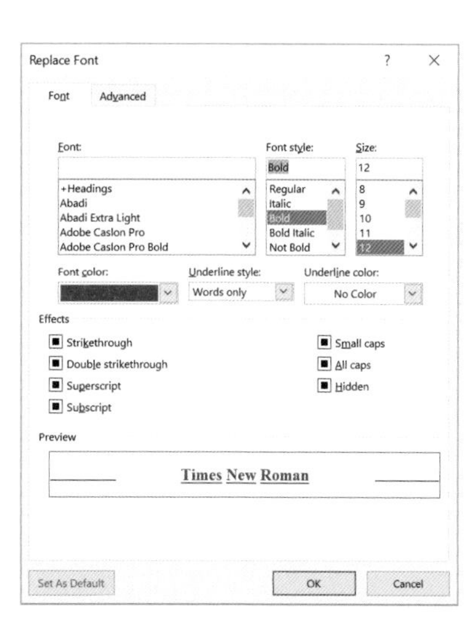

You can also summon the Replace dialog box by using the pop-up menu in the Navigation pane, if available.

The Replace function can make drastic changes to your document, particularly if you use the **Replace All** button.

4. You can now either use the **Find Next** and **Replace** buttons to check each substitution one at a time or, if you're confident to do it all at once, click **Replace All**

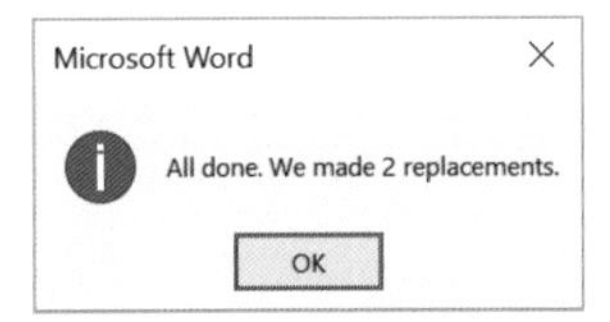

5. A message tells you how many changes were made. If this number worries you at all then use the **Undo** button (or **Ctrl** + **Z**) and then step through the changes one at a time with the **Find Next** and **Replace** buttons

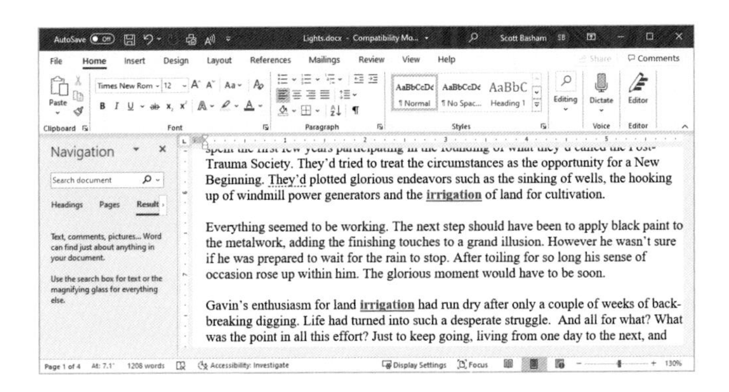

6. In the above example, all instances of the word "irrigation" were made bold, red and underlined

You can also access the Go To feature by using the pop-up menu in the Navigation pane, or with the keyboard shortcut **Ctrl** + **G**.

Go To

The pop-up menu on the **Find** button in the Editing area has a **Go To** option that summons this dialog. It lets you jump easily to another document location, using a range of target options.

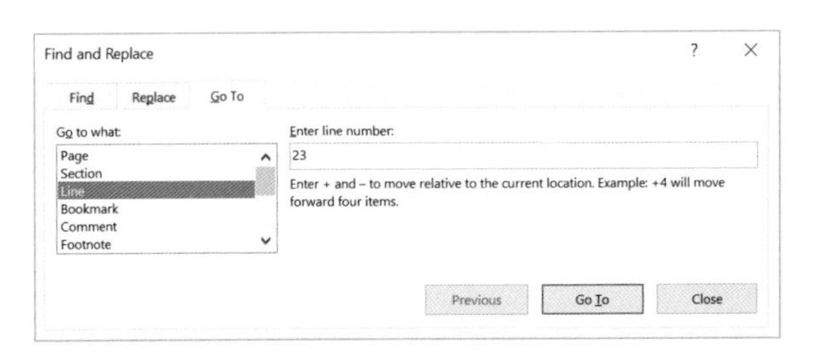

Using special characters

The Find and Replace dialog box also allows you to work with special characters such as paragraph markers or wildcards. It can even match words that sound similar to the search text.

Choose **Advanced Find** and enter your search text. Click **Special** to see a list of special search characters

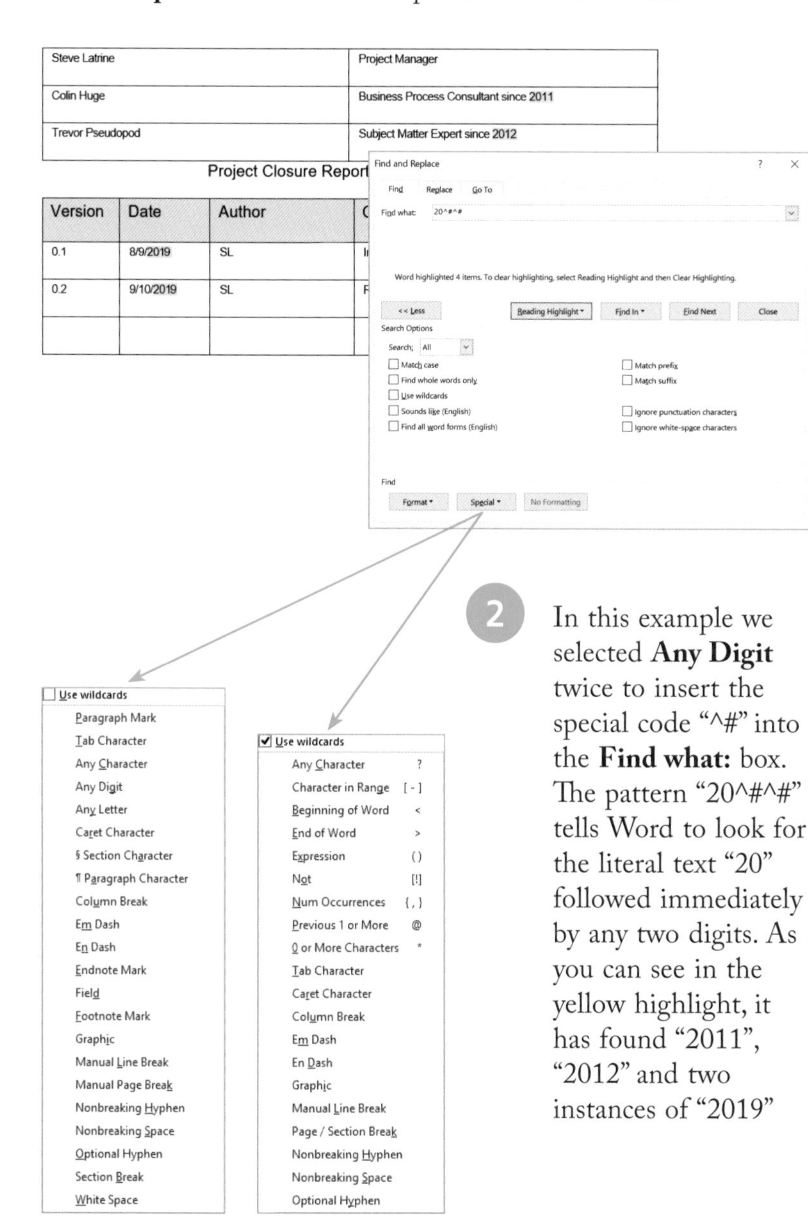

2. In this example we selected **Any Digit** twice to insert the special code "^#" into the **Find what:** box. The pattern "20^#^#" tells Word to look for the literal text "20" followed immediately by any two digits. As you can see in the yellow highlight, it has found "2011", "2012" and two instances of "2019"

If you activate the **Use wildcards** checkbox then the Special pop-up menu offers further options that can help make your searches very powerful. The illustration on the left shows both versions of the menu.

Advanced text effects

WordArt lets you present text using a wide range of visual effects.

Using WordArt

1. Select your text and then click on the **WordArt** icon in the Text area of the **Insert** tab

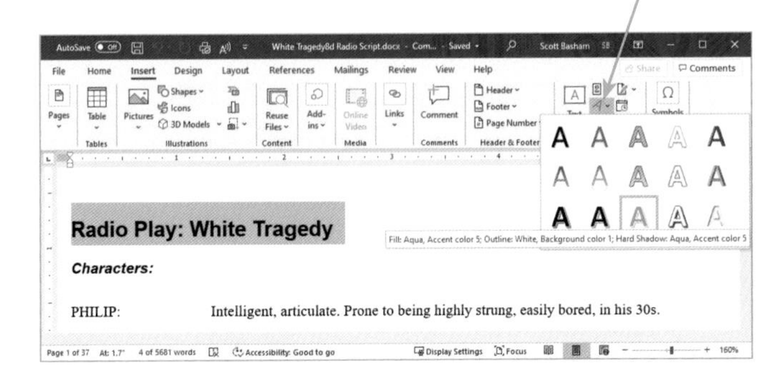

Initially, the new WordArt object is independent of the main text, so you can easily move it by dragging. You can make it part of the main text by selecting it, clicking on its **Text Wrap** icon that appears on the right side, then selecting **In Line with Text**.

2. Choose an effect from the gallery

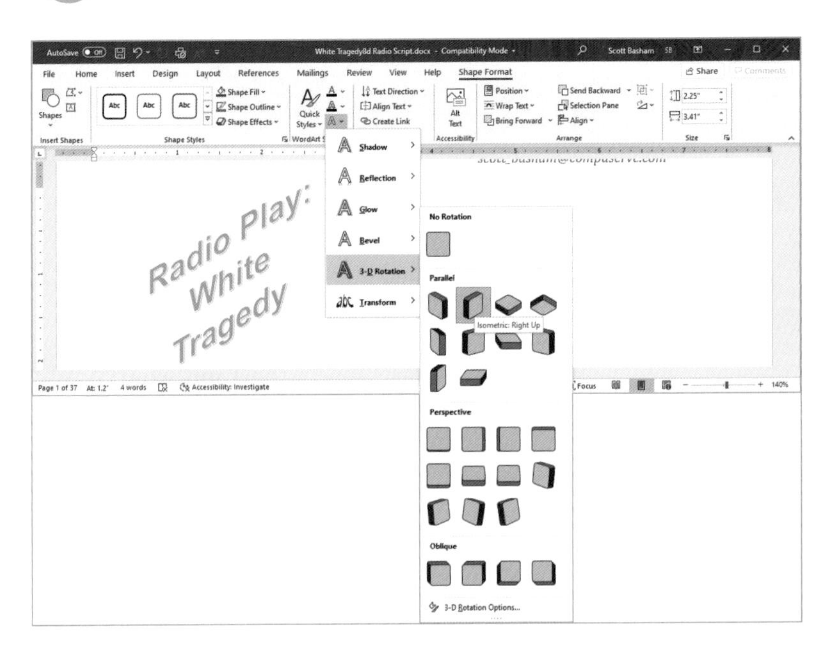

Whenever your WordArt object is selected, the **Shape Format** tab is displayed. This can be used to customize its appearance further.

3. There's a set of WordArt tools in the **Shape Format** tab. Click on the ◲ symbol in WordArt Styles

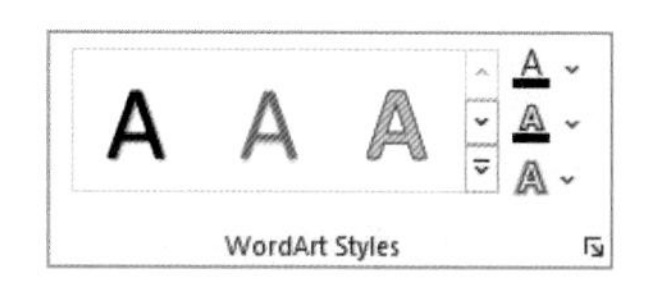

4. Select or change an option to see the results in your document. You can resize the text box for the new object by dragging on its corner handles, or rotate using the top handle

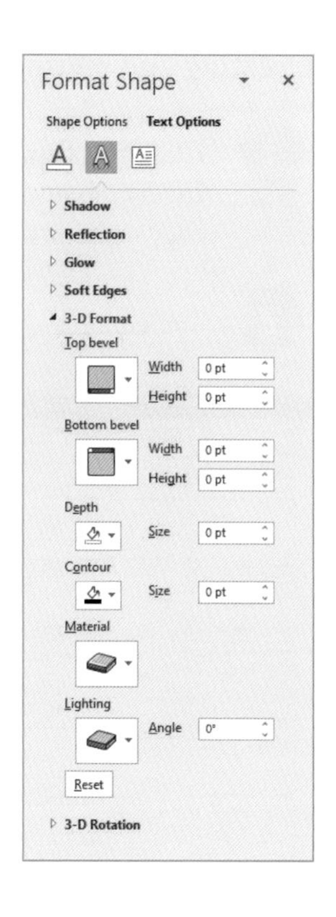

If you spend a lot of time creating an effect, consider saving the result to the Quick Part Gallery – see page 83 in the next chapter for details on how to do this.

Creating a Drop Cap

1. Click anywhere inside a paragraph, then from the Text area on the **Insert** tab, click on the **Drop Cap** tool to select a Drop Cap style

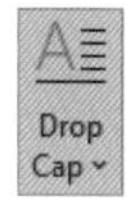

2. The first letter becomes an object that can be resized by dragging on its handles, or reformatted as text

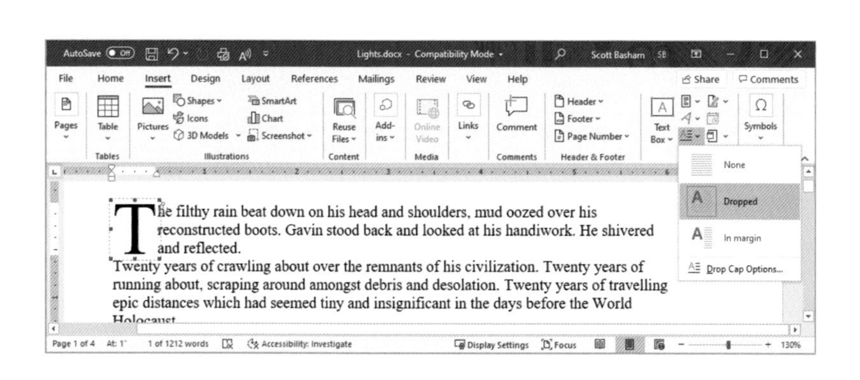

Equations and symbols

Creating and editing an equation

1. Click the **Equation** icon in the Symbols area of the **Insert** tab and select one of the prebuilt equations, or choose **Insert New Equation** to enter one manually

2. The equation appears as a new object on the page

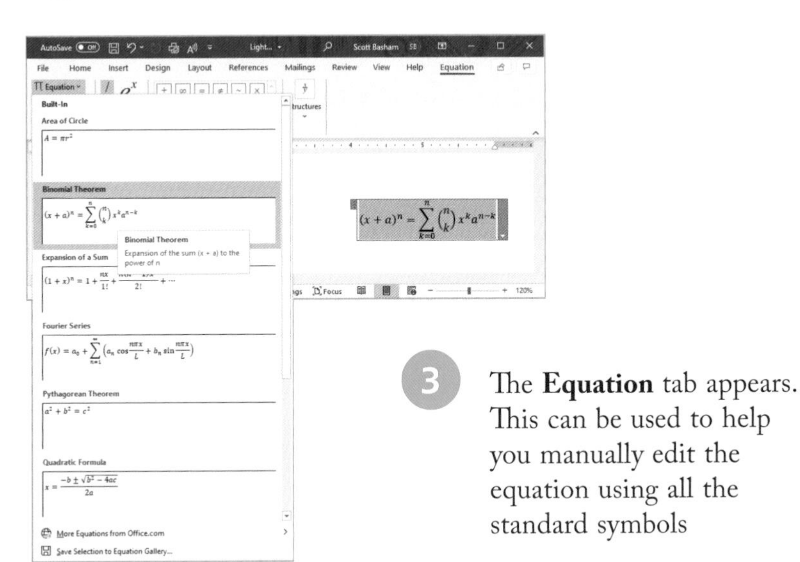

3. The **Equation** tab appears. This can be used to help you manually edit the equation using all the standard symbols

4. Click the **Equation** icon again to see the **Ink Equation** option near the bottom of its list of actions. This lets you write by hand, using the mouse, pen, or touchscreen. Word will interpret this and convert to an editable equation

Hot tip

If you can find something similar to what you need then it's much easier to select an existing preset equation and edit it – compared with entering the whole thing manually.

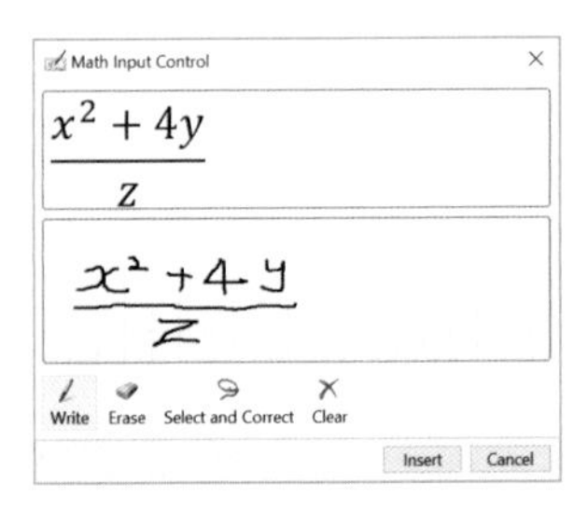

Inserting a symbol

1. Click on the **Symbol** icon in the Symbols area of the **Insert** tab to open the pop-up menu

2. If the symbol you want is in the display of commonly-used items, simply click to insert; otherwise, click on **More Symbols...** for a larger selection

4 Structured documents

Now that we've examined a range of editing techniques, it's time to look at features that make it easier to work with longer, more structured documents. We'll use controls in the Insert, Design and Layout tabs.

The Pages tools

The **Pages** area, on the left-hand side of the **Insert** tab, has three controls for working with pages.

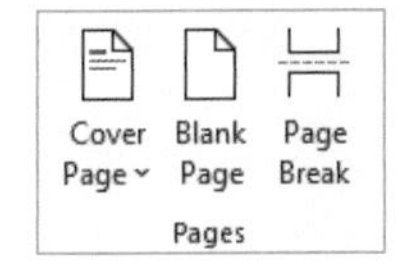

Adding a blank page

Normally, you don't need to do anything to add pages to your document – as you add text and other objects, Word automatically makes room for them by creating new pages as necessary. Sometimes, however, you may want to force Word to create a new blank page in a specific part of your document.

Note that in **Web Layout** view, the concept of pages is very different, as the whole document will exist in a web browser as a single page. In this case, your new blank page will show up as a few blank lines.

1. Click the **Blank Page** icon to add a new blank page

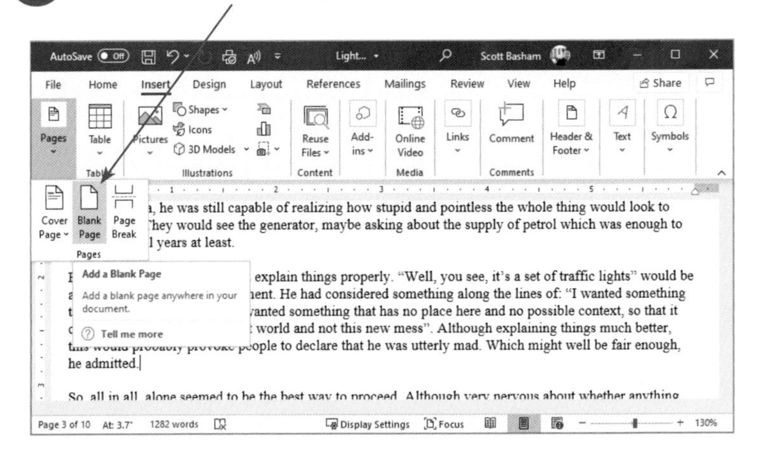

2. Any text before your insertion point will remain on its own before the new blank page. Any text after the insertion point will be moved to after the new blank page

You can repeat this process to add as many pages as you like. In this example, two pages have been inserted mid-way through the document.

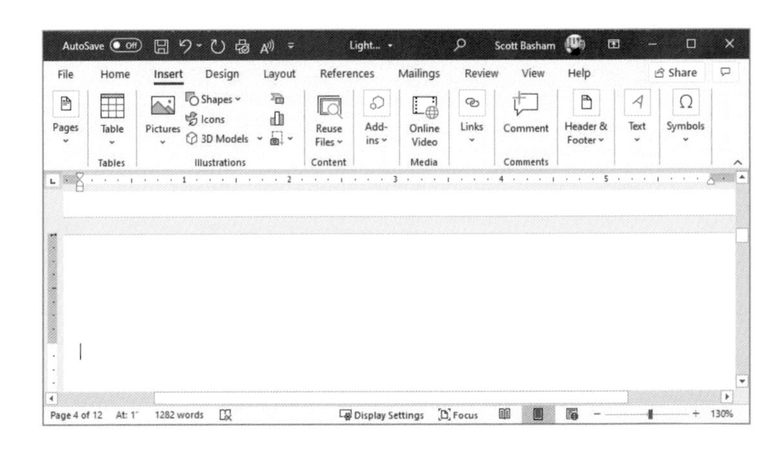

Adding a page break

1. Click the **Page Break** icon. Everything after the current cursor position will move to the next page

2. If the ¶ tool in the **Home** tab is active you'll be able to see the page break as a visible marker

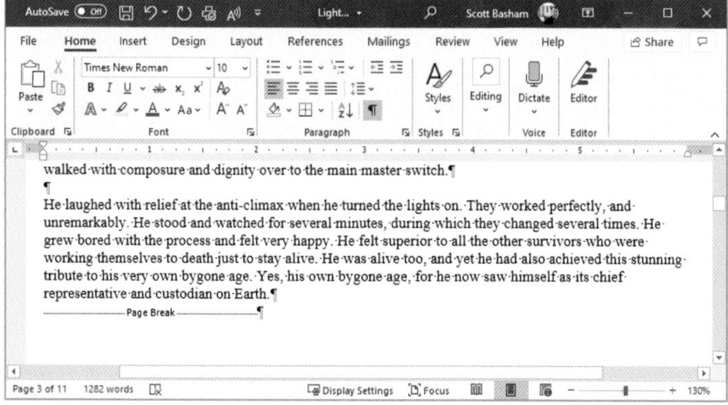

Hot tip

When you're entering text you can type **Ctrl** + **Return** to insert a page break.

Hot tip

Like any other character, the page break can be selected and deleted if necessary.

Adding a cover page

1. Click the **Cover Page** icon and select from the gallery of styles available. The new page is inserted at the start

2. Select the placeholder text and type in your own

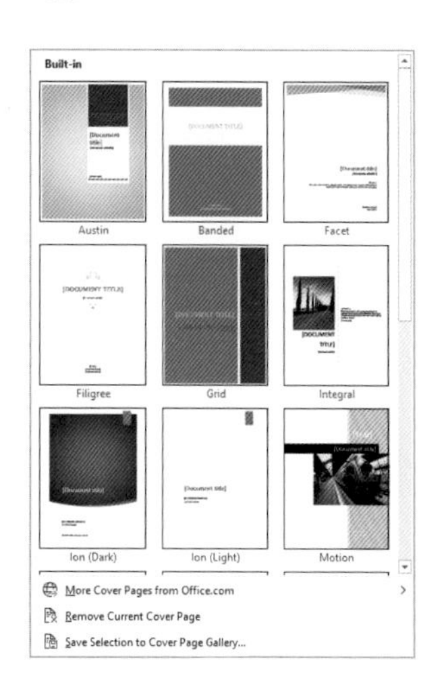

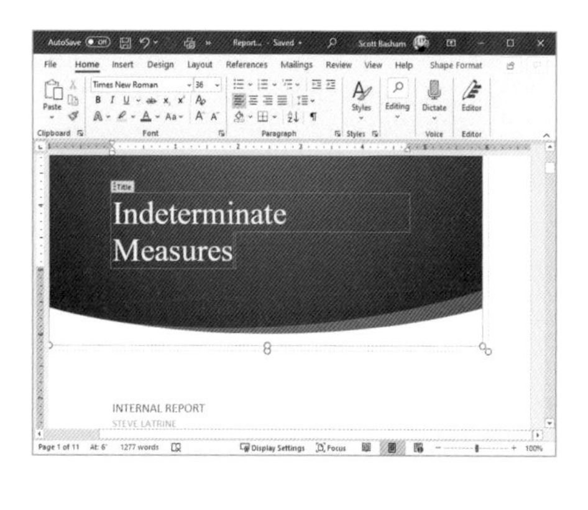

Don't forget

In this example, since you are replacing text, the original formatting is kept. This maintains the look and feel of the cover page design.

Tables and illustrations

These tools in the **Insert** tab allow you to add graphical elements to your document. As soon as you start working with tables or pictorial items, a new tab with relevant controls appears – this will be covered in detail in Chapter 5.

Always check to see which display mode you're using. If it's set to **Draft** or **Outline** then you will not see any graphical elements at all. For graphical editing work you should use the **Print Layout** view, available from the Status bar.

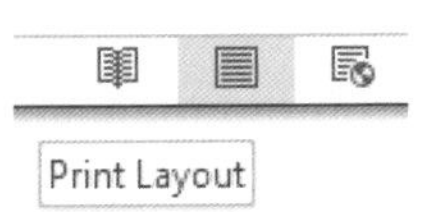

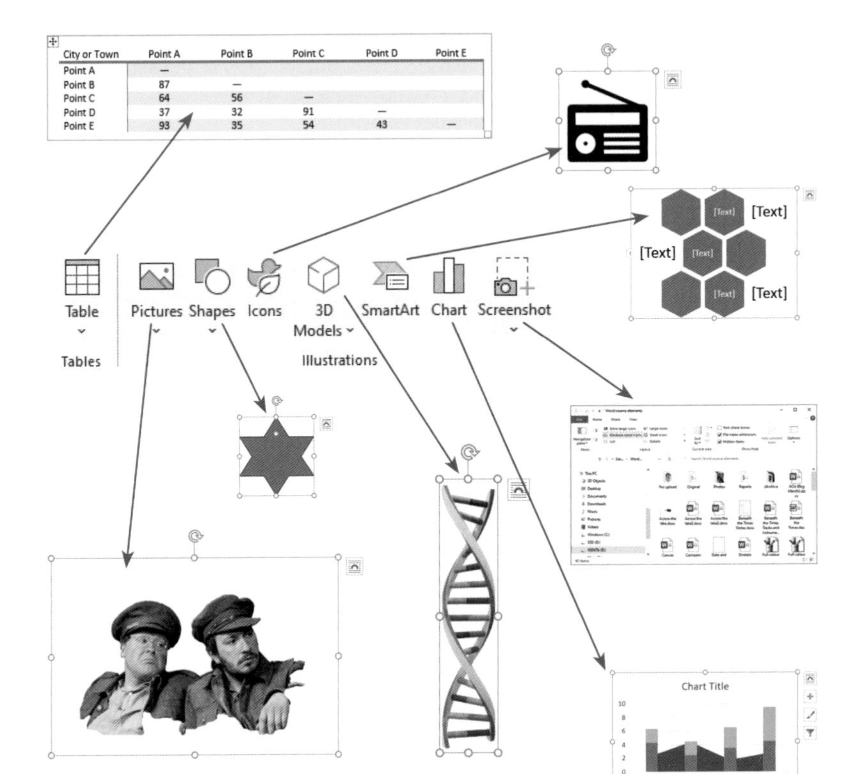

City or Town	Point A	Point B	Point C	Point D	Point E
Point A	–				
Point B	87	–			
Point C	64	56	–		
Point D	37	32	91	–	
Point E	93	35	54	43	–

Icons and 3D Models are examined in more detail in the next chapter, Chapter 5.

Note that some of the predesigned cover pages seen earlier contain graphical elements. If you use one of these it's possible to edit and format these pictorial components, just as if you'd added them yourself.

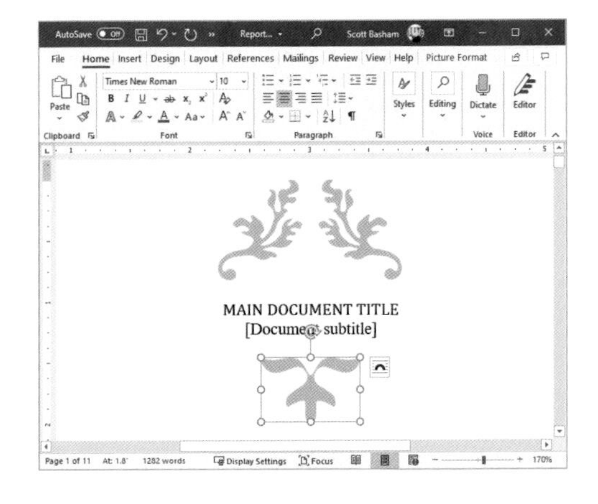

The Links tools

This section of the **Insert** tab lets you add links (hyperlinks), bookmarks, and cross-references.

Bookmarks

Defining bookmarks at key places in your document makes it easy to navigate to them, or even to create hyperlinks from other areas.

Creating a bookmark

1. Navigate to the appropriate position in your document. Click on the **Bookmark** icon in the Links area

2. The **Bookmark** dialog appears. Enter a name for your bookmark and click on the **Add** button. Note that spaces are not allowed in the name

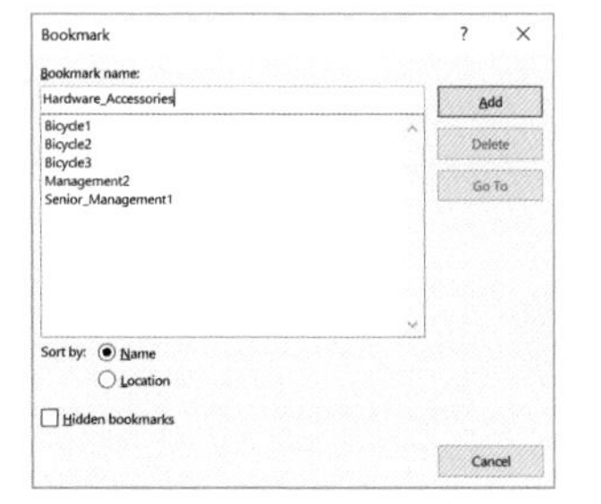

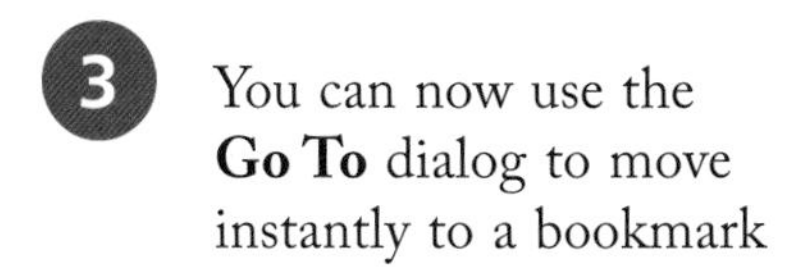

3. You can now use the **Go To** dialog to move instantly to a bookmark

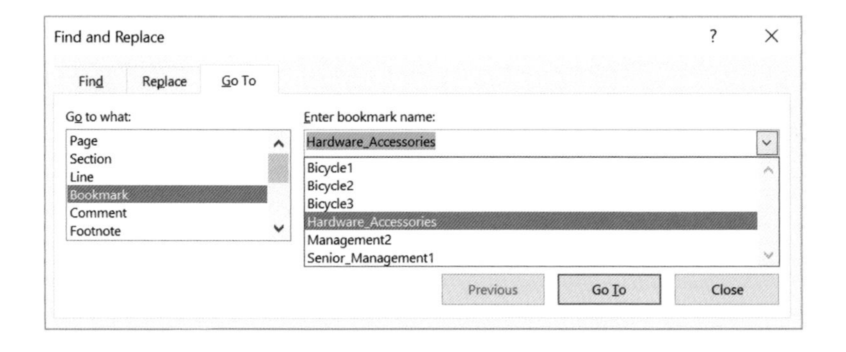

The quickest way to get to the **Go To** dialog is to type **Ctrl** + **G**.

...cont'd

Links

A link, sometimes called a hyperlink, is usually presented as colored and/or underlined text. Clicking on a link will normally take you somewhere else – perhaps to a web page, a different document, or a different position within the current document.

Creating a hyperlink to a document on your computer

1. Place your insertion point wherever you want to add the hyperlink, or highlight the text to be hyperlinked

2. In the Links area of the **Insert** tab, click **Link** – or press **Ctrl** + **K**

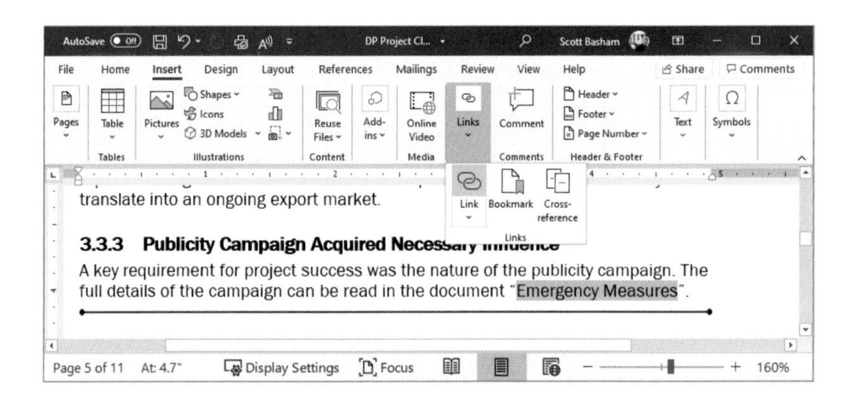

3. For **Link to:** choose **Existing File or Web Page** and locate the desired document. Select this and click **OK**

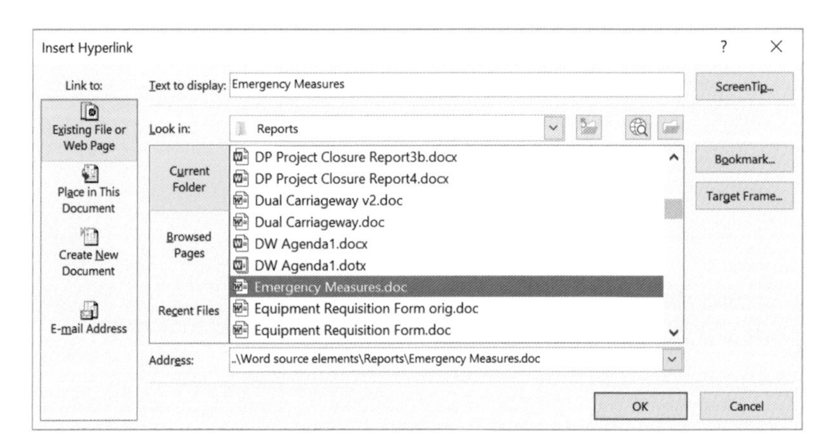

This hyperlinking feature works in much the same way across all Microsoft Office applications.

The hyperlink is inserted into your document. To follow it to its destination, hold down the **Ctrl** key and click the link.

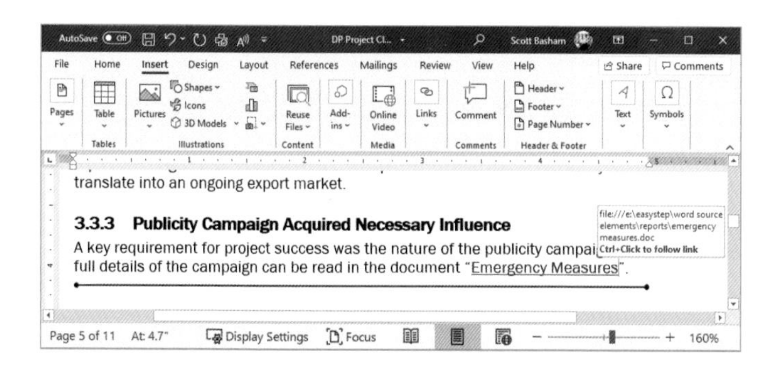

Cross-references

Sometimes you'll want to refer to another location; e.g. "see page 89 for more information". If you actually type in the number "89" then you'll need to go back many times to check to see if that target reference has changed, perhaps because you've added more pages or edited some text. You can avoid this problem by creating automatic cross-references in Word.

1. Place your insertion point wherever you want the cross-reference to appear, then click the **Cross-reference** tool

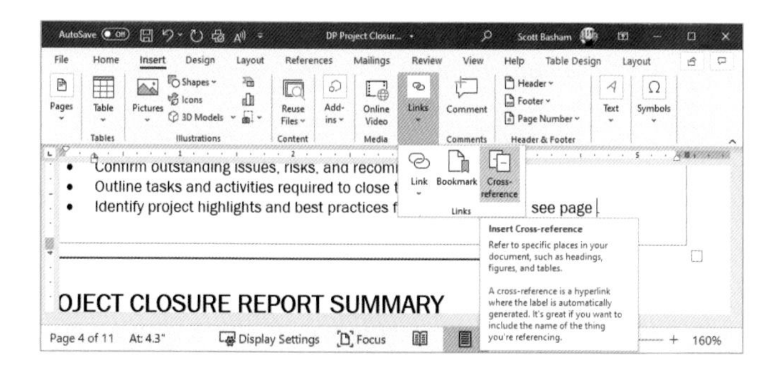

2. Choose the reference type and pick from the list of targets. Click **Insert** to see your reference

- Confirm outstanding issues, risks, and recommendations.
- Outline tasks and activities required to close the project.
- Identify project highlights and best practices for future projects - see page 8.

You can cross-refer to a range of possible targets including headings, bookmarks and tables.

When creating a cross-reference, click an insertion point rather than select text. This is because any text selected will be replaced by the cross-reference.

In the Cross-reference dialog you can also choose the form of the reference. For example, if your reference type is a heading you might want to use the heading number, the heading text itself, or the page number.

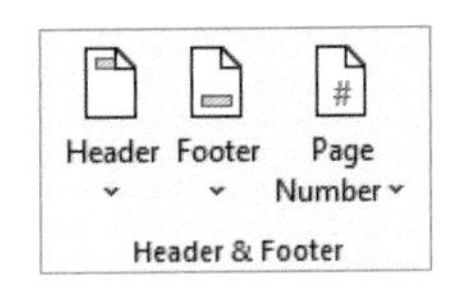

Headers and footers

Headers and footers appear at the top and bottom of each page. There are built-in items available with standard designs for these.

Adding a header or footer

1. In the Header & Footer area of the **Insert** tab click **Header** or **Footer** as appropriate

2. Select the design you want. The header or footer will be added to your document

Editing a header or footer

1. Double-click on the header or footer to enter **Edit** mode. A new set of Header & Footer tools will appear

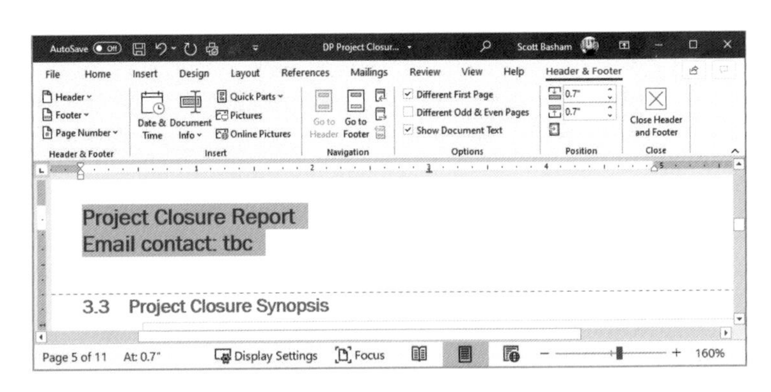

2. You will now be able to edit directly in the header or footer area of the page. With the Header & Footer tools you can adjust the position of the header and footer, add text or graphics, and even decide whether headers and footers should be separately defined for odd and even pages (this can be useful if you plan to print your document double-sided)

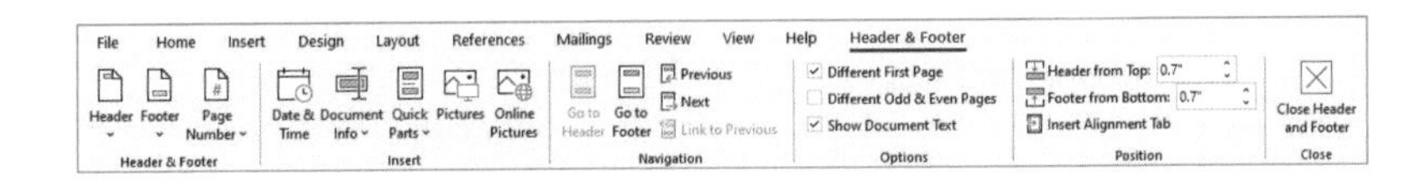

When you're finished working with headers and footers, simply double-click in the main page area to reactivate normal editing. Alternatively, click the **Close Header and Footer** button.

3. There is also a Navigation area in the tab, which allows you to switch between header and footer. If your document is divided into sections, then headers and footers can be defined independently for each section

See page 99 to learn how to divide your document into sections.

Inserting a date and time

1. Place your insertion point then click **Date & Time**

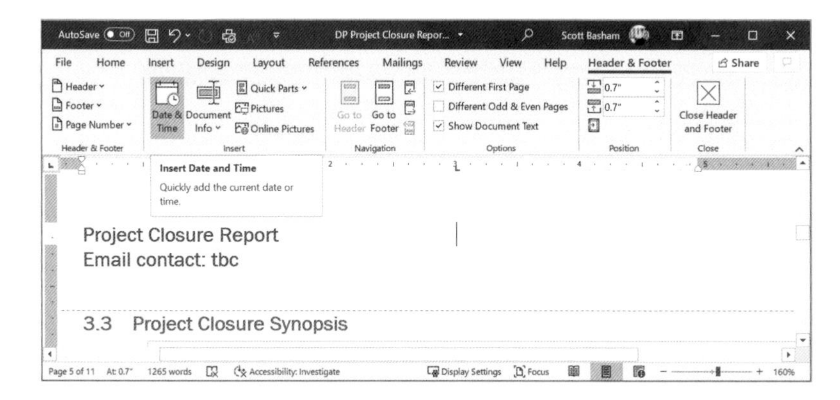

2. Choose from one of the formats listed then click **OK**

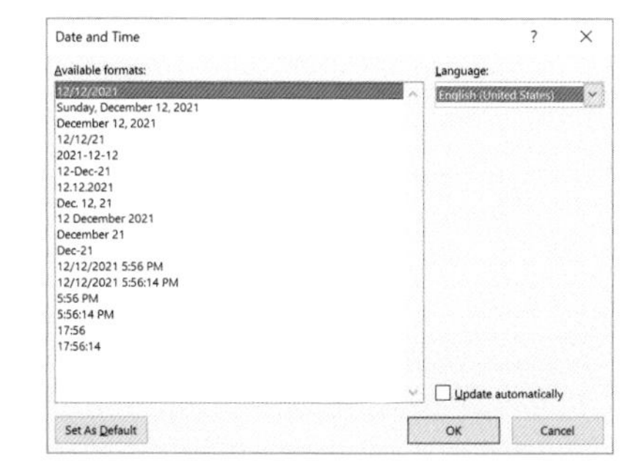

3. The current system date and/or time will be inserted at the current position

If you select the **Update automatically** option in this dialog then the date/time value is updated whenever the document is saved or printed.

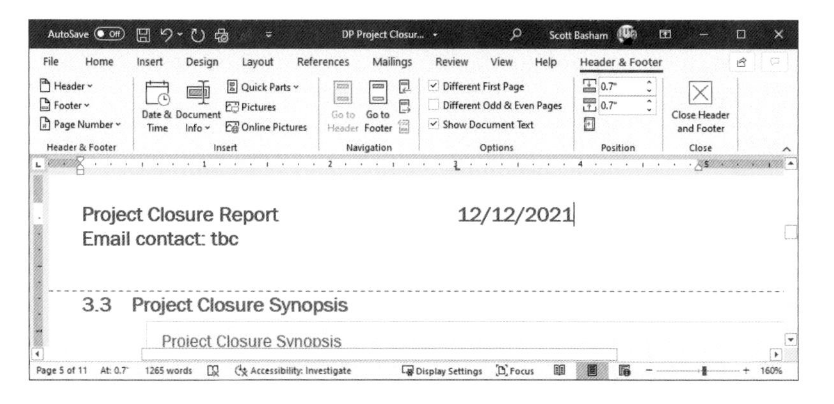

The Text tools

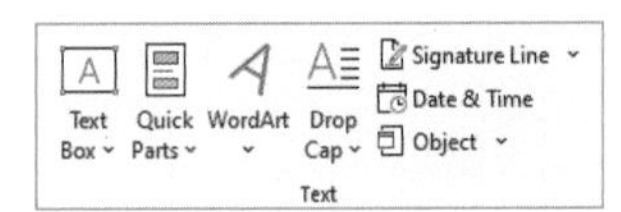

These tools in the **Insert** tab let you add a variety of objects.

Text boxes

These give you a lot of freedom in positioning and formatting small amounts of text. Text can also be flowed automatically between boxes, which can help with more advanced page layouts.

Text boxes, like other shapes, can have text wrap applied to them. This is useful if you have a text-filled page – you can decide how the main text will flow around the edges of the text box. See pages 118-119 for more on text wrap.

Using text boxes, Building Blocks and Quick Parts

1. Click the **Text Box** icon to access the pop-up menu

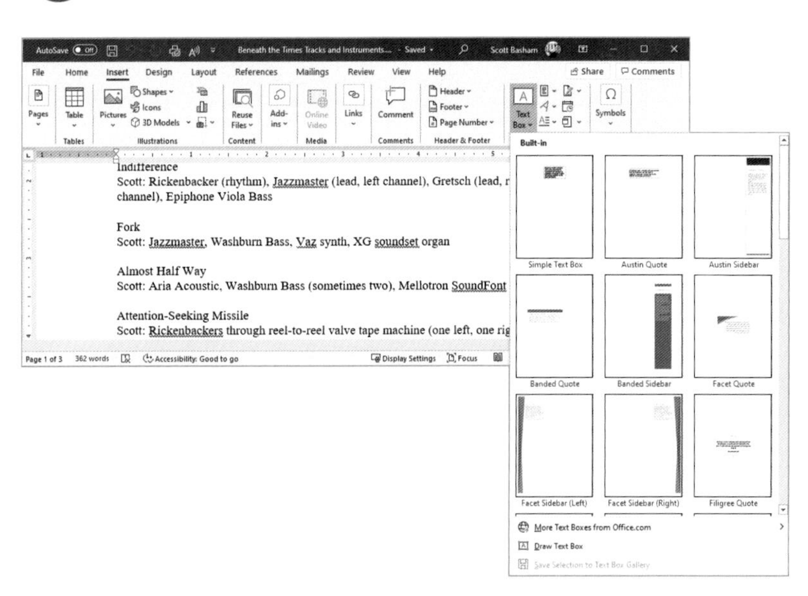

In the gallery that appears you'll see examples of Building Blocks. These are components that can be used in any document. You can define your own Building Blocks or download more from the **Office.com** resource. Other types of Building Block are headers, footers, page number styles, cover pages, watermarks, and equations.

2. If you hover over a design you'll see a tooltip with a brief explanation. Click on one of the designs to insert it into your current page

The text box appears on the page in whichever is the default position for this particular design.

3. To resize the text box, drag on one of its circular handles, either in the corner or halfway along each edge

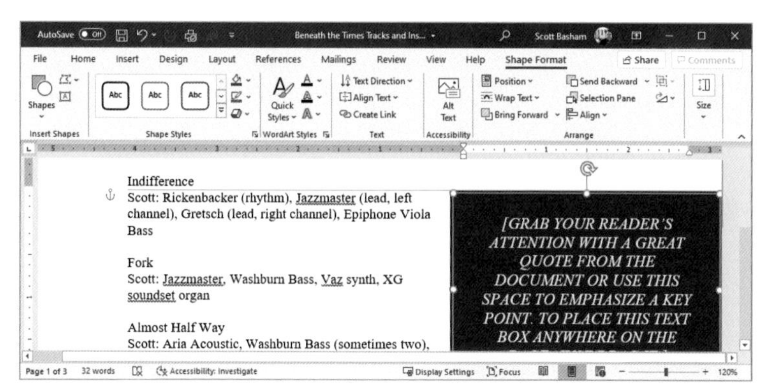

As you drag an object, horizontal and vertical guides may appear. These are called alignment guides – see page 121 for more on how to activate these.

4. If you want to move the text box, then drag somewhere on its edge but not on any of its handles

5. The text box comes with some sample dummy text. Select this and enter your own

6. You can change the appearance of the text, or the box itself, using the controls in the **Home** tab or the Quick Access Toolbar

7. If you've enhanced or changed the design and would like to reuse it later on, make sure the **Insert** tab is active, click on the **Text Box** tool and choose **Save Selection to Text Box Gallery**. Name your design then click **OK**

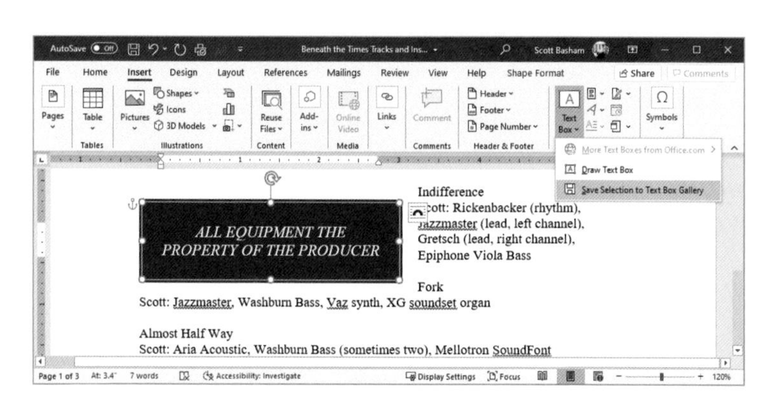

...cont'd

Creating a text box manually

1. Make sure the **Insert** tab is active. Click the **Text Box** icon and choose **Draw Text Box**

2. Your cursor will temporarily change to a cross. Drag a rectangular area to define the box perimeter

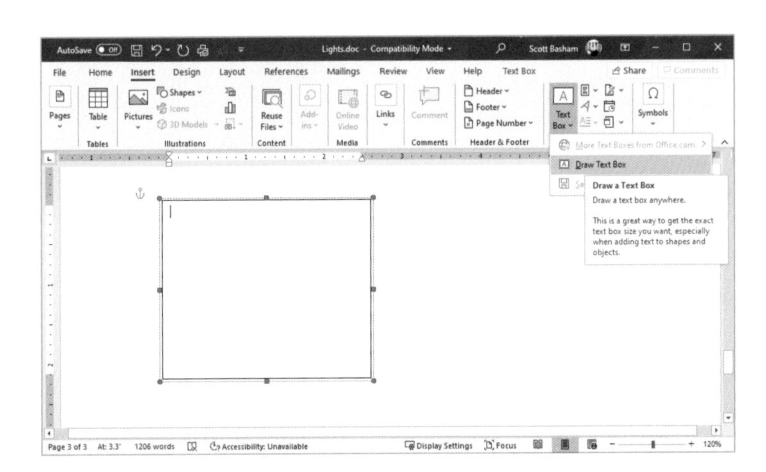

If you're not happy with the size of your text box you can either click **Undo** and draw it again or drag on its corner or edge handles to resize.

3. Click inside to enter text within the box. You can use all the normal editing techniques and formatting controls you learned in earlier chapters

4. When the text box is selected, the **Shape Format** tab will be available. You can use this to control the line and fill style of the box, as well as to change the layering (using **Bring to Front** and **Send to Back**). You can also apply more artistic effects such as shadowing, 3D boxes or geometric transformations

Sometimes the box may be too small for your text. If this happens you can either increase the box size, reduce the text size, or create more boxes and link them using text flow. We'll see how to use text flow next.

Flowing text between boxes

1. Locate a text box that has too much text to display within its defined area

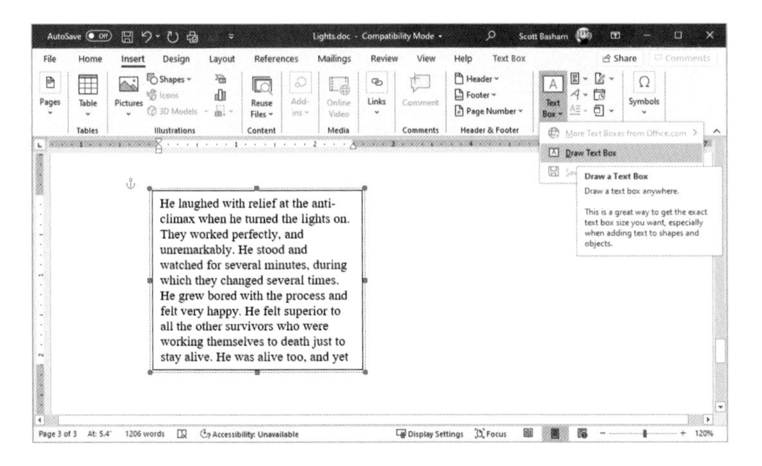

2. Click on the **Text Box** icon in the Toolbar and, in the pop-up menu that appears, choose **Draw Text Box**

3. Click and drag to define the second text box

4. Select the first box and check the **Shape Format** or **Text Box** tab is visible. Click on **Create Link in the Text area**

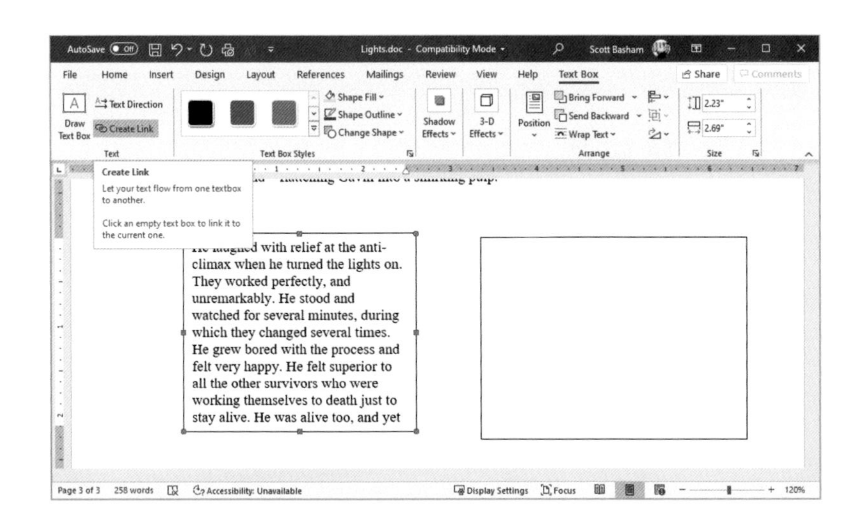

Text flow works not just on text boxes, but on any shapes that are capable of containing text. See Chapter 5 for more details.

You can save a text box as a picture to a file on disk. Simply right-click on the text box and choose **Save as Picture...** from the pop-up menu. Supported file formats are Portable Network Graphics (*.png), JPEG (*.jpg), Graphics Interchange Format (*.gif), TIFF (*.tif), Windows Bitmap (*.bmp) and Scalable Vector Graphics (*.svg).

...cont'd

5. Now, click anywhere within the second text box. The text that didn't fit into the first box will automatically flow into the second

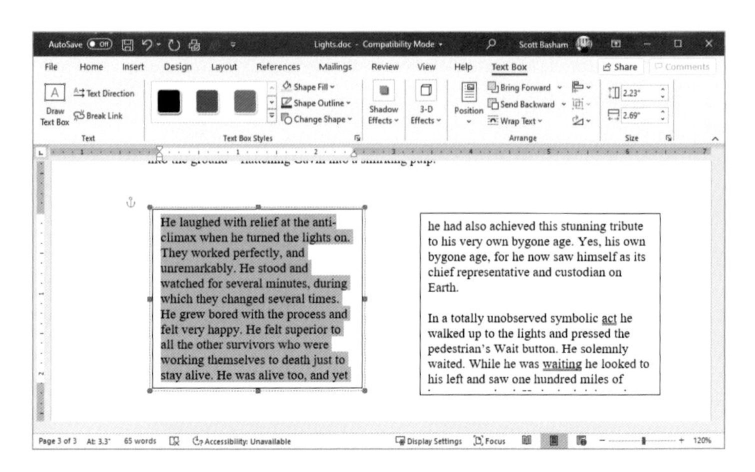

You can reverse this operation by selecting the first text box and then clicking on **Break Link**. All the text will be moved back into the first box. You will now need to edit the text, change its size, or change the size of the text box to see all the text once again.

6. If there is still too much text, or if you decide to add more text, you can repeat this process to create a longer sequence of text boxes with the same text continuously threaded through them

7. The text remains linked, so changing the size and shape of any box will automatically cause the text to reflow. Similarly, adding or removing text may cause Word to readjust the flow between the boxes

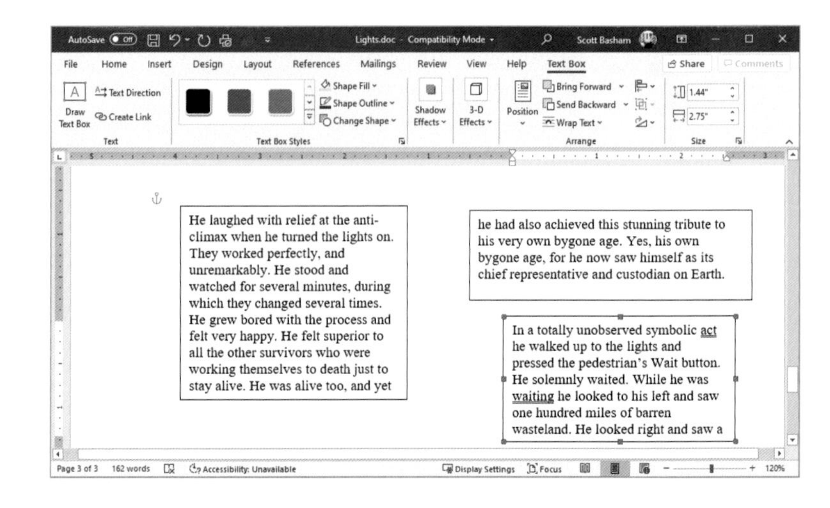

Creating your own Building Blocks

As we saw on pages 78-79, you can select any text or other objects within Word and make these into new Building Blocks.

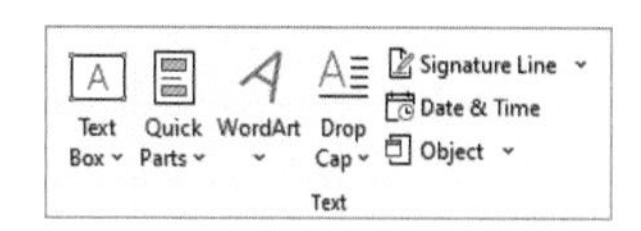

1. Create and format the content that will become your new Building Block

2. Select your content, then click **Quick Parts** and select **Save Selection to Quick Part Gallery...**

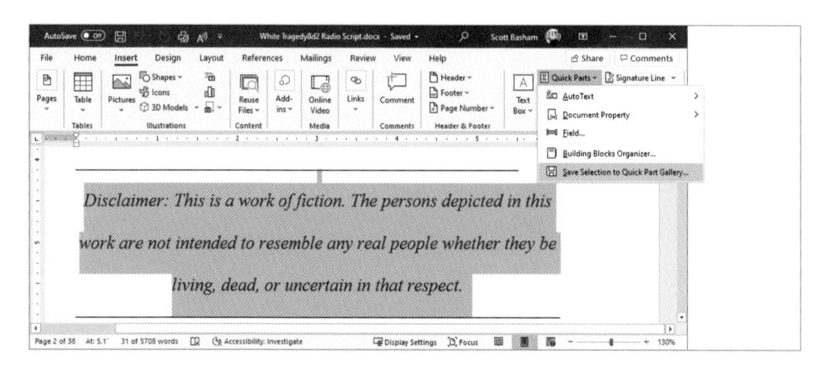

3. The **Create New Building Block** dialog appears. Enter a name and select a gallery to use (in most cases this should be the Quick Part Gallery)

4. Choose a category and enter a text description

5. Next, choose the Word template that will store the Building Block. If you select **Building Blocks.dotx** then the Building Block will be available to all documents

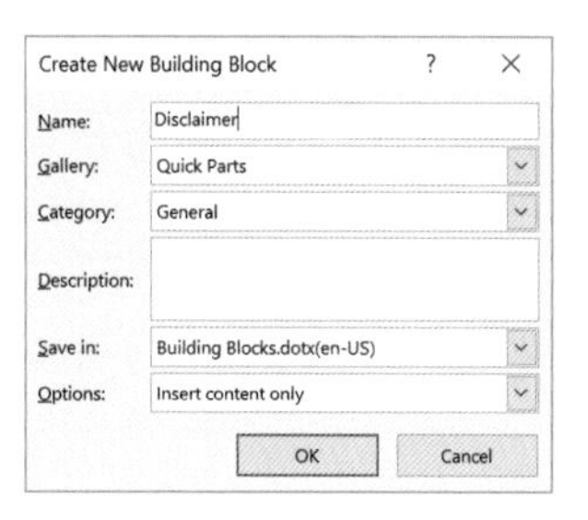

6. The Options available are **Insert content only**, **Insert content in its own paragraph**, and **Insert content in its own page**. Choose the appropriate option and then click **OK**. Your Building Block is now installed and ready for you to use from the Quick Parts tool

Quick Parts are useful if you need to use standard formatted text across many documents. An example may be a disclaimer that has been agreed with the legal department of your company – it may be company policy to include this in any correspondence with customers.

...cont'd

Using your own Building Blocks

Once you have created your own Building Blocks you can use them in the same way as the others.

1. Navigate to the part of your document where you want to add your Building Block, and click an insertion point

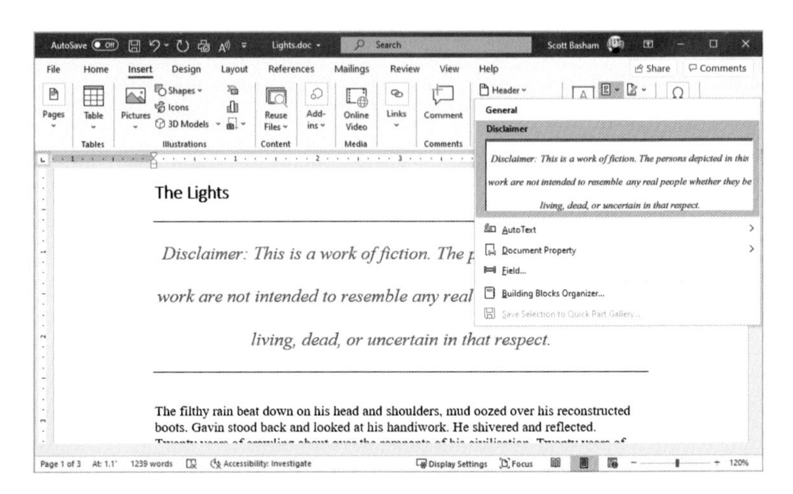

2. Click the **Quick Parts** button and select your Building Block from its gallery. It will be added at the current position

Editing an existing Building Block

If you have an example of a Building Block somewhere in your document, then you can edit this and reattach it to the gallery.

1. Make the necessary changes to the content, then select it
2. Click the **Quick Parts** button and make a careful note of the name of the Building Block you're planning to edit
3. Click on **Quick Parts** and choose **Save Selection to Quick Part Gallery**
4. If you enter exactly the same name and gallery as before then the original Building Block's definition will be overwritten

To replace an existing Building Block, you must enter precisely the same name in the **Create New Building Block** dialog.

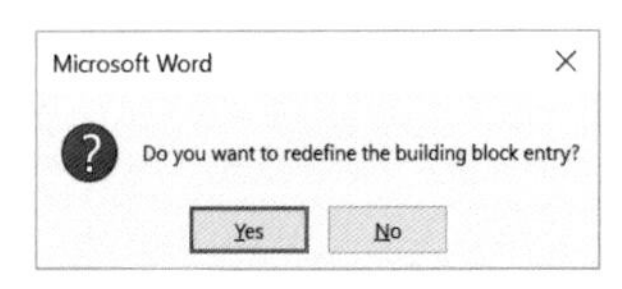

The Building Blocks Organizer

Building Blocks can be very flexible, and there are many different types. In this chapter we have seen tools such as Cover Page, Header, Footer, Page Number, Text Box, and the more general Quick Parts. Each of these has its own gallery containing a particular type of Building Block. Here, we'll see how to manage all these objects in one place.

The Quick Parts tool is in the **Insert** tab, as are most of the tools covered in this chapter.

1. Click on the **Quick Parts** tool and choose **Building Blocks Organizer** to see this dialog

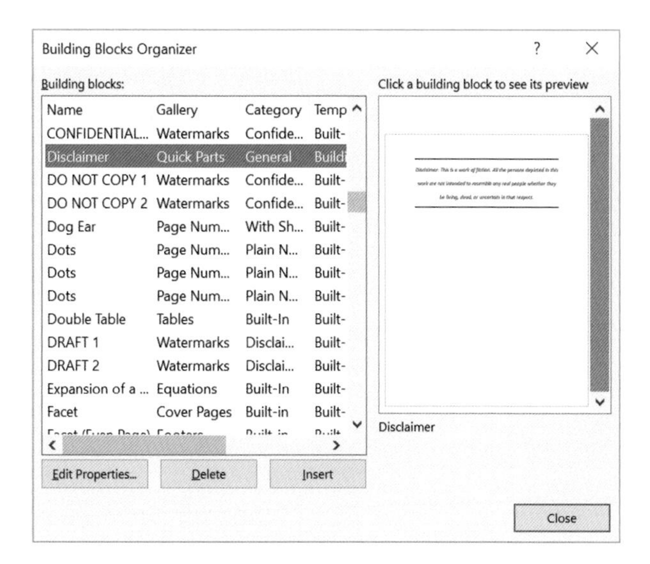

2. If you scroll down through the predesigned elements you should be able to find Quick Parts objects you created yourself. Click **Edit Properties...** to change an item's attributes

If you previously saved a customized text box as a Quick Part you might want to use this dialog to change its Gallery attribute to **Text Boxes**. It'll then appear directly in the pop-up menu that you see when you click on the Text Box tool.

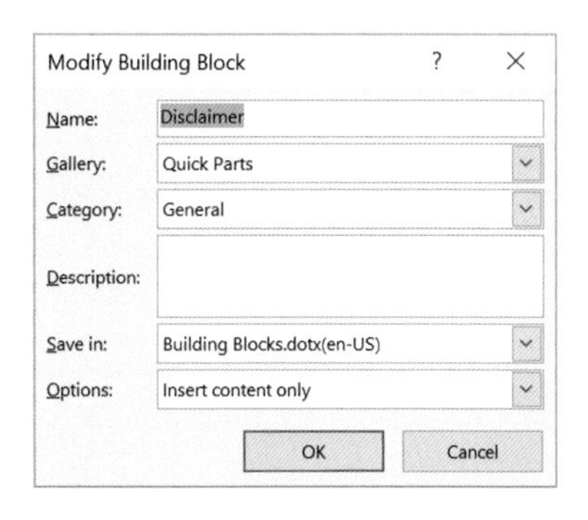

Tables

Tables allow you to organize and manage text in rows and columns. They provide a more visual way of working than you'd have with normal text formatted via tab stops.

Inserting a table

1. Click on the **Table** icon in the **Insert** tab

2. In the grid that appears, click and drag to define an initial table size. Don't worry too much about getting this right first time, as it's easy to change the size later on

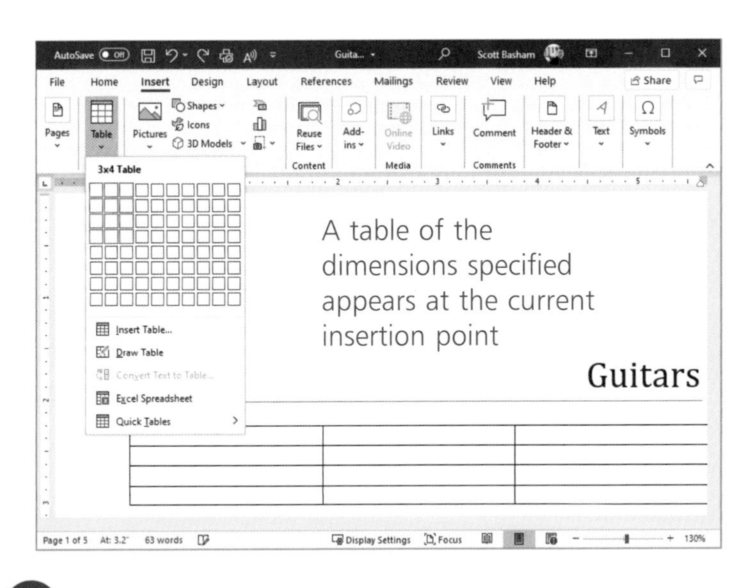

3. Alternatively, if you click the **Table** icon and then choose **Insert Table** from the sub-menu, this dialog box appears. You can then specify the table dimensions numerically. Click **OK** to go ahead and create the table

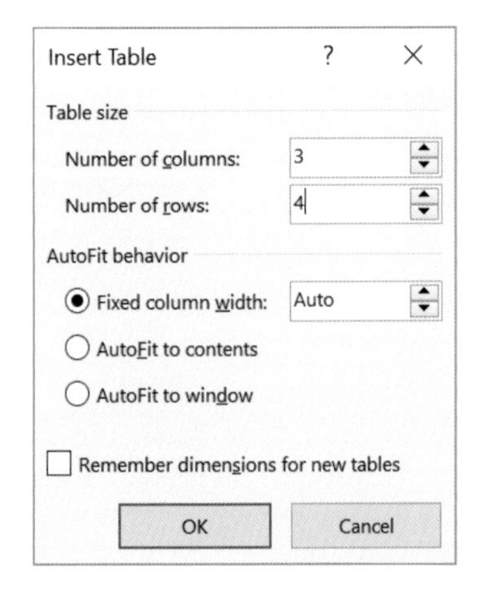

If you already have some text formatted using tab characters, then it's easy to convert this to a table automatically. To do this, select the text, click the **Table** icon and choose **Convert Text to Table...**.

Resizing a table

1. Click and drag on the boundary between rows or columns to resize them. Your cursor will turn into a double-headed arrow as you do this

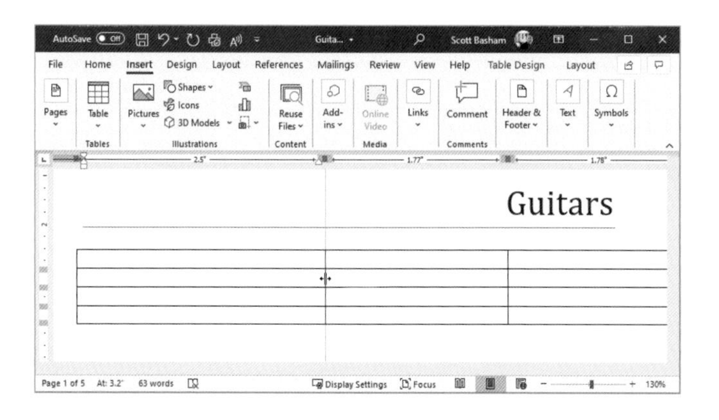

When resizing in this way, if you hold down the **Alt** key, you'll see a constantly-updating numeric display of the column widths.

Drawing a table

You may prefer to use the **Draw Table** tool to create tables. This gives you more flexibility, particularly when you're trying to create irregularly-shaped tables.

1. Click the **Table** icon and choose **Draw Table**

2. Click and drag to draw a rectangle that defines the overall table size

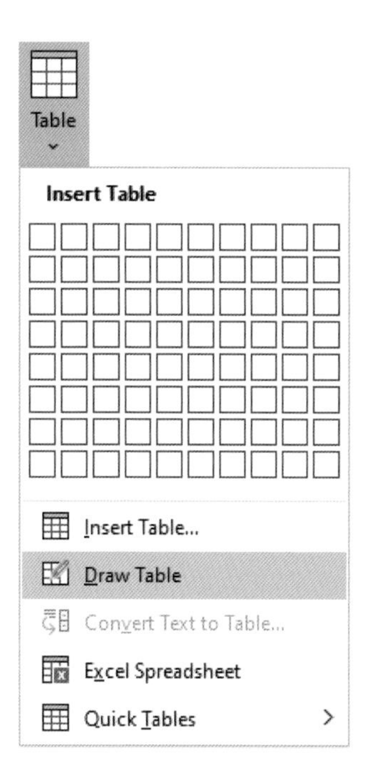

The rectangle you drew represents the table perimeter. Your next task is to draw in the rows and columns. The special **Layout** tab is automatically activated and its **Draw Table** tool is selected ready for you to start work.

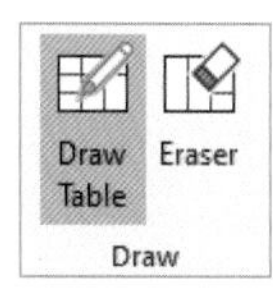

As soon as you have a table or part of a table selected, two tabs will appear: **Table Design**, and **Layout**.

...cont'd

3. Click and drag horizontally across the table to draw in the rows. As you drag, a dotted or red line appears, giving you a preview of the new line. If you accidentally draw the line in the wrong place, simply use **Ctrl** + **Z** to undo, and then try again

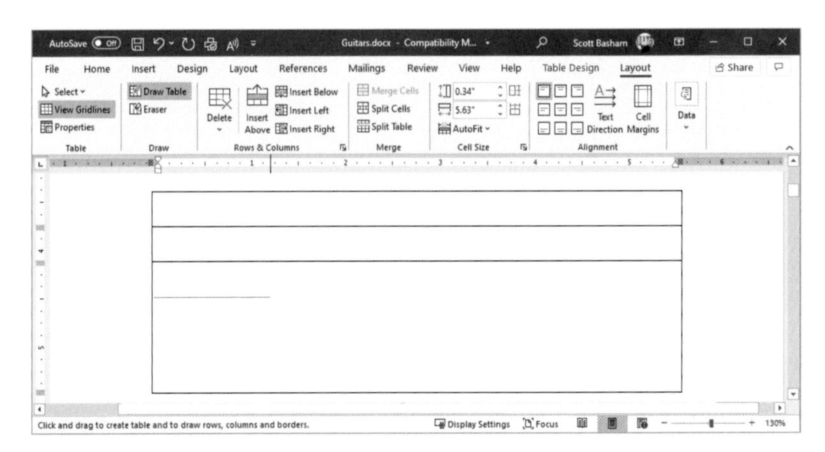

All these features are still available to you even after you add text into the cells of your table. Sometimes it's useful to see how much text you need before you finalize the table's dimensions.

4. Now, drag vertically to draw in the column boundaries

5. You can even drag diagonally to create a new line that will divide cells in two, as in the example below

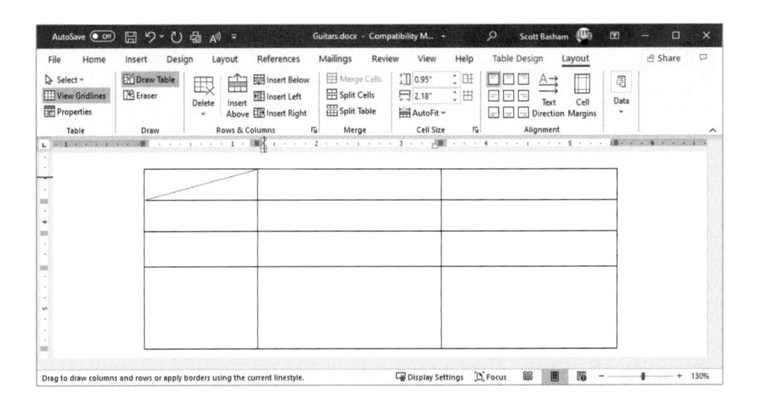

Note that if you drag from inside to an area outside of the table, then nothing will be changed. However, if you begin and end dragging completely outside the table, then a new independent table will be created.

6. Sometimes you will want to remove lines to create an irregular table where some of the cells are much larger. To do this, select the **Eraser** tool and then click directly on the part of the line you wish to remove

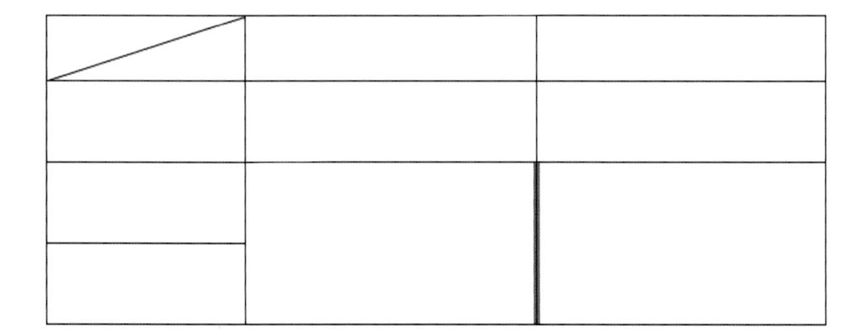

A single click will normally remove the shortest segment at the current mouse position. If you want to remove larger sections of a line, or even a whole line, then click and drag over the desired area.

7. Once you have erased a fairly large area, switch back to the **Draw Table** tool. You can now add in more lines to this area

8. In the example below you can see how flexible this technique is, allowing for a complex patchwork of odd-sized cells to be created

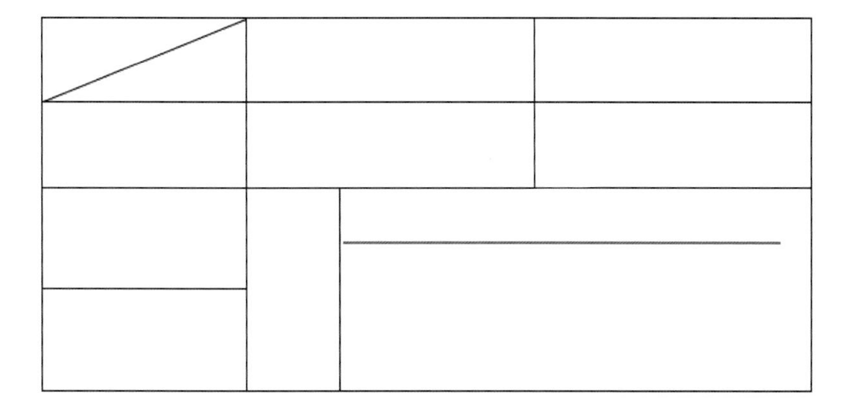

Table cells are normally filled with text, and can have their background shaded and different line styles applied. It's also possible to place other items such as graphics inside a table cell.

...cont'd

Formatting your table

You can use all the formatting techniques learned in earlier chapters on your table text. Often, you'll start by dragging across an entire row or column to select it prior to formatting.

Guitars

Name	Type	Price
Rickenbacker 330	Hollow Body Electric	$1871.00
E		$499.99
S		$283.65

Calibri (Bo 18 Insert Delete New Comment

Bold (Ctrl+B)

If you have changed the dimensions of individual rows or columns but now want to make your table more regular again, then select the relevant area, right-click and choose either **Distribute Rows Evenly** or **Distribute Columns Evenly**.

Inserting and deleting rows or columns

1. To insert a row, first select an existing row just above or below where you want it to be

2. To the left of the row, a circular icon with a plus sign inside will appear as you hover over with the mouse. Click this icon, and the new row will be inserted

Guitars

Name	Type	Price
Rickenbacker 330	Hollow Body Electric	$1871.00
Epiphone Viola	Bass	$499.99
Squire Telecaster	Solid Electric	$283.65

3. To insert additional rows, keep clicking on the icon

4. To add multiple rows in a single action, first click and drag to select the number of rows you wish to add. When you click the circular icon, Word will add the same number of rows

5. You can add columns in a similar way. Select one or more columns then move your mouse to the top left or top right of the area you've selected. The circular **Add** icon will appear, allowing you to add in the columns

Merging cells

Each cell can contain text that is formatted and aligned independently of other cell text (if desired). Sometimes it's useful to group or merge cells together so that they behave as a single cell.

1. Select the cells you wish to merge (note that these must be next to each other), then right-click and choose **Merge Cells**

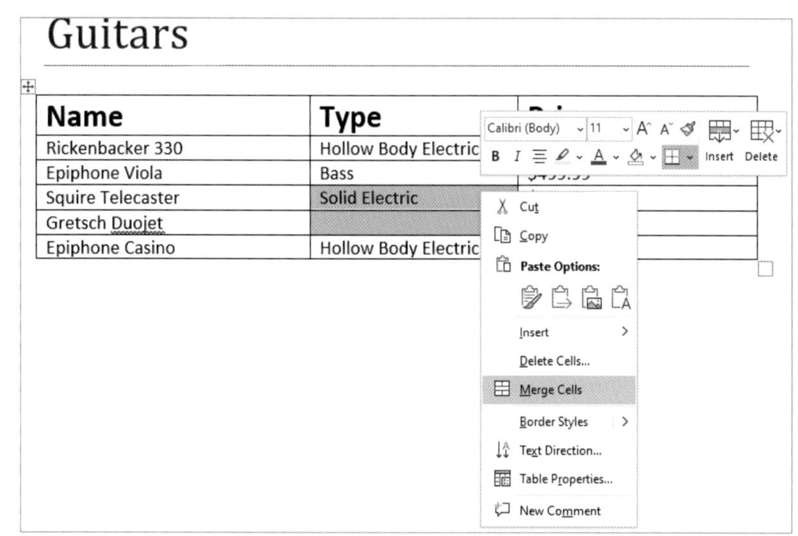

If you accidentally merge the wrong cells then type **Ctrl** + **Z** or click on the **Undo** button in the Quick Access Toolbar.

Your selected area will now be a single cell. All the text that was in the original cells will be present in the new cell.

2. Select the new cell, then make sure the **Layout** tab in Table Tools is active. In the Alignment area choose **Align Center**. Note that the centering acts across the whole area, so it really is behaving as if it were a single cell

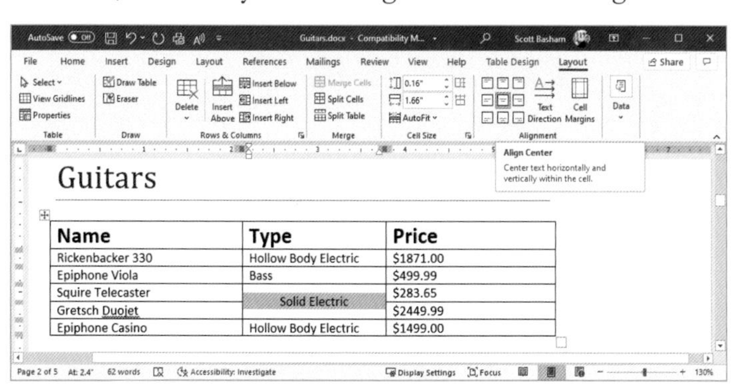

...cont'd

Table Properties

1. Make sure your insertion point is somewhere inside the table (or select part or all of the table), right-click and then choose **Table Properties**

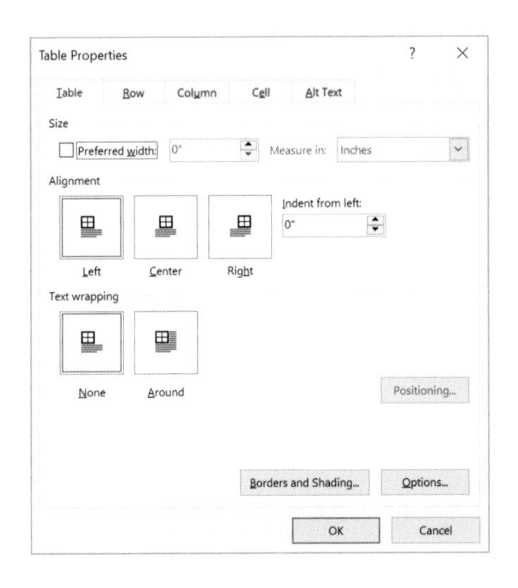

From this dialog you can define properties for the entire table, or at the row, column, or cell level.

You can also use the **Borders and Shading...** button to set visual properties for the whole table.

From the **Cell** tab of the **Table Properties** dialog you have individual control over the vertical alignment of text within each cell. Horizontal text alignment can be controlled via the Paragraph area in the **Home** tab, or both together from the Alignment area of the **Layout** tab.

Table Styles

1. Select or click within your table to make sure the **Table Design** tab is active, then look for the large area named **Table Styles**. As you hover over each style you'll see a preview of your table

2. Click on the style to apply it permanently to your table

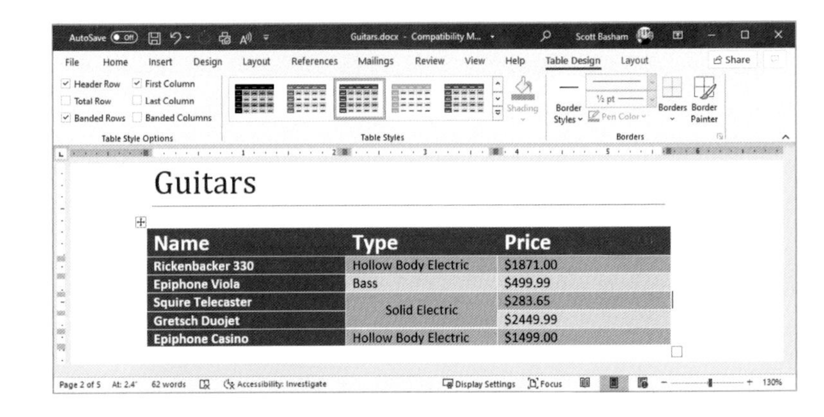

Word includes a wide selection of preset table styles, helping you to quickly apply an effective design without spending hours fiddling with formatting settings.

The Table Design tab

1. Click anywhere in your table and make sure the **Table Design** tab is active

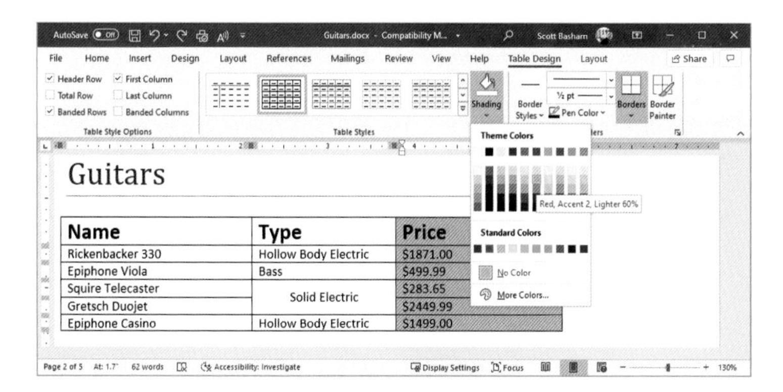

2. Select one or more cells to apply background colors via the **Shading** icon

3. Choose a border style to activate the **Border Painter**. This turns your cursor into a paintbrush that you can use to change the border style of any lines in your table

The Layout tab

If you activate the **Layout** tab you'll see that there are tools for operations on tables, rows, columns, and individual cells.

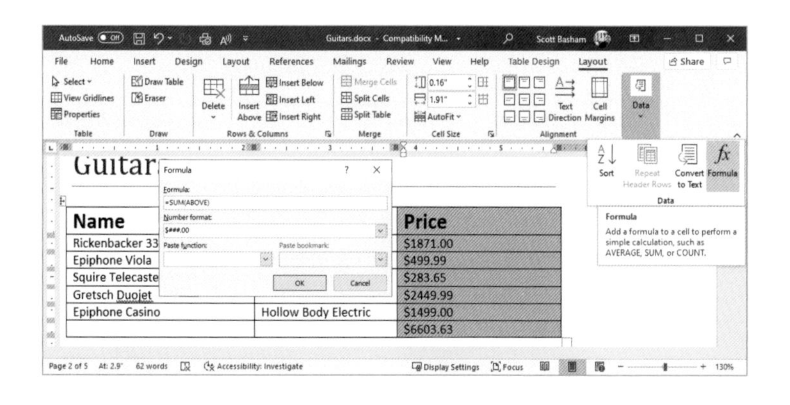

Many of the features in the Table Layout controls are also present in the pop-up menu when you right-click within a table.

In this example, **Formula** (from the **Data** icon) was used to calculate the sum of the values in the cells above the one selected.

Themes

Themes can control your overall document design by defining its main colors, fonts and effects. If you use a theme's colors, for example, then changing the theme will change these automatically.

Selecting a theme

1. Make sure the **Design** tab is active

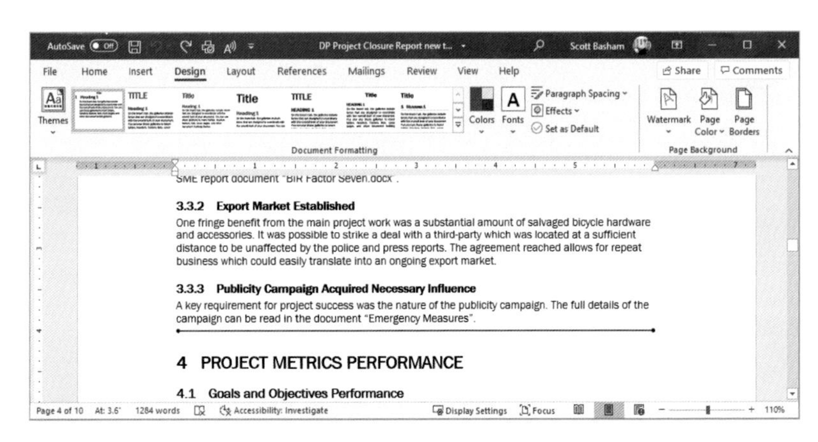

2. Click the **Themes** button and browse through the themes in the gallery. As you hover over a theme, your document will preview its settings. Click once to set the theme

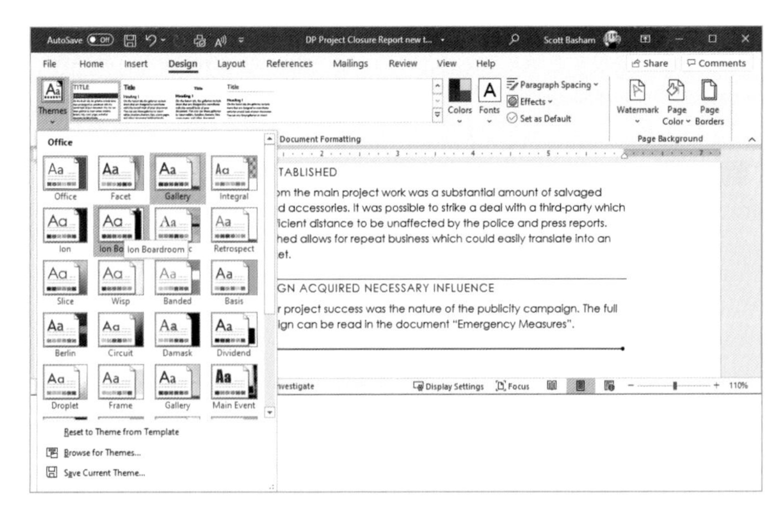

3. All aspects of the document under theme control will be updated to reflect your choice

If your current document does not use theme fonts, colors and effects then applying a new theme will have no visible effect. To remedy this, whenever you choose a font, color or effect, make sure you use an option that is listed under Themes.

Using a theme's colors

1. To change just the colors that belong to the theme, click on the **Colors** icon in the **Design** tab. A gallery of color swatches appears

2. Choose a different option. If your document used theme colors then these will be changed automatically

3. From now on, whenever you select a color you will be able to choose one from the theme's current selection

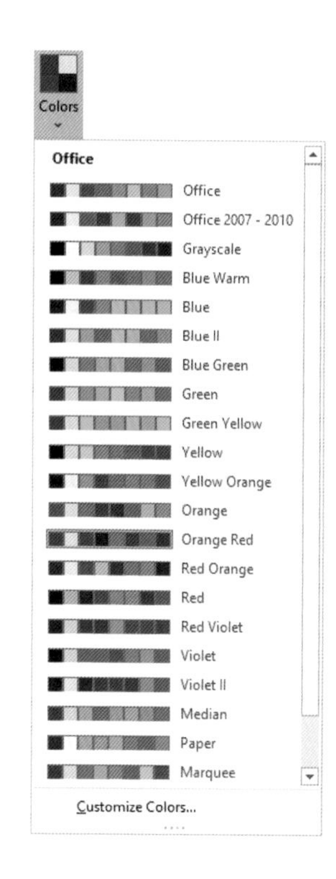

If you really want to use a color that is not available in this list, then click **Customize Colors...**. This will allow you to either create new theme colors from a preset selection or mix your own using different models, or even enter a direct Hex code if you happen to know what you need.

Using a theme's effects

1. You can also change a theme's effects independently of its fonts and colors. To do this, click on the **Effects** button in the **Design** tab and select a different option. As you hover over an option, the effect will be previewed

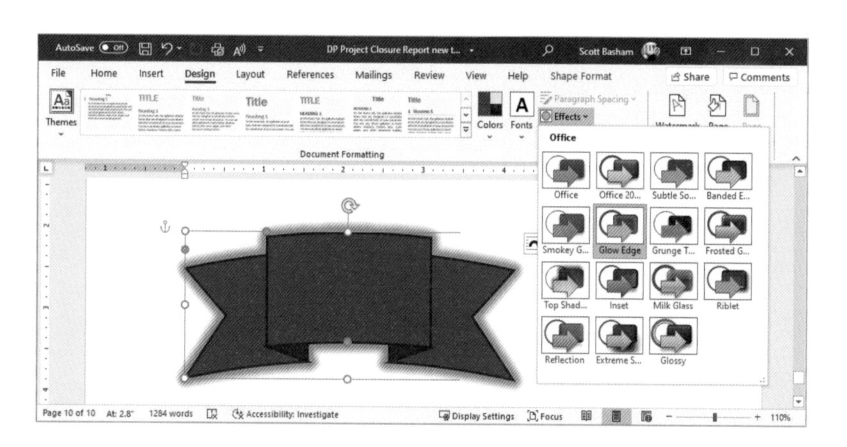

...cont'd

Using a theme's fonts

1. Make sure the **Design** tab is active, then click on **Fonts** in the Document Formatting area. Each option contains one font for headings, and a second for main body text

2. Choose a different option. If your document used theme fonts then these will be changed automatically

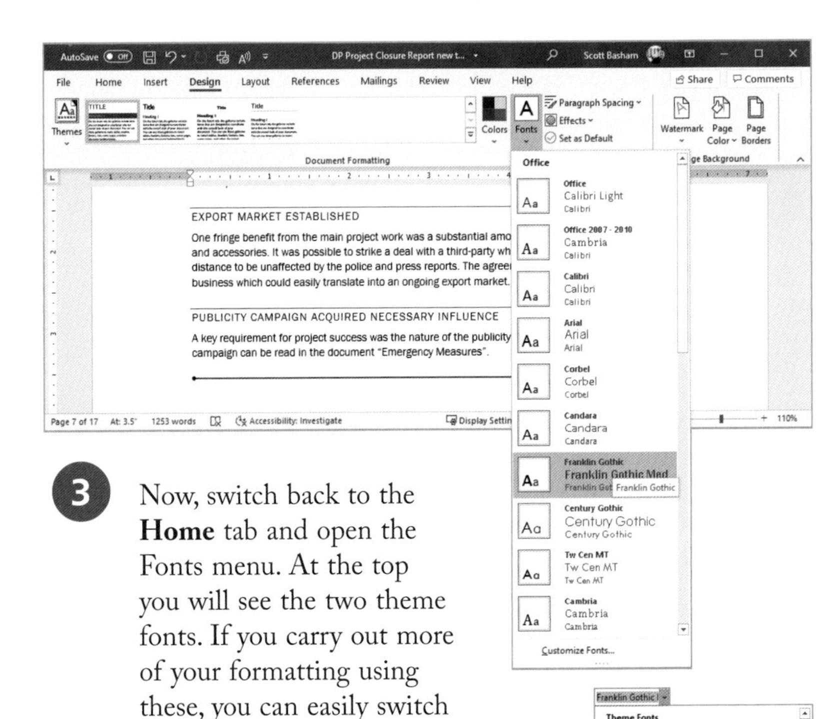

As you hover over an option, any text currently using theme fonts will preview the new settings.

3. Now, switch back to the **Home** tab and open the Fonts menu. At the top you will see the two theme fonts. If you carry out more of your formatting using these, you can easily switch themes later – your text will change accordingly

A small cloud icon next to a font name indicates that it is not currently installed. If you simply click on the item it will be automatically downloaded and then selected.

4. It's a very good idea to make sure your text styles are defined using theme fonts – if your document uses those styles throughout, then it's very easy to experiment with different designs

Page Setup

This set of tools includes controls for margins, size and orientation, as well as line numbering, adding breaks, and hyphenation.

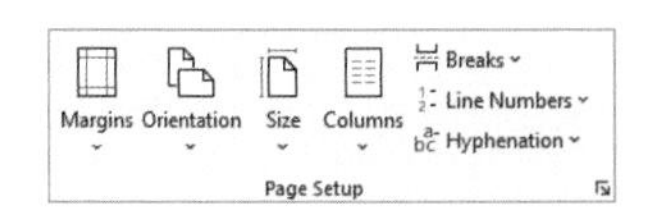

Margins and columns

1. Make sure that the **Layout** tab is active. In the Page Setup area click on the **Margins** icon to choose from the gallery, or click **Custom Margins...** to define these via a dialog box

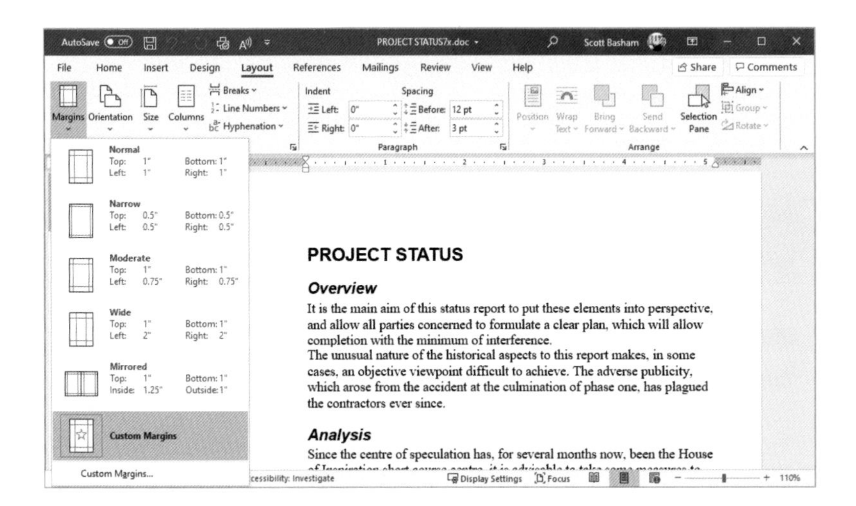

2. By default, your text is set out in a single-column spread across the page. To change to a multi-column layout, click the **Columns** icon and choose the number you want. Your text will be reformatted in the new layout

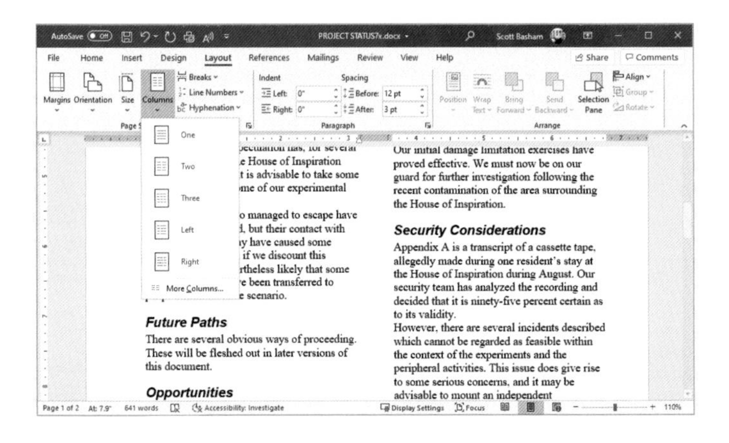

If the option you want is not in the menu, click on **More Columns...** to summon a dialog box. This gives you full control over the number of columns and their individual sizes.

Breaks

Different types of break

At the start of this chapter we saw how to add a simple page break. The **Layout** tab also has a tool for this, but it's much more powerful.

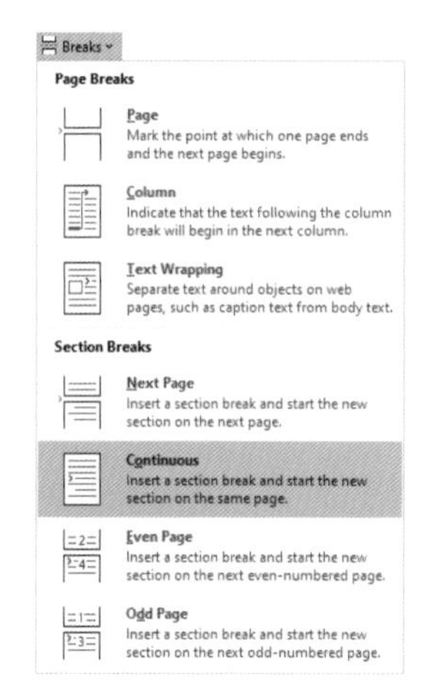

For this example make sure you choose the **Breaks** tool present in the **Layout** tab (and not **Page Break** from the **Insert** tab).

1. Position your insertion point then click the **Breaks** tool

2. As you can see, there's a number of different options. To help organize our document we'll create a section break – choose the **Continuous** type

3. At first sight nothing seems to change. However, if you click on the ¶ tool in the **Home** tab you'll see the break

4. Now, click in the text after the break and change the number of columns. Note that this affects just the current section; i.e. the text after the break

5. If you add more section breaks to your document, then you'll be able to set columns for each section separately

The quickest way to add a simple page break is to press **Ctrl** + **Return**.

The **Columns** control is also found in the Page Setup area of the **Layout** tab.

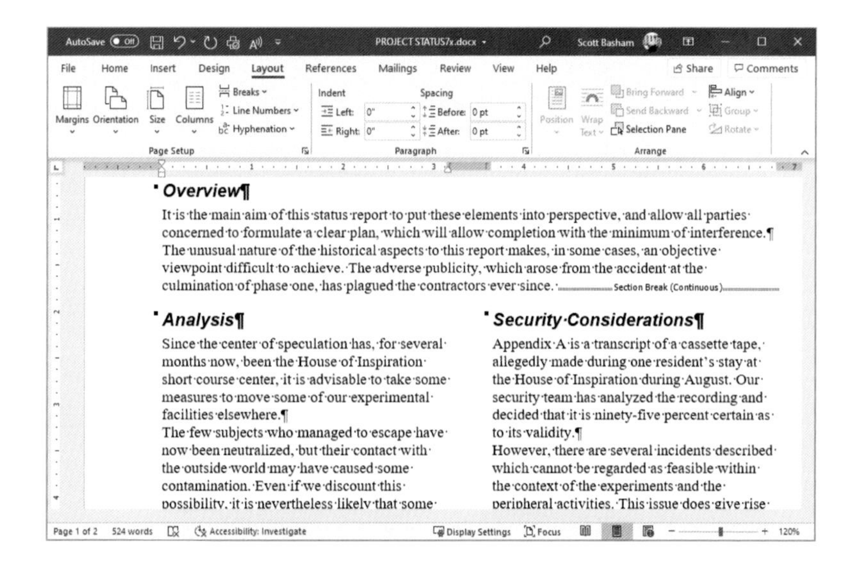

Sections

Dividing a document into sections

It's useful to divide your document into sections using the **Next Page** section break so that the next section starts on a new page. This helps organize your work, and different sections can have their own page numbering, plus different headers and footers.

1. Divide your document into sections by clicking the Breaks tool and choosing a **Next Page** section break. On the first page after a section break, double-click anywhere within the footer to see the **Header & Footer** tools

2. Click the **Link to Previous** icon (in the Navigation area of the **Design** tab) to deactivate it. You can now set a different footer for this section

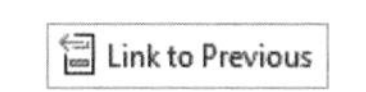

3. If you have an automatic page number then right-click on it and choose **Format Page Numbers...**

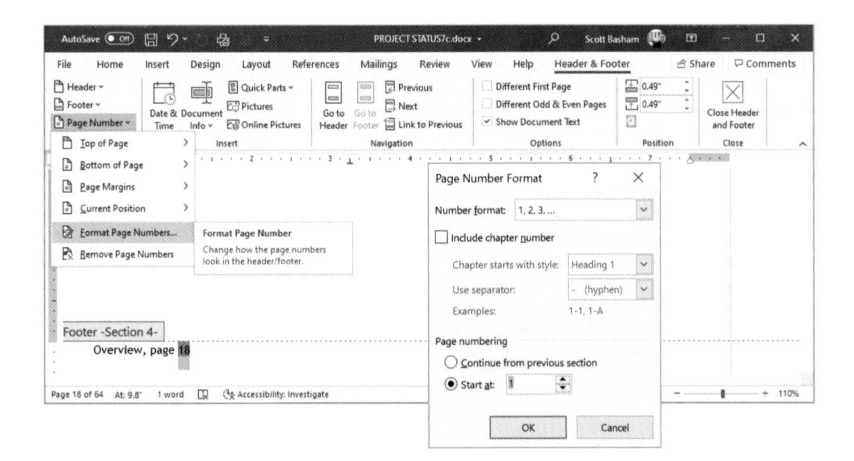

4. Change the **Page Numbering** option to restart at page 1

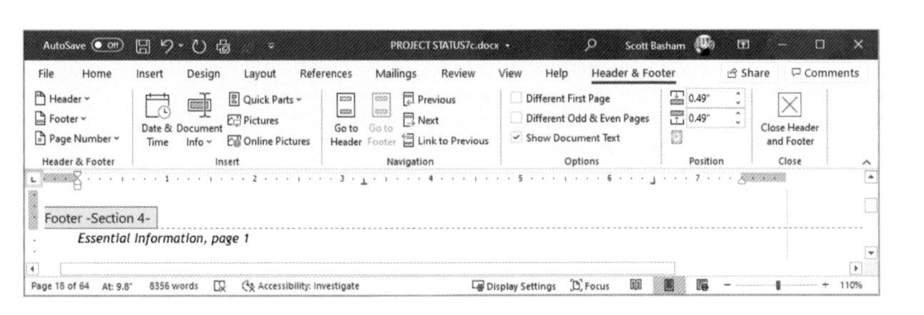

It's worth spending some time customizing each section. In this example, the footer text in the new section has been changed. The document's earlier footer used the text "Overview", but for this section it's changed to "Essential Information".

...cont'd

Line numbers

You can add line numbers to your whole document or to sections, and you can also switch this on and off for individual paragraphs.

1. Either select your whole document or just click within a section, depending on where you'd like line numbering

2. Click **Line Numbers** (**Layout** tab) and choose an option

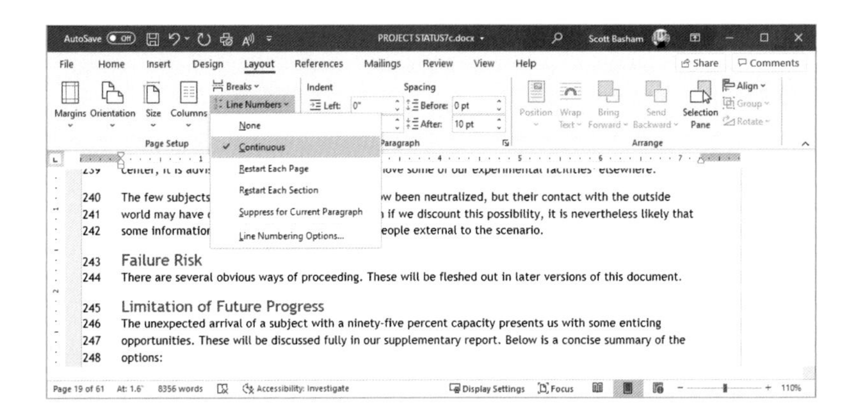

Hot tip

The **Layout** tab also reproduces the indent and spacing settings that are available in the Paragraph dialog (accessible from the **Home** tab). The dialog itself can also be summoned using the icon in the lower-right corner.

Indent Spacing
Left: 0" Before: 0 pt
Right: 0" After: 0 pt
Paragraph

The Page Setup dialog

1. Click on the small icon in the lower-right corner of the Page Setup tools area

2. This dialog contains controls for adjusting the margins and page orientation, as well as advanced options for setting multiple pages per printed sheet

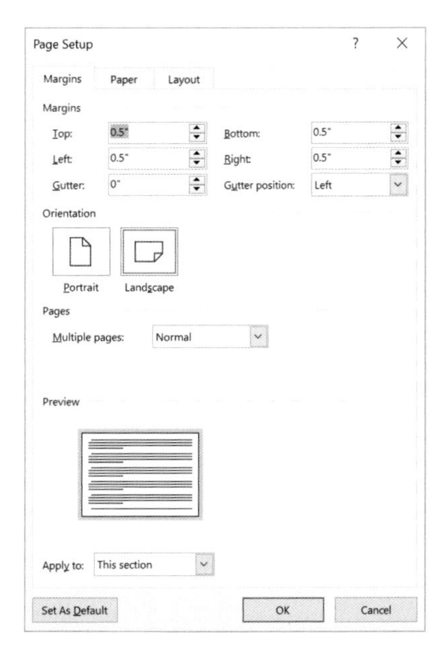

Don't forget

If your screen doesn't match this illustration then make sure the **Margins** tab within the dialog is active.

3. Click the **Paper** tab to define the size and printing options

4. The **Layout** tab lets you make settings for either the whole document or individual sections. You can also access line numbering and border options

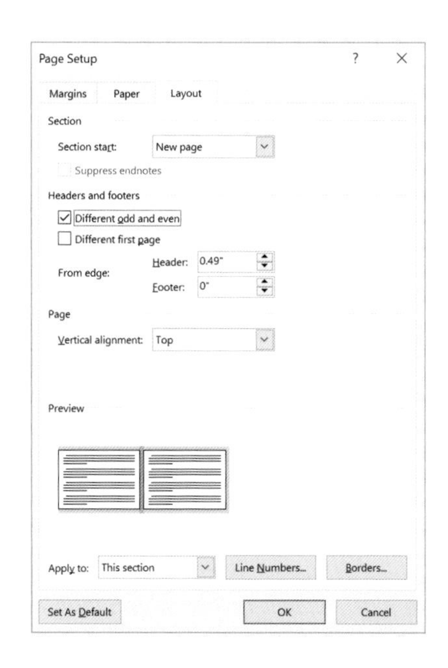

Hyphenation

Word can automatically hyphenate your text for you. This can allow more text to fit on the page, particularly useful if lines of text are not very long. You can also choose manual hyphenation, where Word will prompt you for each potential instance. Hyphenation can be appropriate when working with a layout that uses many columns, such as a magazine or newspaper design.

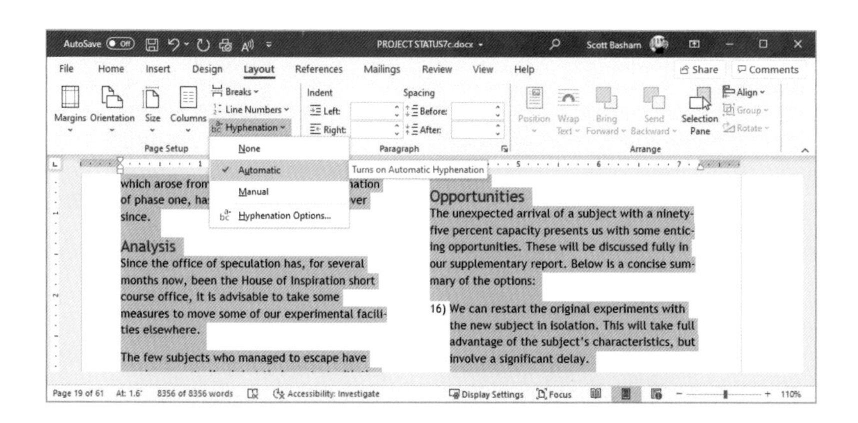

With automatic hyphenation, Word uses special information in its dictionary to decide where within a word a hyphen can be placed. This dictionary is specific to each installed language used by Word.

Click the Hyphenation tool and choose **Hyphenation Options...** to see the following dialog. This gives you finer control over exactly how much hyphenation takes place:

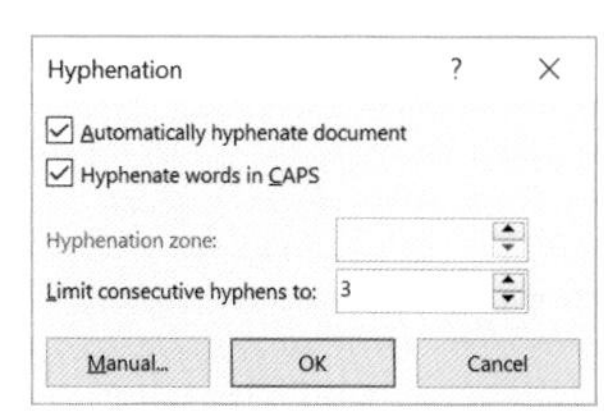

Page background

These controls can be found at the right side of the **Design** tab.

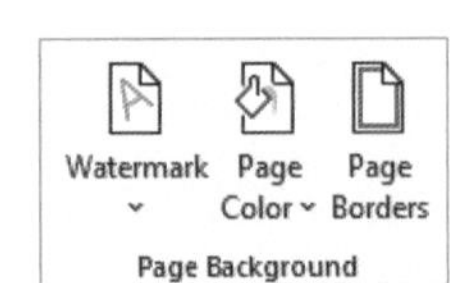

Watermark

You can add either a text or a picture watermark using the **Watermark** tool. This will appear as a background to the page, and can be lightened so that it does not dominate too much.

Page Color

Using the **Page Color** tool you can set your page to a solid color, or even a graduated fill. This can be a good option if your document is to be read online but is perhaps best avoided when printing, due to the amount of ink required.

Page Borders

You can add a range of borders to the edges of your page.

1. Click on the **Page Borders** icon in the **Design** tab

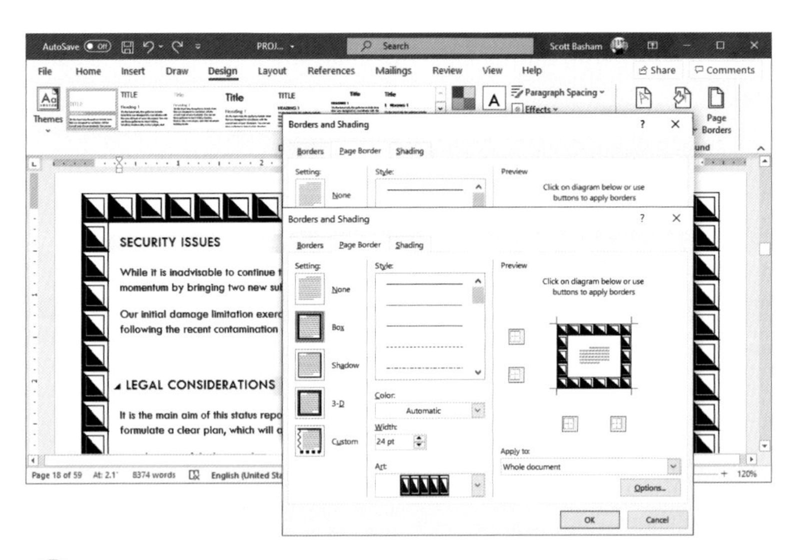

2. Choose your setting and experiment with the line style, color, and width. The **Art** pop-up lets you select from a range of graphic designs. As you work, the **Preview** section on the right will give you some visual feedback

3. You can choose different borders for different sections or apply a border to the whole document, as in this example

The **Shading** tab in this dialog allows you to apply background shading to the current paragraph.

5 Pictures and graphics

This chapter looks at Word's graphical features, from photos and video through to charts, diagrams, icons, 3D models and screenshots.

Pictures

The Illustrations area

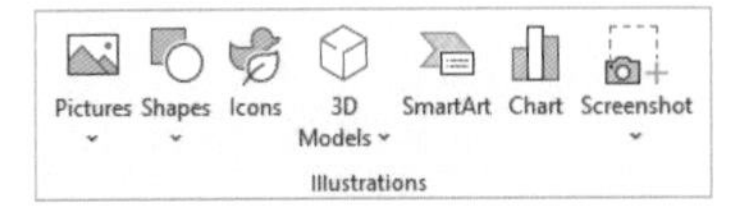

The **Illustrations** area of the **Insert** tab allows you to add a range of different graphical objects.

Word can import many types of graphic file format, and these fall into two main categories. Draw-type graphics are represented as mathematical objects. They can usually be scaled up or down with no loss in quality. The other type is bitmapped; i.e. stored as a structure of dots or pixels. Be careful not to enlarge bitmapped images too much, as the pixels get bigger and more noticeable.

Adding a photo from a file on disk

In this example we'll import an image created by a digital camera. We'll assume that we have some photo files available on the hard disk or other storage medium.

1. Navigate to the appropriate part of your document, click on **Pictures** in the **Illustrations** area of the **Insert** tab and choose **This Device**

2. Use the standard Windows controls at the top and the left of the dialog to locate the photo files

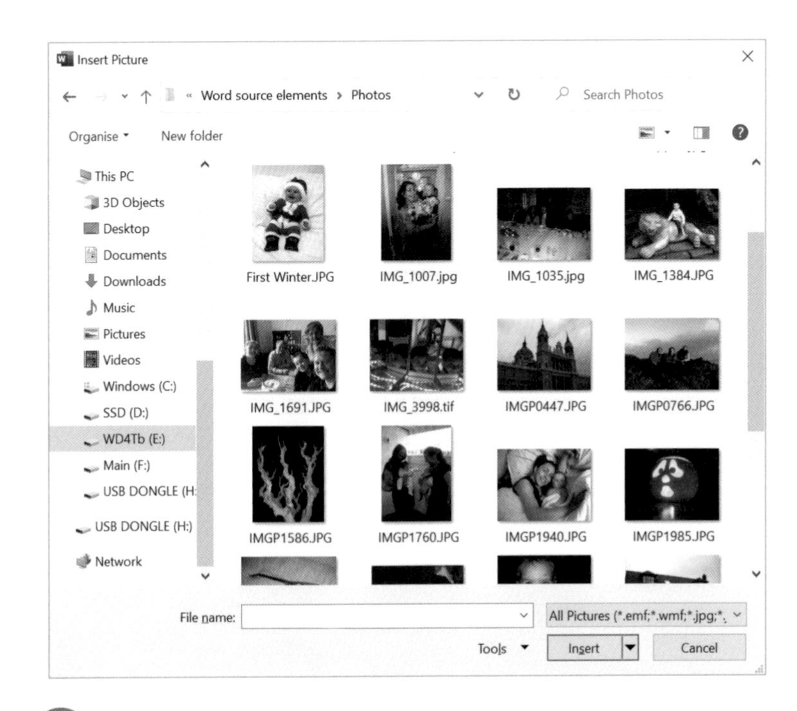

3. Once you have found the image you want, select it and then click the **Insert** button

If you move your mouse over one of the images you'll see additional file details such as the image's dimensions.

4. The image is brought into the current page. Note that it has eight circular "handles", which can be dragged around if you want to manipulate the image

Drag on a corner handle to resize, keeping the picture in proportion. Drag one of the handles halfway along an edge to stretch just vertically or horizontally.

Drag the circular arrow icon to rotate the image; any other handle will resize it

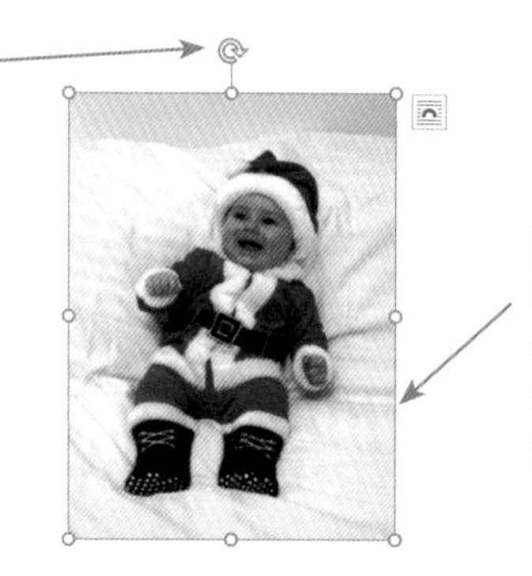

Drag directly on an edge (not on a handle) to move without resizing

5. Sometimes you'll want to cut away unnecessary parts of the picture. Click on the **Crop** tool and you'll see some heavy black corners and edges. Dragging inwards on these will prepare the image for cropping

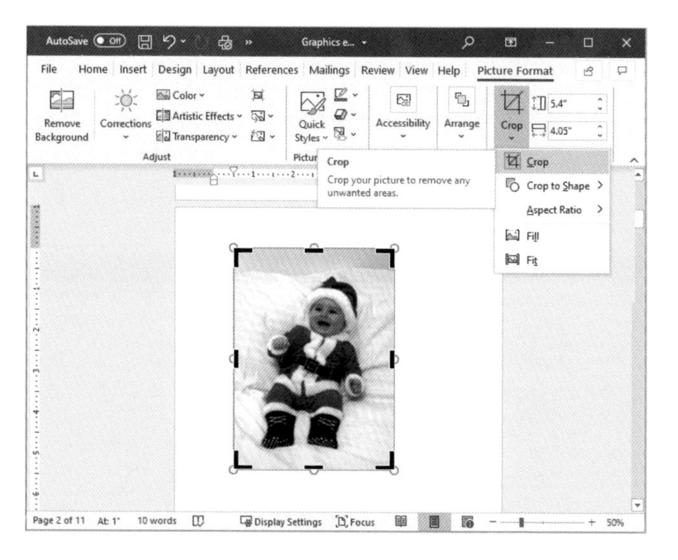

6. When you're happy with your adjustments, click on the **Crop** tool again and choose **Crop** to apply the changes. If you change your mind later, simply reselect **Crop** and drag the black handles outwards again

In the Crop tool's pop-up menu there are also **Crop to Shape** options, and many preset shapes to choose from.

...cont'd

Remove Background

If your photo has a prominent main object that is easily distinguishable from its background, then you can get help from Word to remove the background automatically.

1. Select the photo, then click the **Remove Background** tool in the **Adjust** area of the **Picture Format** tab

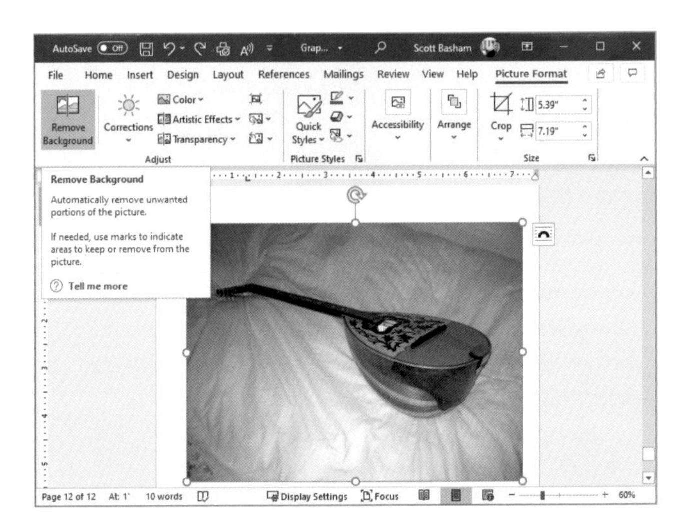

The **Picture Format** tab only appears when a picture is selected in your document.

2. The magenta-colored area indicates Word's guess at what is the background. If it hasn't got it quite right, then use the **Mark Areas to Keep** and **Mark Areas to Remove** tools to subtract from or add to the magenta area

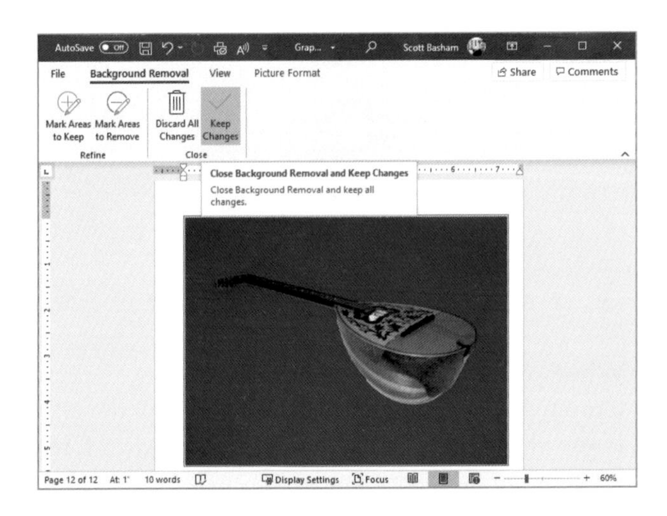

3. When you're satisfied that the correct area is defined, click the **Keep Changes** icon and the background will be removed

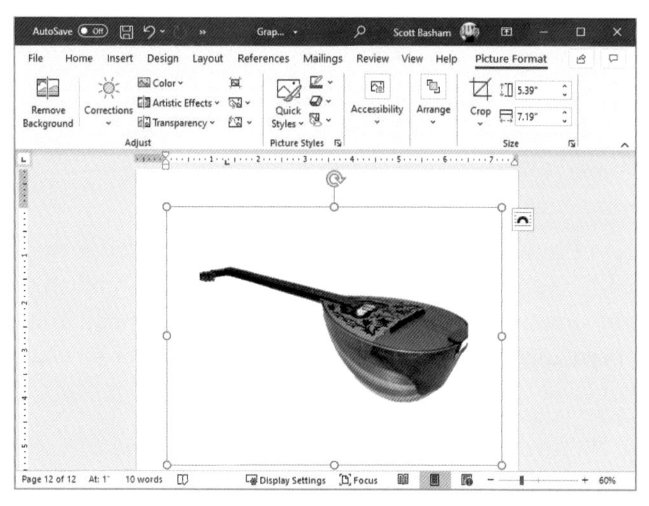

Most of the tools described here are in the **Picture Format** tab. If you select a picture, the tab – although available – may not be currently active. In this case, simply click on the tab title (depicted below) to select it.

Review View Help Picture Format

Artistic Effects

Although Word isn't a fully-blown photo-manipulation package, it does have a range of tools for both creative and corrective work.

1. Select the photo and click the **Artistic Effects** tool

2. The pop-up menu contains options for treating your photo using creative filter effects, as you can see in this example. Hover over an option to see a live preview

Similar to **Artistic Effects**, the **Corrections** tool gives you a number of options for sharpening/softening and for adjusting the brightness and contrast of a photo.

...cont'd

The Adjust tools

There are some useful tools in the **Adjust** area of the **Picture Tools/Format** tab, although three might not have visible captions:

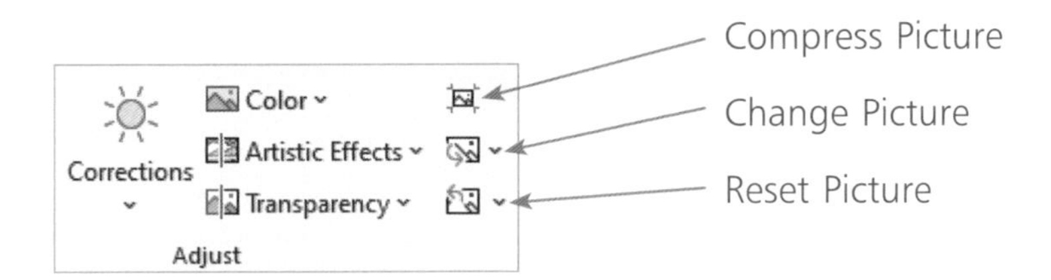

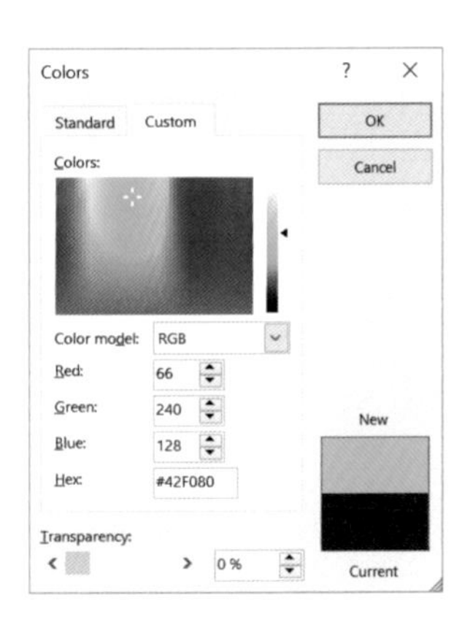

Compress Picture gives you the opportunity to reduce the file size used for your image (and consequently reduce upload and download time if copying across the web or via email). You can do this by permanently removing cropped-out areas, or by changing the detail level (resolution).

Change Picture lets you substitute in a new picture file, whilst preserving attributes such as size and crop information.

Reset Picture removes all the formatting, effectively returning the image to how it was when first imported.

Picture Styles

The **Quick Styles** icon in the **Picture Styles** area lets you apply a wide range of visually-interesting effects such as Shadow, Glow, Reflection, Rotation or a combination of these in a preset style.

Word's **Colors** dialog box can be called up from a number of places, usually by selecting a **More Colors...** icon in another dialog. It allows you to select a color from a palette, or define using RGB (Red, Green, Blue) or HLS (Hue, Lightness, Saturation). You can also enter a color Hex code directly if you want to make a precise choice.

The Format Picture pane

As well as the tools in the **Format** tab, there is a task pane window that gives you more control over your picture settings.

1. Select a photo and click the **Picture Styles** icon

2. The **Format Picture** task pane will appear. Make sure the **Shadow** tools are active to see the controls available

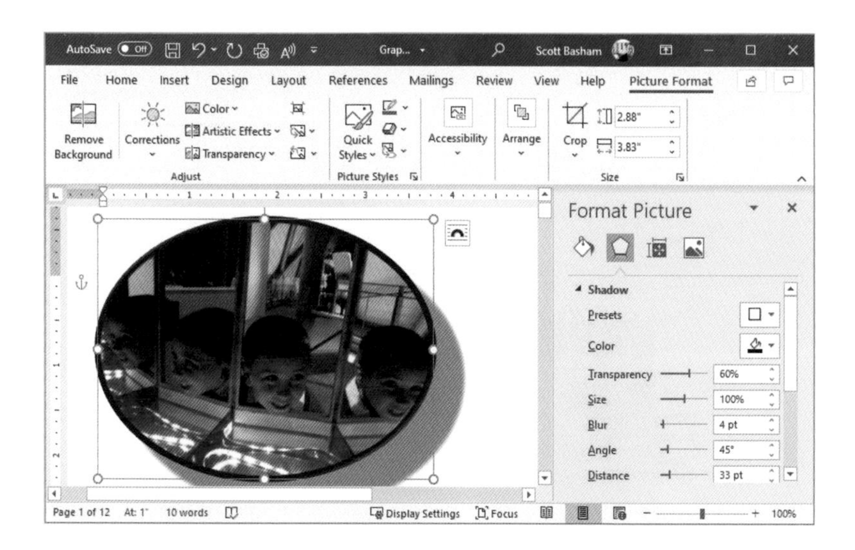

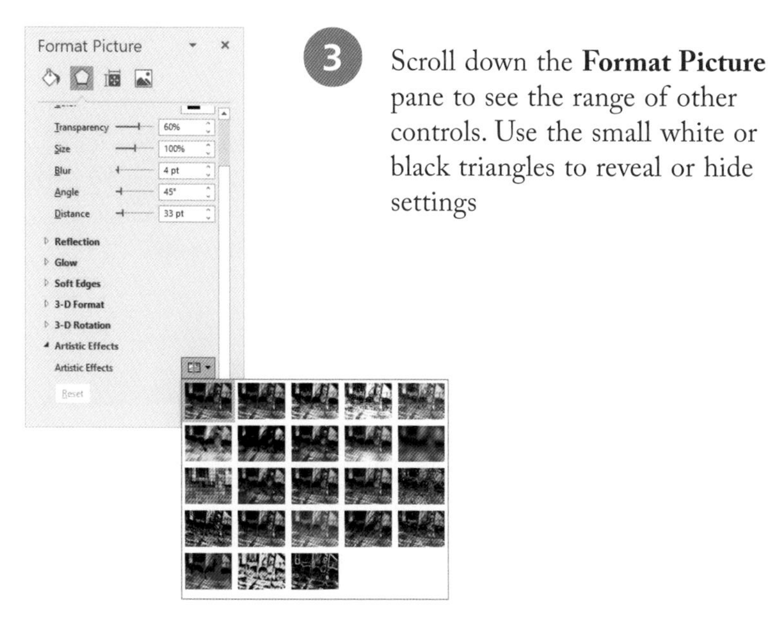

3. Scroll down the **Format Picture** pane to see the range of other controls. Use the small white or black triangles to reveal or hide settings

The **Format** task pane's controls will change to reflect what is currently selected. If, for example, you select a picture, it appears as a **Format Picture** panel.

Side panels can be undocked by dragging on their title away from the current position. Once free from the main window, they can be positioned and resized easily. To re-dock, simply drag onto the left or right side of the tabbed controls area.

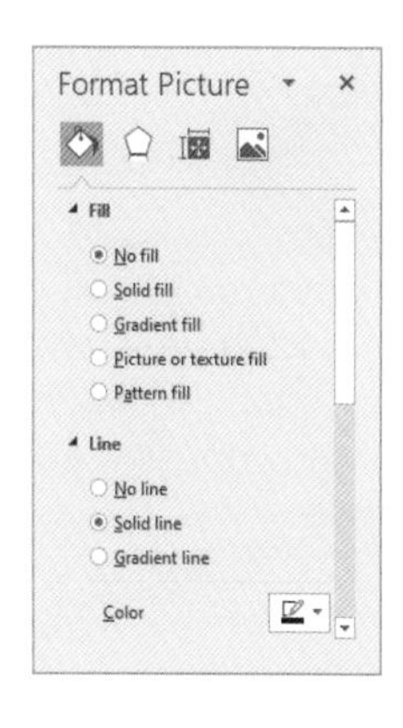

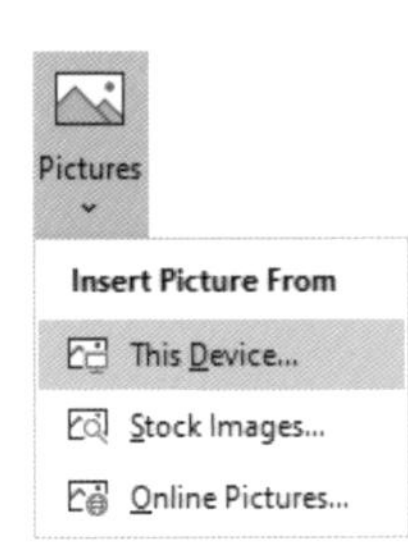

Adding a draw-type picture from a file

In this example we'll import and manipulate a draw-type object.

1. Navigate to the appropriate part of your document, then choose one of the options under **Pictures** in the **Illustrations** area of the **Insert** tab

2. Once you've found a suitable draw-type graphic, select it and then click the **Insert** button

Draw-type graphics can generally be edited with no appreciable loss in quality, as they are stored as a set of mathematical objects. WMF (Windows MetaFile) and SVG (Scalable Vector Graphics) are examples of draw file types.

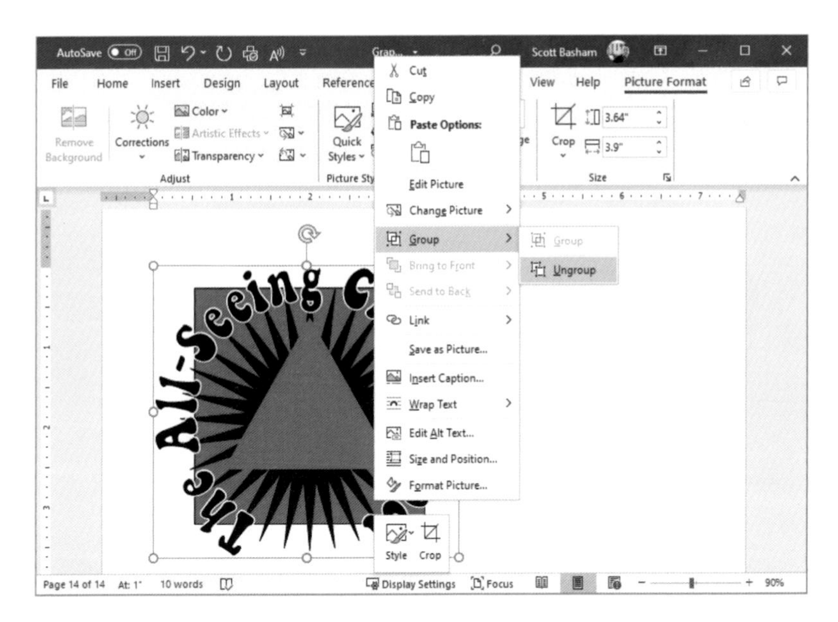

3. If the graphic consists of a number of shapes, then it's usually possible to edit its individual components. To do this, right-click to access the pop-up menu. Click on **Group** to see a sub-menu, and select **Ungroup**

You can also convert an imported draw-type picture by right-clicking on it and choosing **Edit Picture**.

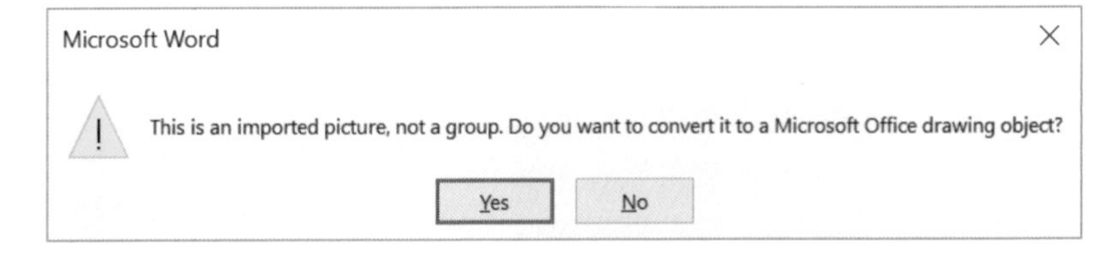

4. If you see the dialog box pictured above, click **Yes**

5. Often, this will be sufficient for you to start editing individual elements. Experiment by clicking on different areas of the graphic to see what you can select. Once an element is selected it can usually be moved, resized, rotated, or formatted using different colors or line styles

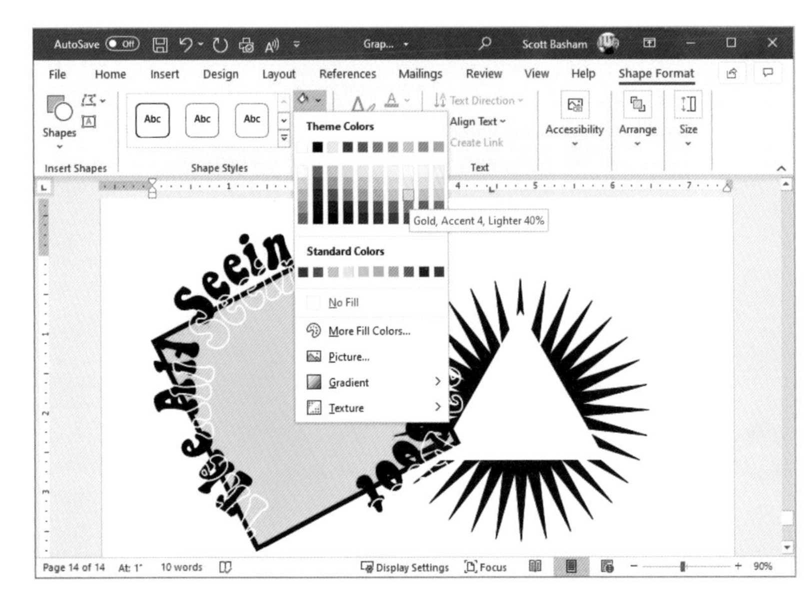

6. Sometimes a draw-type graphic consists of items that are grouped together. If it does, you can break it down further by right-clicking and choosing **Group** and then **Ungroup**

7. The graphic is now split into a set of smaller objects

8. Experiment by editing one or two objects. You can use the **Shape Format** tab to apply new borders, color or styles

9. When you've finished you might want to regroup. To do this, select all the objects then right-click, choose **Group** and select **Group** again from the sub-menu

Paint-type graphics cannot be manipulated in this way. They are represented as a grid of rectangular pixels (picture cells) rather than objects, and so cannot be broken down into simpler elements.

The easiest way to select all the objects within the general graphics frame is to click on one (to establish selection within the frame), then type **Ctrl + A** for **Select All**.

Converted draw-type graphics exist within a rectangular frame area. It is sometimes a good idea to drag on one of its circular edges or corner handles to make it larger. This gives you more room in which to move and edit elements.

Online Pictures

1. Move your insertion point to the place in your document where you'd like to put the picture

2. On the **Insert** tab click **Pictures** then **Online Pictures...**

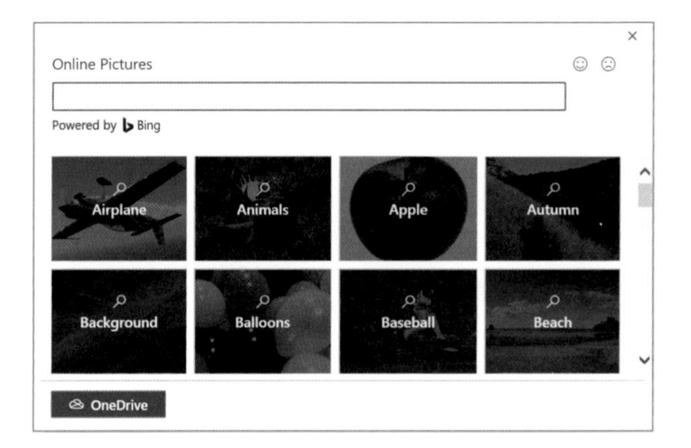

3. You can either select from the categories available or enter some search text in the dialog that appears. When you've found a suitable picture select it then click on the **Insert** button

4. The picture is imported into the current position. It can now be manipulated just like other photos

In the **Online Pictures** dialog, once you select a category (such as Animals in this example) then a filter icon appears on the left side above the images. If you click this you can filter the results by size, type, layout or color.

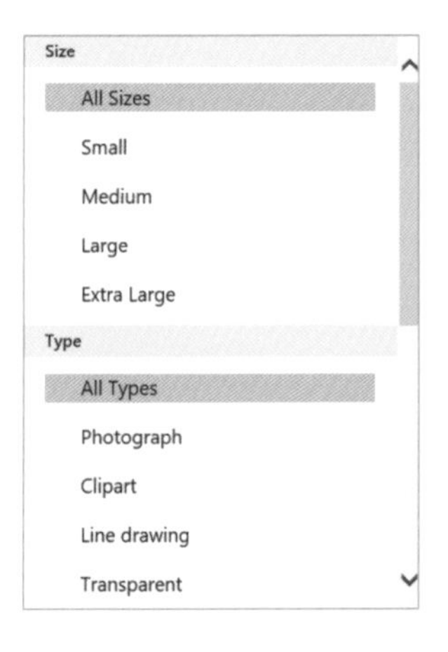

Shapes

Word offers a large selection of standard graphic shapes that can be drawn and then customized.

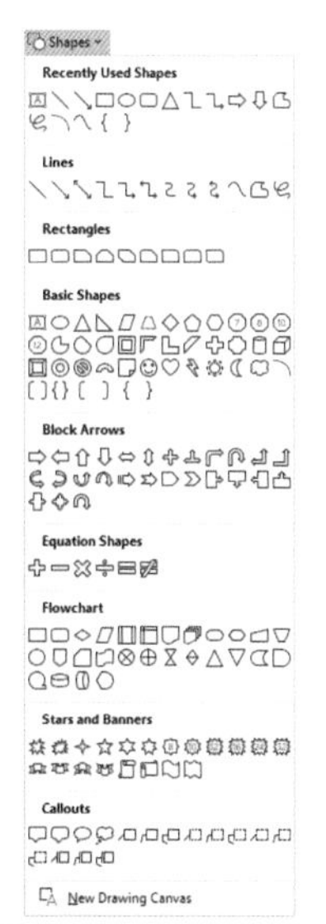

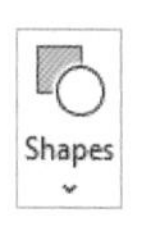

1. Click on the **Shapes** icon in the **Insert** tab. A gallery of standard shapes appears. These are draw-type graphics, so you can resize and manipulate them in many ways without any loss in quality

2. Select one of these. This example uses **Callout: Down Arrow**

3. Click and drag diagonally to create the initial shape. If it's the wrong size or position this can be changed easily

You can rotate shapes just like other graphic elements by dragging on the circular arrow tool that appears above the item when it's selected.

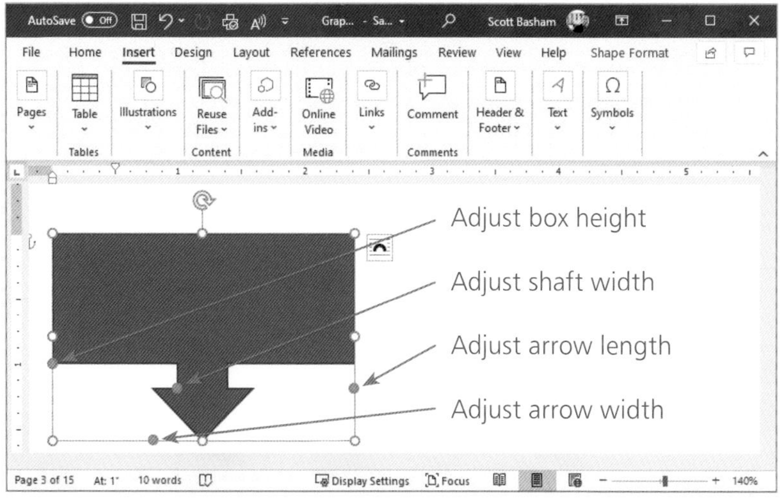

4. You can move the object by dragging directly on it. Drag on a white circular handle (corner or edge) to resize it

5. Drag on a yellow circular handle to change a single aspect of the shape. Precisely what this changes depends on the shape, so it's worth experimenting. In the above example, the yellow handles let you customize the dimensions of the box and the arrow part individually

Right-click on a shape and choose **Edit Points**. You'll then be able to change the shape by dragging its vertices. Click and drag along a line to add a new point. Right-click a point to choose between **Smooth**, **Straight** or **Corner**.

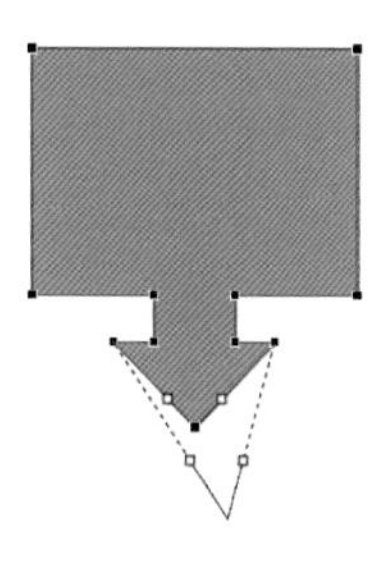

3D Models

Here, we'll see how you can import and even manipulate 3D objects within your Word documents.

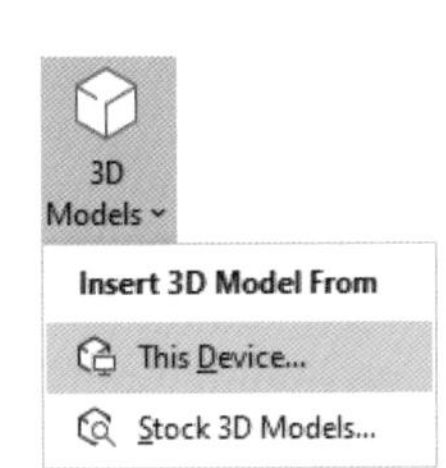

1. Click on the **3D Models** icon in the **Insert** tab and select either **This Device...** or **Stock 3D Models...**

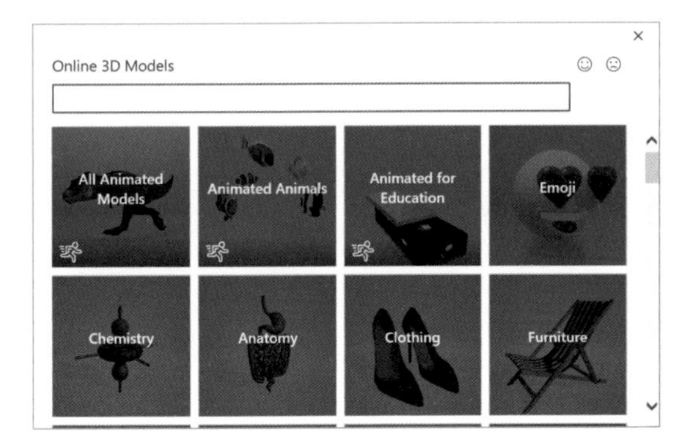

Word can import 3D models from the following file formats: Filmbox (*.fbx); Object (*.obj); 3D Manufacturing (*.3mf); Polygon (*.ply); StereoLithography (*.stl); and Binary GL Transmission (*.glb). It can import both static and animated models.

2. In this example we are selecting from **Online Sources**. Choose a category to see the options available or, alternatively, enter some text in the Search box and click the magnifying glass icon

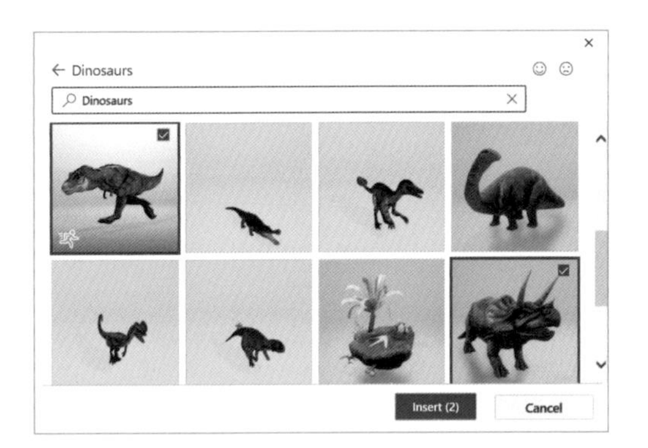

If you select multiple items, the **Insert** button at the bottom of the dialog box keeps track of the total number that will be imported with one click.

3. When you have selected the desired 3D graphic, click the **Insert** button. You may have to wait for a few moments while Word processes the file

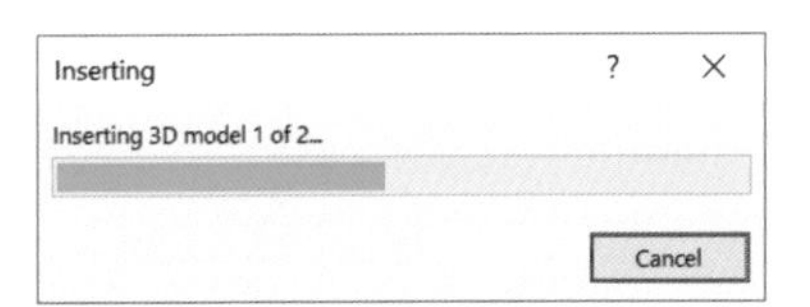

4. Your 3D graphic will appear at the current document position. You can move, resize and use the normal rotation tool just as you can for ordinary graphic elements

Drag directly on this icon to control 3D Rotation

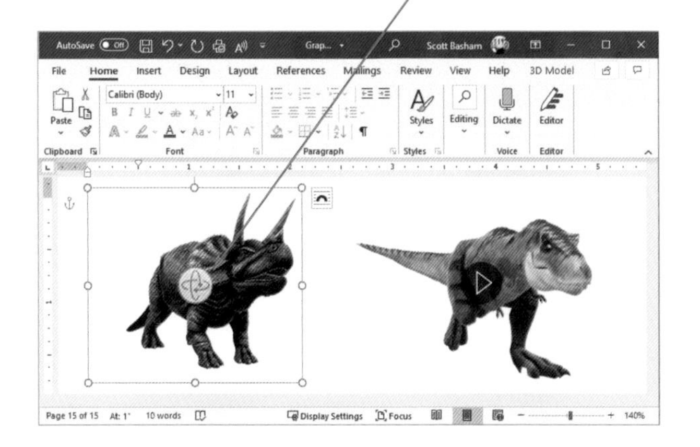

5. In the center of the graphic is a special **3D Rotation** tool. If you drag on this you can rotate the graphic about its other two axes. By using this in combination with the normal **Rotation** tool you can turn the model in any direction you like. In the example below we made six copies of our dinosaur so that we could compare different rotational views

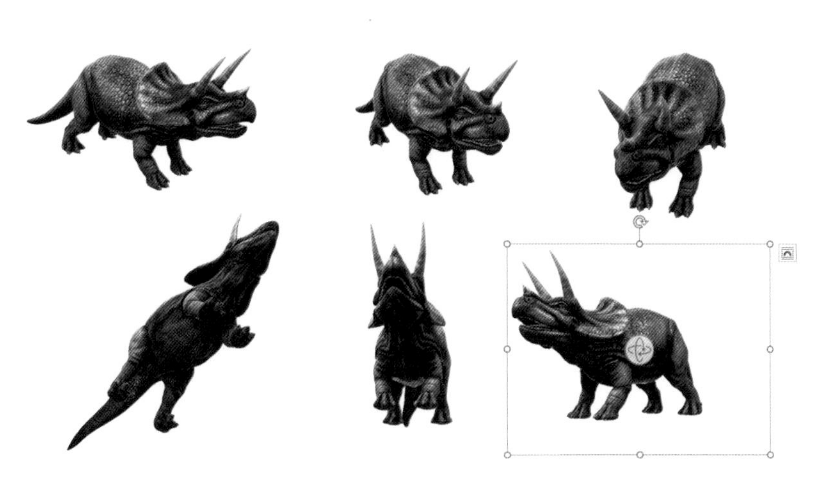

When you have a 3D object selected, the **Format** tab shows two extra tools. **3D Models** lets you import another graphic, while **Reset 3D Model** will switch it back to its initial view and (optionally) change it back to its initial size.

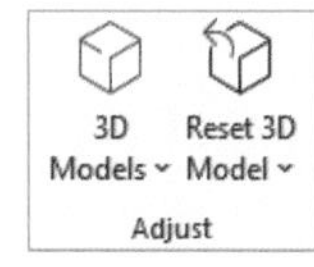

Icons

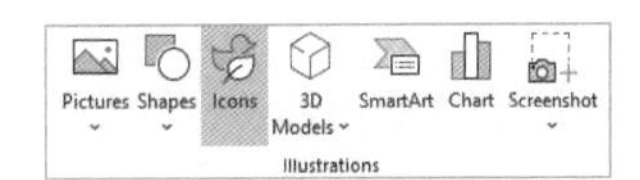

Icons are usually simple bold graphics used to convey a concept in a visually-striking way, independent of language.

1. To add an icon to your document, first make sure the **Insert** tab is active and click on **Icons**. The following dialog box appears

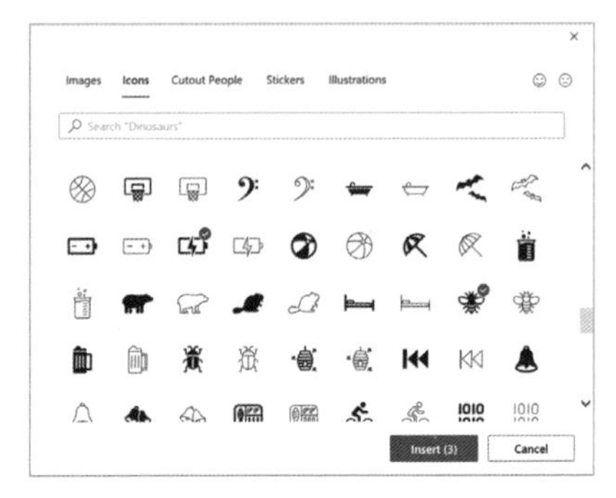

As with pictures, you can select multiple items and then import in one operation by clicking the Insert button. In the example in Step 1, three icons have been selected.

2. Select a category from the list at the top, and then browse through the available icons

3. Select your icon then click the **Insert** button

4. The icon will appear at the current position in your document. It can be moved and sized just like any normal graphic. Because it is a draw-type graphic, it can also be edited further. To do this, right-click on the icon and choose **Convert to Shape**

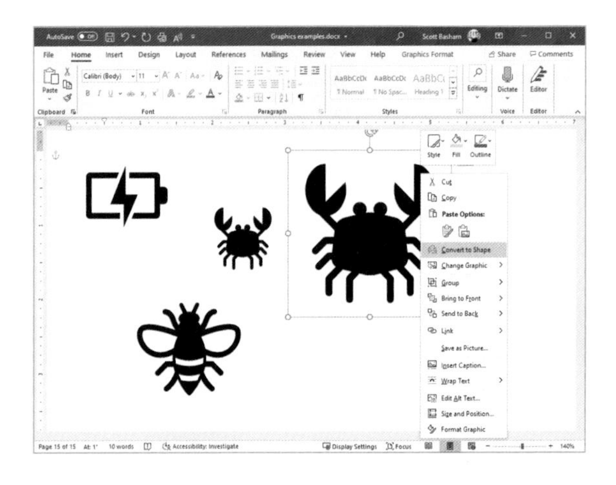

You can save any of these graphic objects to a file on disk. Simply right-click on the object and choose **Save as Picture...** from the pop-up menu. Supported file formats are Portable Network Graphics (*.png); JPEG (*.jpg); Graphics Interchange Format (*.gif); TIFF (*.tif); Windows Bitmap (*.bmp); and Scalable Vector Graphics (*.svg).

5. Now that the icon has been converted, you can right-click and choose **Edit Points** from the pop-up menu

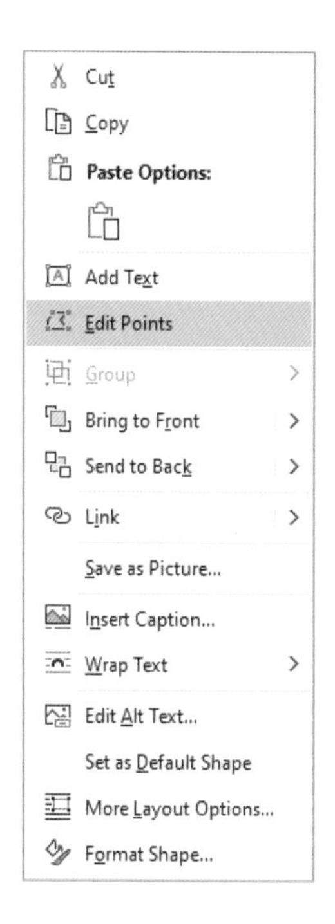

6. The shape can now be manipulated as a set of straight lines and curves connecting points that are marked as black squares. If you select one of these you can adjust curvature by dragging on the white square "handles" that appear. Dragging further from its counterpart black square changes the sharpness of the curve

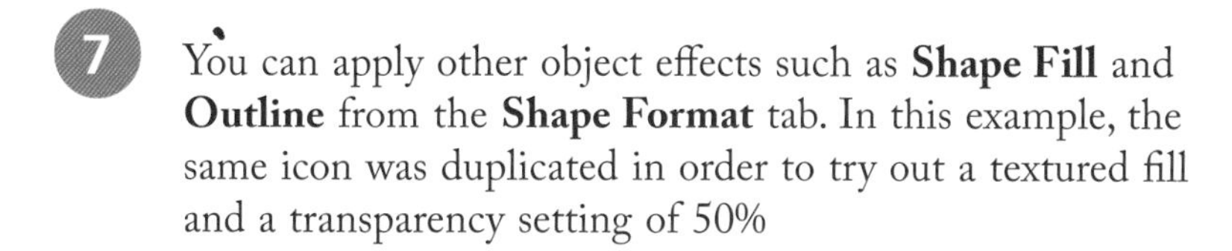

7. You can apply other object effects such as **Shape Fill** and **Outline** from the **Shape Format** tab. In this example, the same icon was duplicated in order to try out a textured fill and a transparency setting of 50%

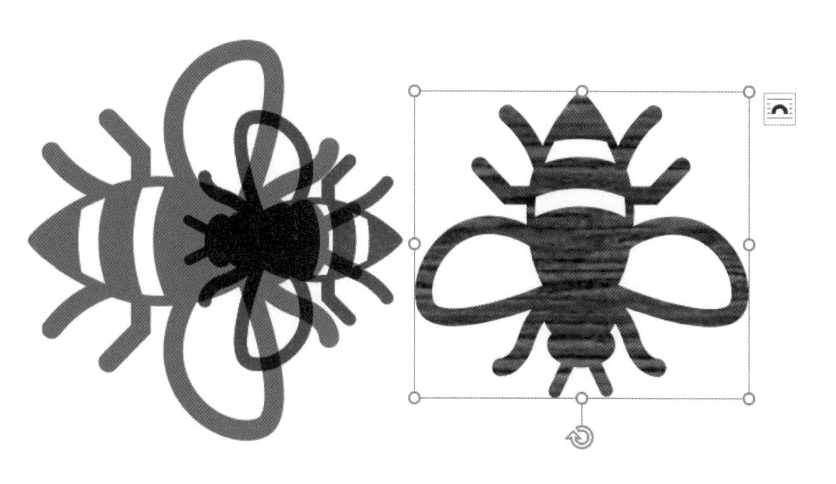

Because icons are drawing objects you can perform actions such as resizing, rotating, and scaling without any loss in quality.

Layout Options

1. Select any object and then click on the **Layout Options** icon to see the following settings

The **Layout Options** icon appears at the top right of any object you select, and provides a quick way of controlling how it interacts with its surroundings.

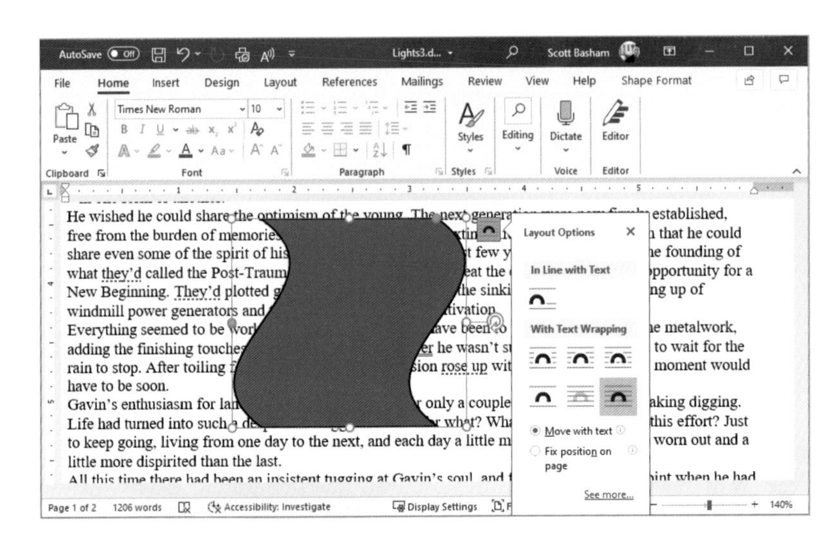

2. If your object overlaps text, you may be interested in using text wrap. **Tight** is sometimes all you need for surrounding text to closely follow the shape's contours

3. Right-click on the object and a menu will appear. Choose **Wrap Text** then **Edit Wrap Points**. You'll then see the text wrap border defined as straight black lines connected by small black squares that work as handles

The **Arrange** tools on the right of the **Shape Format** tab can be used to align objects, and move them in front of or behind other objects.

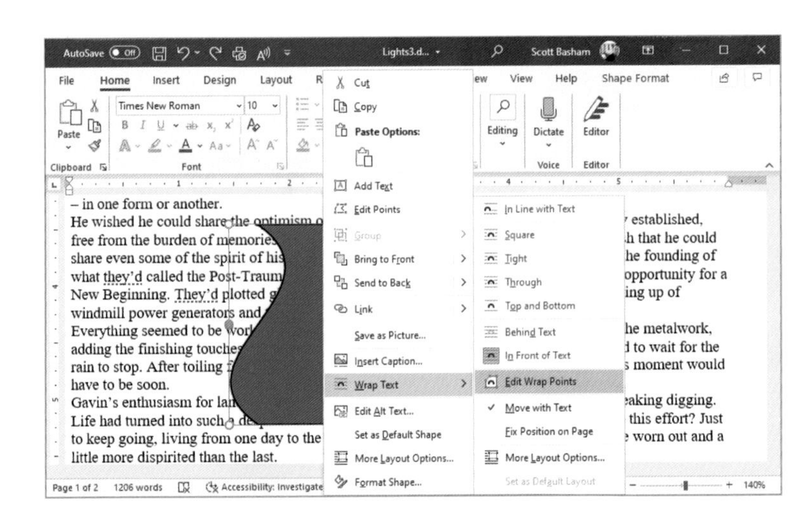

4. Drag one of these handles to move the boundary line. If there's text nearby then you'll see it move so that it's always outside the perimeter

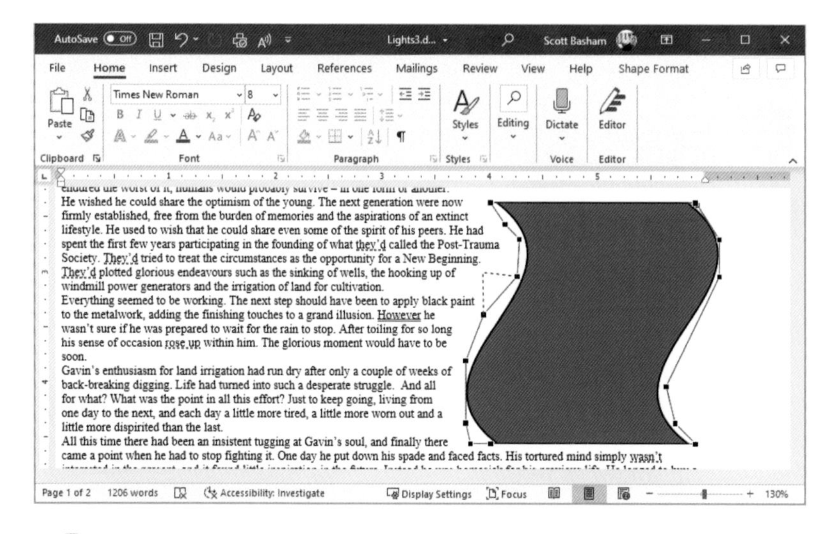

To delete a text wrap handle, hold down the **Ctrl** key and click directly on the handle.

5. Click and drag on the border, but not on an existing handle, to create a new handle. Using these controls you can alter the way text flows around any irregular shape

6. Click on an object's **Layout Options** icon and choose **See more...** to see a dialog where you can numerically set position, text wrap, and size. Some of these options are also available from the **Layout** and **Format** tabs

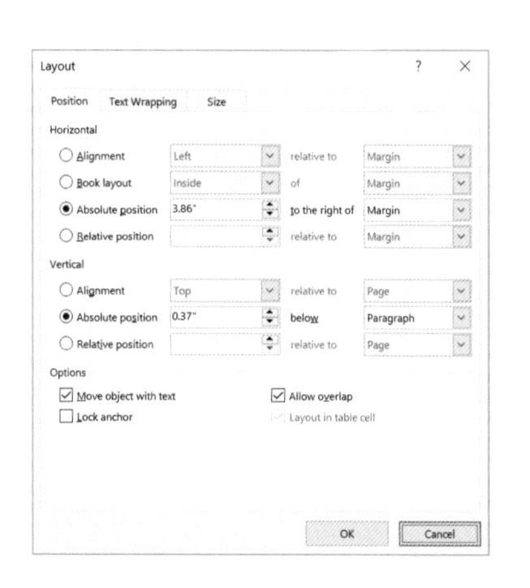

...cont'd

Adding text inside a shape

Most shapes can be used as text boxes, and all the normal text formatting options are available within these.

1. If there's currently no text in the shape, then right-click and choose **Add Text**

2. Enter the text (or paste from the Clipboard)

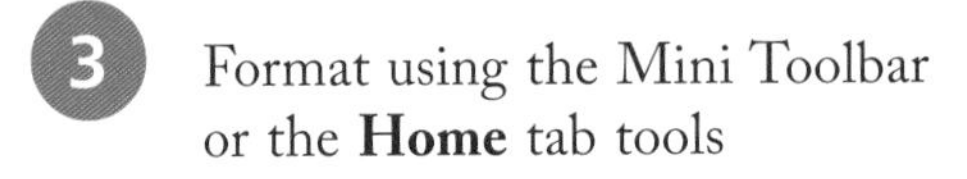

3. Format using the Mini Toolbar or the **Home** tab tools

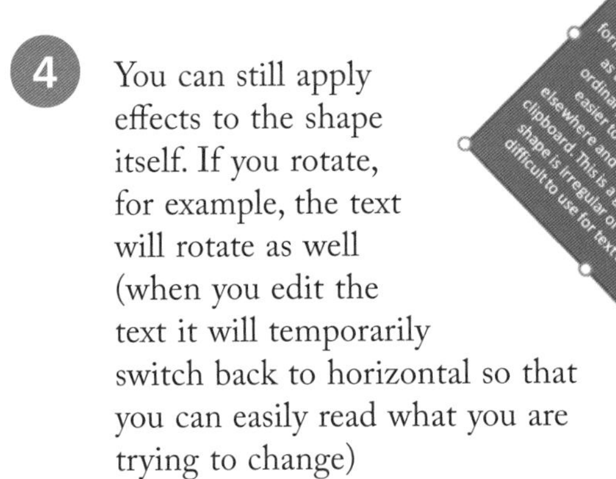

4. You can still apply effects to the shape itself. If you rotate, for example, the text will rotate as well (when you edit the text it will temporarily switch back to horizontal so that you can easily read what you are trying to change)

Canvas objects

When you ungroup a complex object it will, by default, become a series of smaller items within a rectangular canvas object. You can move the whole thing or set layout options by clicking on the canvas border, or manipulate the individual items inside by selecting them in the normal way.

It's usually worth resizing the canvas object to make it larger. Make sure you give yourself enough room to easily manipulate the graphic objects within. You can always shrink the canvas again later.

Controlling layout

Alignment guides

1. Go to the **Layout** tab, click **Align** and make sure **Use Alignment Guides** is selected

2. Move an object to see temporary vertical and horizontal guides – these assist with alignment to other objects

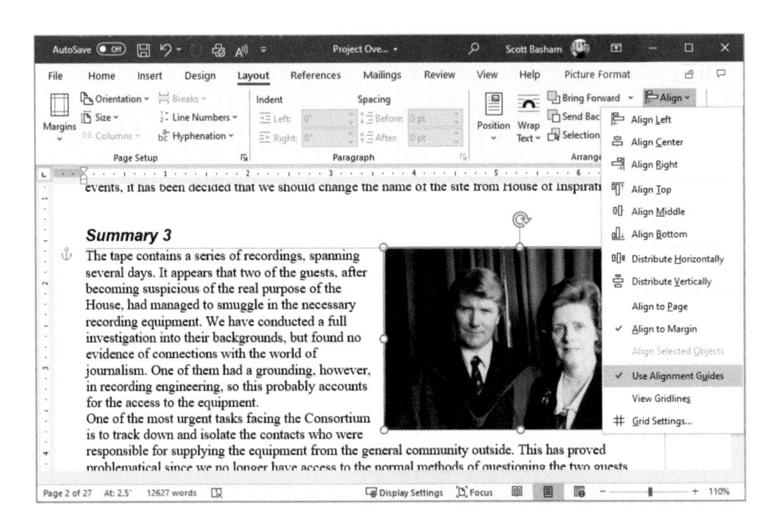

The alignment guides are magnetic and so help you to easily align the object you're moving with other items such as margins, graphics, or the center of the page.

Live layout

Word gives you a real-time preview of your document as you move, resize, or rotate a picture – so you can see exactly the effect of your changes without any delay.

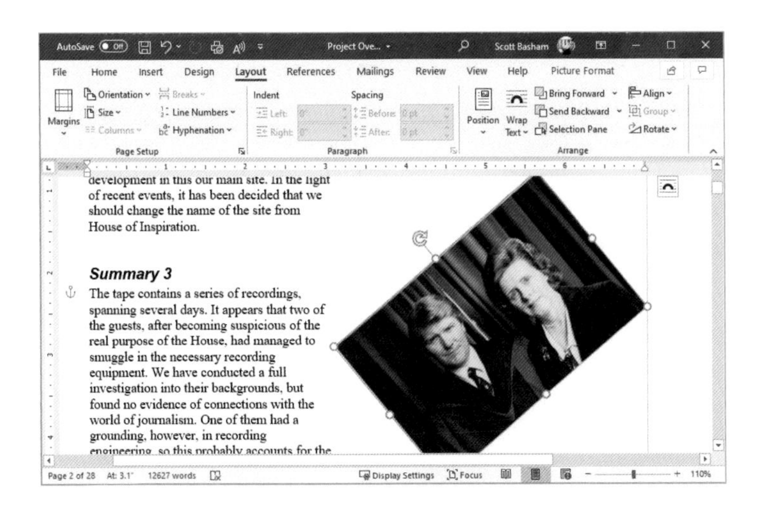

Online Video

As long as your computer is online, you can easily add videos to your documents from a variety of sources.

1. Click **Online Video** in the **Media** area of the **Insert** tab

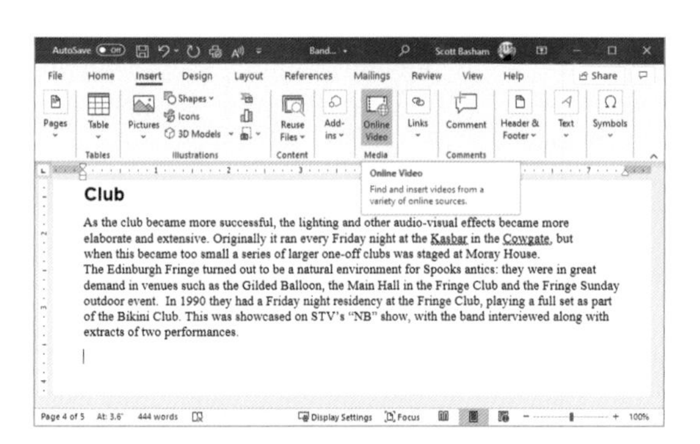

Websites showing online videos sometimes have controls that display the relevant embed code, which you can copy and paste into the bottom section of the Insert Video dialog.

2. The **Insert Video** dialog appears. Either enter a video web address URL or a video embed code directly

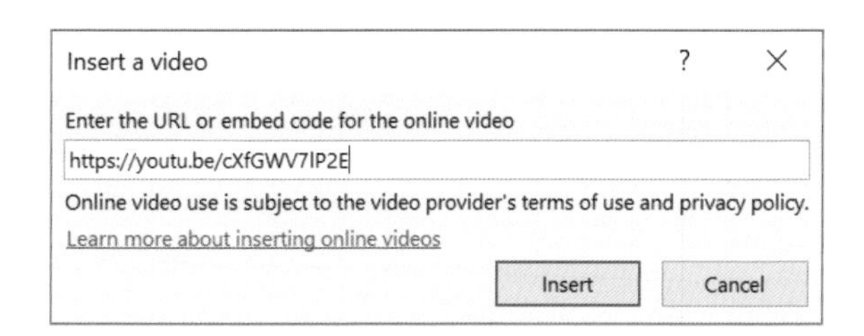

Word does not actually embed the video in the document – instead, it stores a link to its source website. This keeps your documents small, but it also means that you need to be online whenever you attempt to play the video.

3. Click the **Insert** button. The **Video** object is added to the current location. You can move, resize, or play it by clicking the white triangle

SmartArt

SmartArt graphic items allow you to present concepts and information in a visual way.

1. Click on the **SmartArt** icon in the **Insert** tab. The following dialog appears. Choose an item and click **OK**

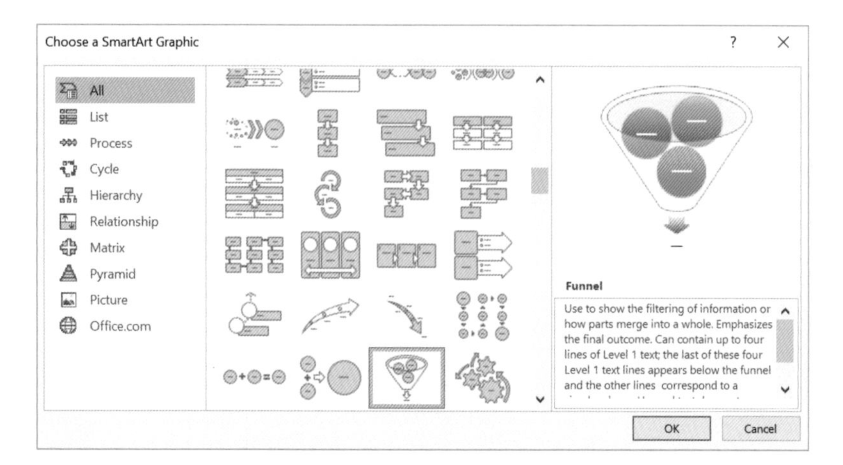

2. Click on **Text Pane** in the **Create Graphic** area of the **SmartArt Design** tab to make it visible. Enter your text in the window on the left, and it will appear in the diagram

3. You can work on parts of the object by selecting individual items and then formatting, moving, resizing, or performing other types of edit

You can radically alter your design at any time by changing the selection from the **Layouts** and **SmartArt Styles** areas of the **SmartArt Design** tab.

...cont'd

The SmartArt tools

Whenever SmartArt objects are selected, the **SmartArt Tools** appear, divided into two tabs: **SmartArt Design** and **Format**.

In the **SmartArt Design** tab, click to activate the **Text Pane** icon. Use the **Create Graphic** controls to promote/demote the text lines, or **Tab** to indent directly

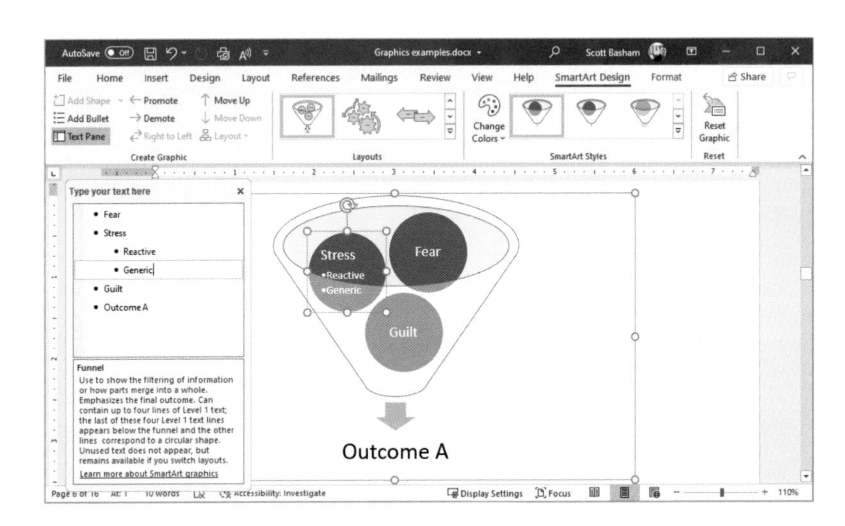

SmartArt objects are ways of presenting text lists in graphical form. Often you'll edit the text directly on the object, but sometimes it's more useful to view and change it in the separate Text pane.

2 Activate the **Format** tab to experiment with different visual effects

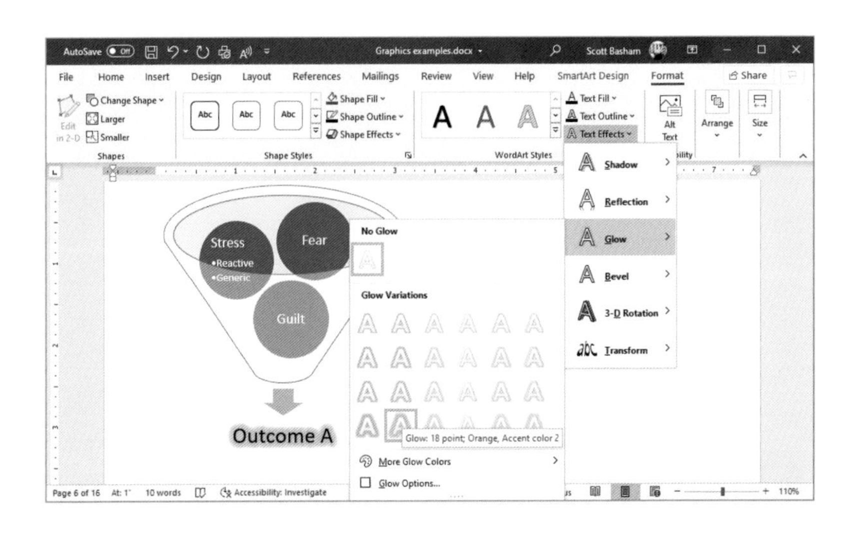

Depending on what you select, these **Format** controls can apply to the whole object or to individual parts.

Charts

If you've used Microsoft Excel you may be familiar with the concept of presenting tables of figures in chart form.

1. Click on the **Chart** icon in the **Insert** tab. The following dialog appears, with a large selection of chart variants

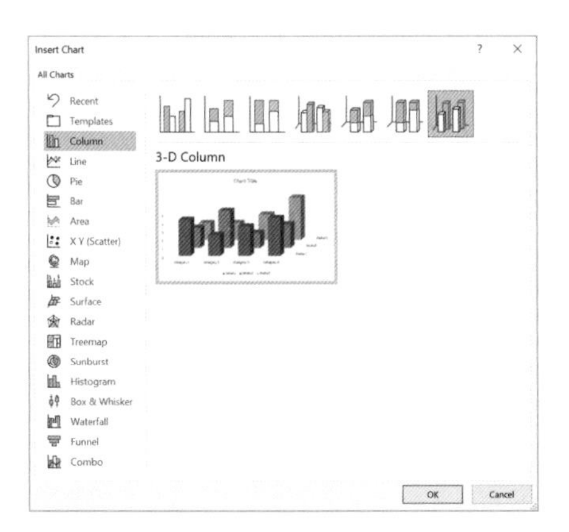

2. Choose a chart type and click **OK**

3. A default chart appears. You can select and customize this using the **Chart Design** tab, which appears automatically

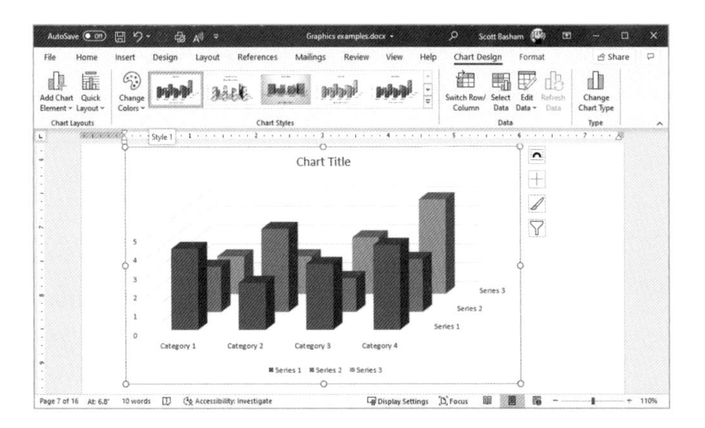

4. A separate window opens, displaying some sample chart data. You can edit this so that the chart uses your own text and figures

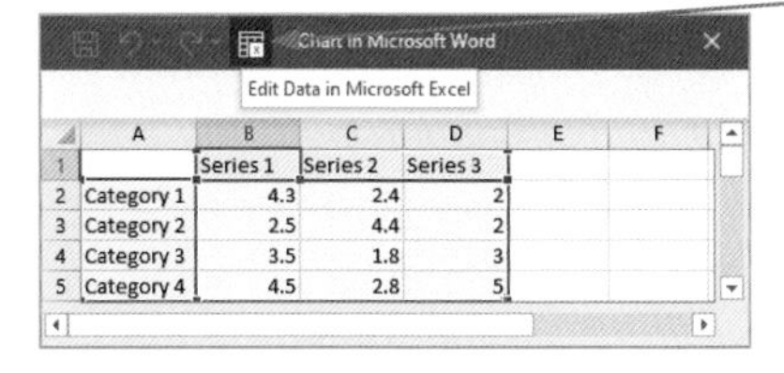

	A	B	C	D	E	F
1		Series 1	Series 2	Series 3		
2	Category 1	4.3	2.4	2		
3	Category 2	2.5	4.4	2		
4	Category 3	3.5	1.8	3		
5	Category 4	4.5	2.8	5		

If you don't like the chart type you selected it's easy to go back and select another, so enjoy the freedom to experiment.

You can save a chart as a picture to a file on disk. Simply right-click on the chart and choose **Save as Picture...** from the pop-up menu.

If Excel is installed on your computer, you can click the **Edit Data in Microsoft Excel** icon to access its full range of features.

Screenshots

Many technical and training documents make use of screenshots. These are images taken directly from a computer screen, perhaps demonstrating a particular task within a program. Some people use the **PrtScn** key, which places an image of the entire current screen in the Clipboard (**Alt** + **PrtScn** snapshots just the currently-selected window). Since this functionality is rather limited, others might use special utility software. However, there's also support for doing this directly within Word.

1. Click the **Screenshot** icon in the **Insert** tab. The pop-up will show you thumbnails of the current windows – either choose one of these or select **Screen Clipping**

If you choose **Screen Clipping** then you'll be able to click and drag to define a rectangular area to crop within the screen display area.

2. The screenshot is inserted as a picture into your document. Note this is a bitmap (rather than a draw-type) graphic, so be careful if you plan to resize it. If you increase its size too much then the image will become "blocky", with the pixels clearly visible

3. Repeat the process if you need to include a series of screenshots

4. Remember to save your document. The screenshots are stored internally within the Word document, so you don't need to worry about locating separate graphic files on your computer or online

6 Document views

Here, we'll look at six different ways of viewing your document, some additional visual features, and using Word to create web pages.

Read Mode

Use Word's **Read Mode** if you're viewing, rather than writing or editing, a document.

In **Read Mode**, Word reformats the entire document to make the best use of the available screen space. Material is organized into screens rather than pages, so a break between pages may not be in the same place as a break between screens.

Activating Read Mode

1. Make sure the **Read Mode** icon (shaped like a book) in the Status bar is selected

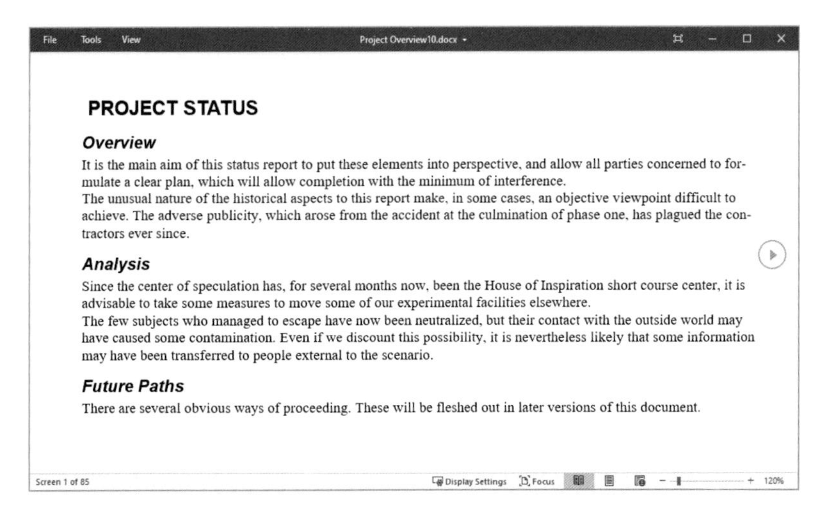

PROJECT STATUS

Overview

It is the main aim of this status report to put these elements into perspective, and allow all parties concerned to formulate a clear plan, which will allow completion with the minimum of interference.
The unusual nature of the historical aspects to this report make, in some cases, an objective viewpoint difficult to achieve. The adverse publicity, which arose from the accident at the culmination of phase one, has plagued the contractors ever since.

Analysis

Since the center of speculation has, for several months now, been the House of Inspiration short course center, it is advisable to take some measures to move some of our experimental facilities elsewhere.
The few subjects who managed to escape have now been neutralized, but their contact with the outside world may have caused some contamination. Even if we discount this possibility, it is nevertheless likely that some information may have been transferred to people external to the scenario.

Future Paths

There are several obvious ways of proceeding. These will be fleshed out in later versions of this document.

Read Mode is ideal when working with a tablet or touch-enabled computer, as the left- and right-arrow icons are easy to operate with your finger. You can also use swipe left or swipe right gestures to move through a document.

2. Use the left- and right-arrow icons, or the scroll bar at the bottom, to move between screens. The Status bar shows you the number of the current page

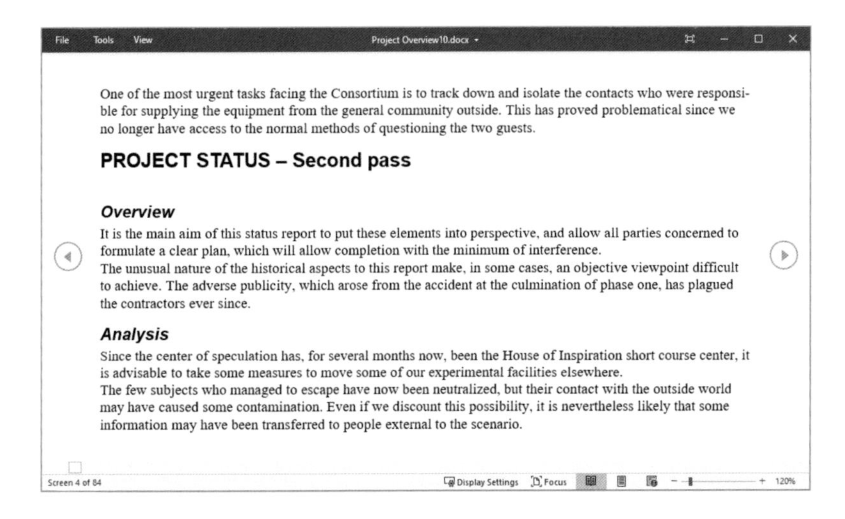

One of the most urgent tasks facing the Consortium is to track down and isolate the contacts who were responsible for supplying the equipment from the general community outside. This has proved problematical since we no longer have access to the normal methods of questioning the two guests.

PROJECT STATUS – Second pass

Overview

It is the main aim of this status report to put these elements into perspective, and allow all parties concerned to formulate a clear plan, which will allow completion with the minimum of interference.
The unusual nature of the historical aspects to this report make, in some cases, an objective viewpoint difficult to achieve. The adverse publicity, which arose from the accident at the culmination of phase one, has plagued the contractors ever since.

Analysis

Since the center of speculation has, for several months now, been the House of Inspiration short course center, it is advisable to take some measures to move some of our experimental facilities elsewhere.
The few subjects who managed to escape have now been neutralized, but their contact with the outside world may have caused some contamination. Even if we discount this possibility, it is nevertheless likely that some information may have been transferred to people external to the scenario.

In **Read Mode** you can type a number then press **Enter** (or **Return**) to jump immediately to that page; e.g. **6** + **Enter** to move to page 6.

3. There is a Reading Toolbar in the top-right corner. As well as the usual minimize, maximize and restore controls, you can also click to auto-hide the Toolbar and menus

4. From the **View** menu you can show or hide the Navigation and Comments areas, and choose **Page Color** and **Layout** options

Click the icon a second time to restore the Toolbar and see the top-left corner menus again. You can also use the icon to temporarily show the Toolbar and menus.

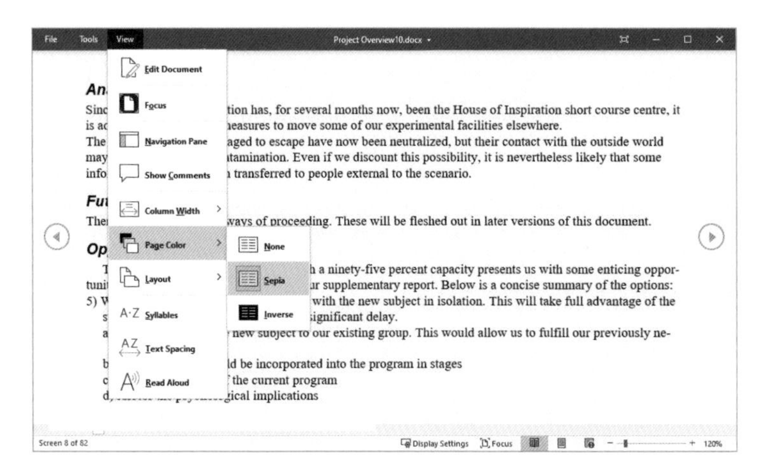

5. Pictures will display at Normal size for the document. However, double-clicking with the mouse, or a double tap on a touchscreen device, will temporarily enlarge an image. Tap or click elsewhere to return to the Normal size

If you click on the **Magnify** icon, the picture will expand to maximum size. Then, you can click on either the icon a second time to reduce the image or elsewhere on the screen to go back to reading your document.

...cont'd

Provided you haven't hidden the Reading Toolbar, there are abbreviated menus in the top-left corner of the screen: **File**, **Tools** and **View**. If you open the **Tools** menu you can use the **Find** feature to locate text within a document.

6. If you close and then later reopen your document, Word remembers the location so that you can carry on reading from where you left off. To do this, click on the message that automatically appears

7. If you select and then right-click (or hold down your finger on a touchscreen device) you'll see a pop-up menu of useful options including Search and language translation. You can also add comments or highlights

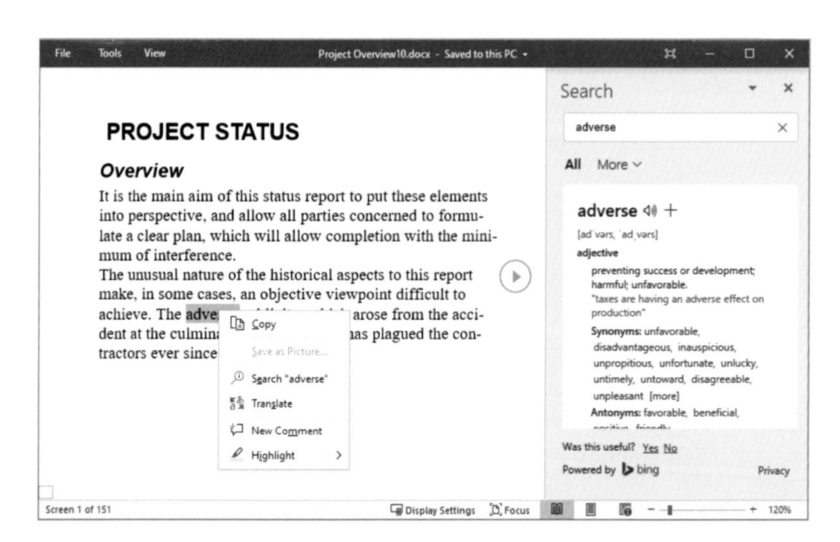

Search allows you to view a word's definition, listen to its pronunciation, and also to explore web resources such as Wikipedia and Bing.

8. You can use the zoom slider in the bottom-right corner to scale the text anywhere from 100% to 300% in size

If you have a touchscreen device, you can zoom using the standard pinch and stretch gestures. This is very useful, particularly if you've hidden the Status bar with its zoom slider.

Accessing the other views

As you've seen already, you can use the **View** icons in the Status bar to switch views. However, this only gives you access to the three main views: **Read Mode**, **Print Layout** and **Web Layout**. There are two other views: **Outline** and **Draft**. To access any of the five views you need to go to the **View** tab.

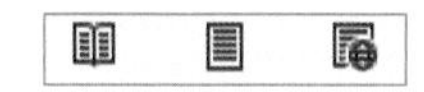

If you're currently in **Read Mode**, first you'll need to switch back to either **Print Layout** or **Web Layout** view before you'll be able to access the **View** tab. Once there you can choose **Outline**, **Draft** or any of the other views.

Print Layout view

1. Go to the **View** tab and select **Print Layout** from the Views area, or click on the **Print Layout** icon in the Status bar

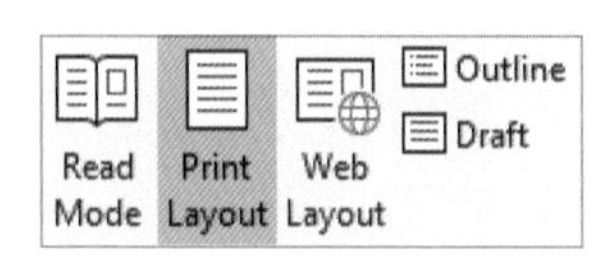

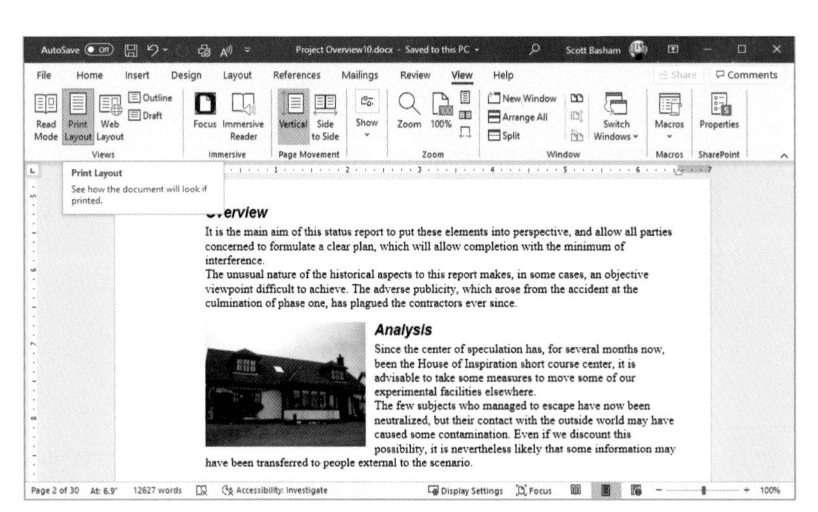

2. This is the best view for general work as it gives you the full range of editing controls, together with a very accurate preview of how everything will look when printed. Scroll through your document and make some changes

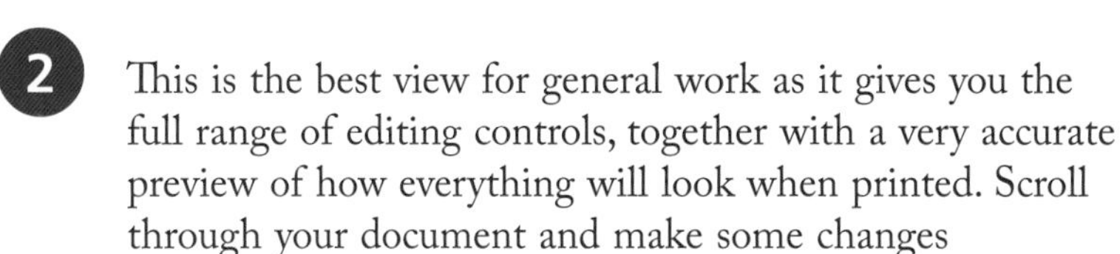

A sixth way of viewing your document is to use **Focus Mode**. See page 139 for more details on this.

3. Temporarily switch to **Read Mode** to see how both the display and the available controls change

4. When you save your document, Word will make a note of which of the main views (**Read Mode**, **Print Layout** or **Web Layout**) you used most recently, and switch to it the next time you open the file

...cont'd

Web Layout view

Web Layout view gives you a good idea of how your document would look if saved as a web page and then viewed in a browser such as Microsoft Edge.

Web pages often make use of hyperlinks for navigation, both within an article and to other articles and websites. See pages 74-75 for more on creating hyperlinks.

Go to the **View** tab and select **Web Layout** from the Views area, or click on the **Web Layout** icon in the Status bar

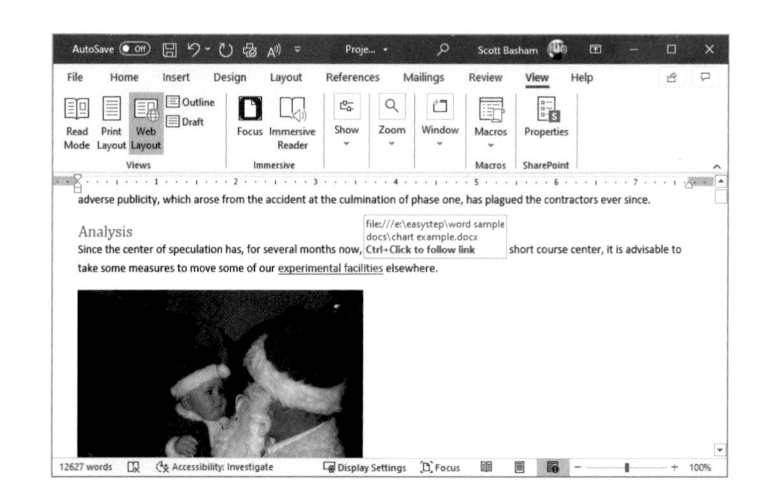

Although you've created a web page, for it to be available on the web it must be copied onto a server run by a web hosting service or Internet Service Provider. If you have an account with one of these then the company will be able to give you instructions on how to upload your files to their site. Microsoft also offers OneDrive Cloud storage based on your account (see page 143).

2 To turn this into a web page, make sure you choose **Web Page** (*.htm, *.html) as the file type when saving

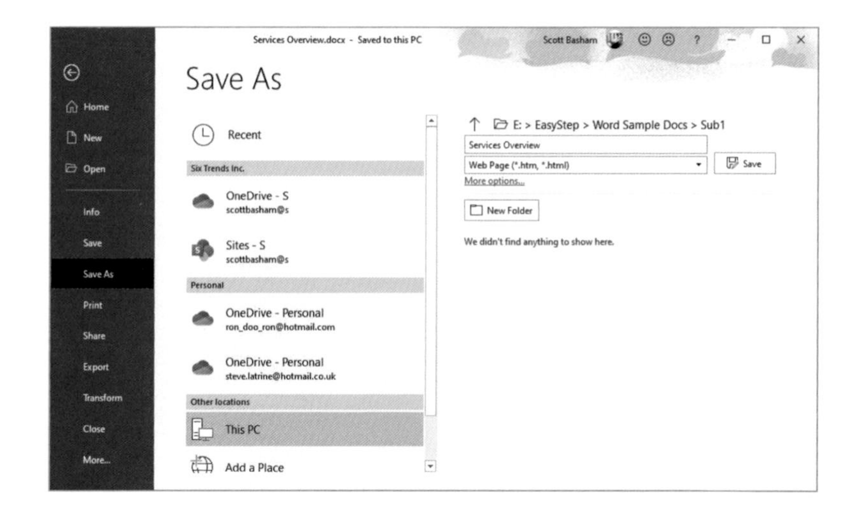

Outline view

1. In the Views area of the **View** tab, click the **Outline** icon

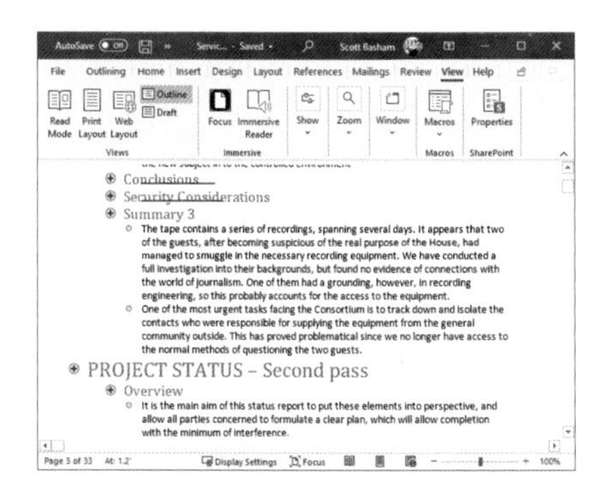

Outline view is useful if you structure your document using headings and subheadings that are allocated to indented levels. The controls in the **Outlining** tab let you change levels, move lines up/down, or "collapse" items so that lines on lower levels are temporarily hidden from view.

Outline view is only suitable if your document uses at least two levels of heading and subheading – otherwise there is not enough structure for it to add any real value. Remember, Word's **Print Layout** view can also collapse and expand standard headings.

Draft view

1. In the views area of the **View** tab, click the **Draft** icon

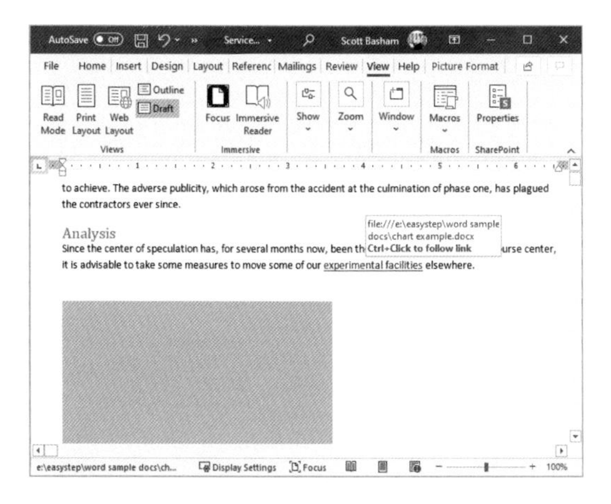

The screen now shows a simplified view of your text, with elements such as graphics, headers and footers not visible.

2. This view is useful if your computer is slow, or if you just want to concentrate on the text with no distractions

3. You can continue to edit your text in this view. However, if you wish to see how your document will look when printed, return to **Print Layout** view by clicking the icon in the Views area of the **View** tab (or in the Status bar)

Gridlines

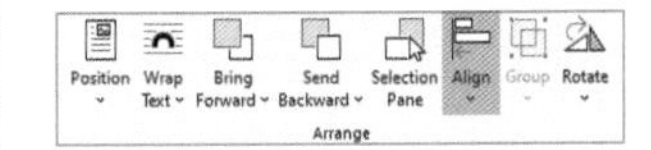

Defining and customizing gridlines

Gridlines are useful for helping you to align objects and resize them in a regular way.

1. When you're working with a drawing object, the drawing tools appear automatically. Make sure the **Shape Format** tab is active, click the **Align** icon in the Arrange area, and then choose **Grid Settings...**

Gridlines can be easily switched On and Off from the Show controls in the **View** tab. To customize your grid, however, you need to follow the instructions on the right.

2. Here, you can set the size of the grid using the settings in the **Grid and Guides** dialog. You can also control how many visible vertical and horizontal lines will be displayed. For example, if you set **Vertical every:** to 2 then a visible line will appear for every second actual gridline. This is useful if you don't want your page cluttered with too many gridlines

3. Select **Display gridlines on screen** and then click **OK**

Gridlines do not print – they are there just to help you arrange items on a page. When the grid is active, objects will "snap" to the nearest gridline as if it were magnetic.

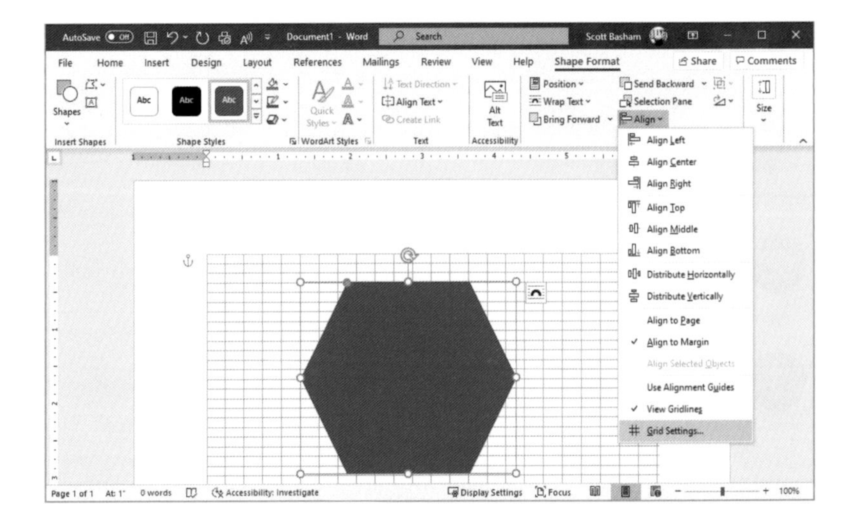

The Navigation pane

The Navigation pane can use the headings in your document to create a structured list located to the left of the main page area. This can be used to navigate easily through a long document.

Activating the Navigation pane

1. In the Show area of the **View** tab, click the **Navigation Pane** checkbox to switch it On

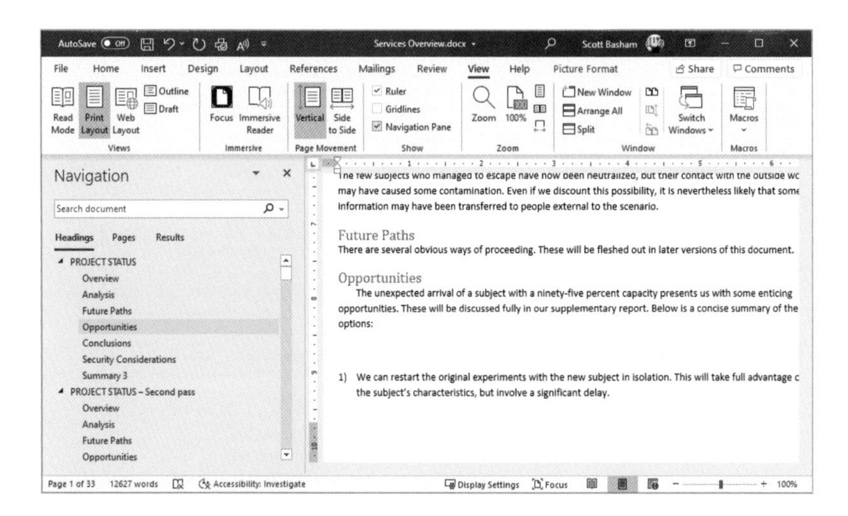

2. The Navigation pane appears, with its own scroll bars. It has three tabbed pages: **Headings**, **Pages** and **Results**. The first will list any headings or subheadings. If you click on one of these then the main document window will automatically move to this line, scrolling if necessary

3. The second tabbed page – **Pages** – will display the pages in your document as thumbnails (small images) so that you can scroll visually through the document

4. The third tabbed page – **Results** – allows searching based on text or objects such as pictures, tables, or equations

5. When you're finished with the Navigation pane, either click the **Close** icon in its top-right corner or switch Off the option in the **Show** area of the **View** tab

A quick way to summon the Navigation pane with the **Results** tab active is to type **Ctrl** + **F**, as this is the shortcut for Find.

...cont'd

The Navigation pane can be used in a variety of ways. Here, we'll see some advanced examples using a document that has been structured with several levels of headings.

If your document has no headings then there's nothing to display in this part of the Navigation pane. You'll see a message explaining this, suggesting that you should apply some heading styles to your document's headings.

Browsing headings

1. Make sure the Navigation pane is visible. If not, select the **View** tab and click on the checkbox labeled **Navigation Pane**

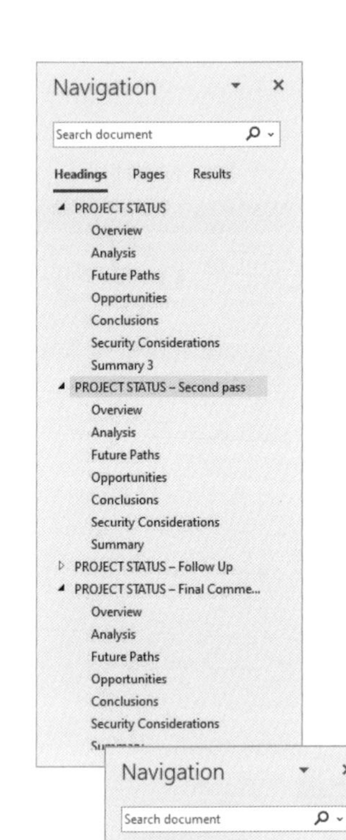

2. Make sure the first of the three options is selected at the top of the pane. This lists just the headings in your document

3. The network of headings and subheadings is displayed as a tree structure. If you click on the small triangle in this area, the sub-structure beneath this line will be collapsed (hidden) and revealed in turn

4. You can drag headings up and down to a different location, effectively restructuring your document very easily

5. Right-click on a heading to see options for adding, deleting, promoting, demoting, selecting, and printing headings

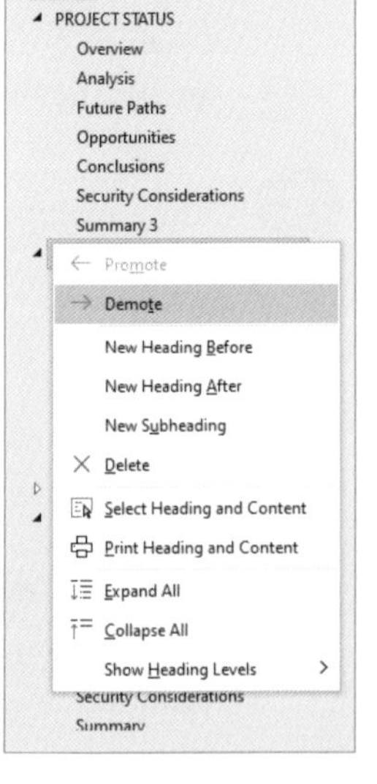

Browsing pages

1. Make the Navigation pane visible then click the second icon labeled **Pages** near its top. This allows you to browse by scrolling through small thumbnail images of each page

2. You can resize the Navigation pane by dragging horizontally on the vertical border between it and the main page. Also, you can drag on its title bar to make it a free-floating window

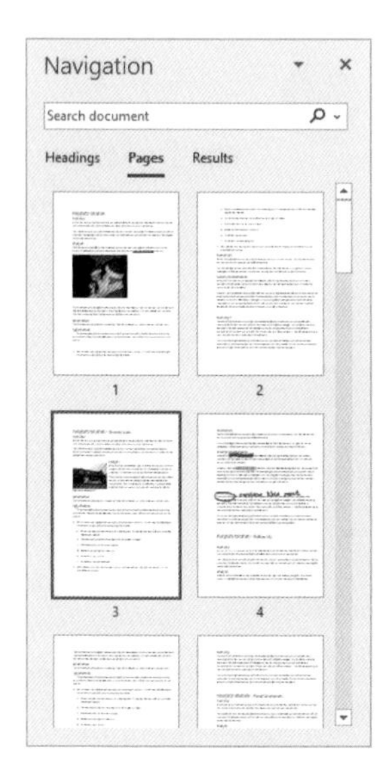

3. If you click on any thumbnail, the main window will scroll to the corresponding page

Browsing search results

1. If you click the small triangle beside the magnifying glass at the top of the pane you can browse through objects such as graphics, tables, or equations, as well as text

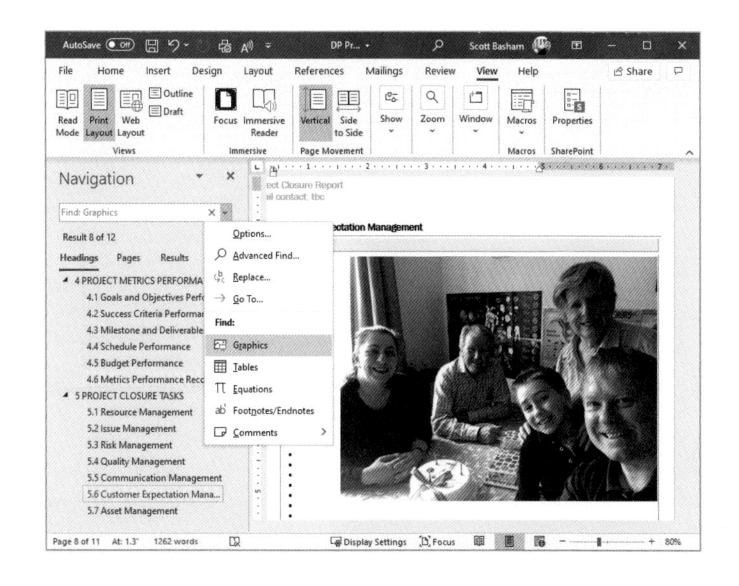

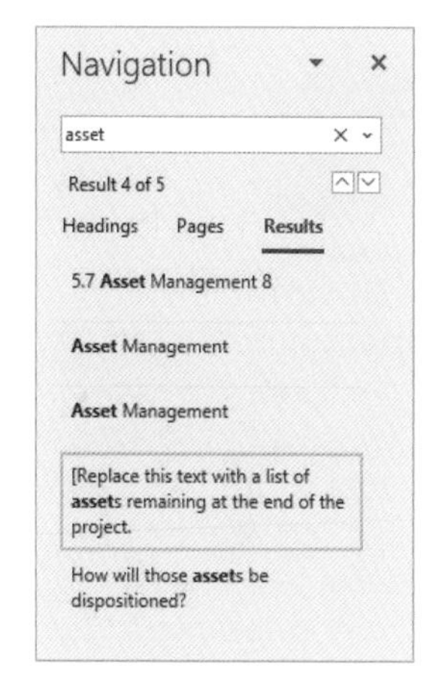

If the **Results** tab is active and you're searching for text, you can see your results in context. Click on one of these and the main page will scroll to the appropriate location.

The Document Inspector

Before distributing your document to others, it's a good idea to check its content carefully. Sometimes your document might contain hidden information, or details you'd rather not include. The **Document Inspector** can help you with this.

1. Click on the **File** tab

2. The Home screen should appear by default, so select **Info** on the left side. Click on the **Check for Issues** button then select **Inspect Document** from the pop-up

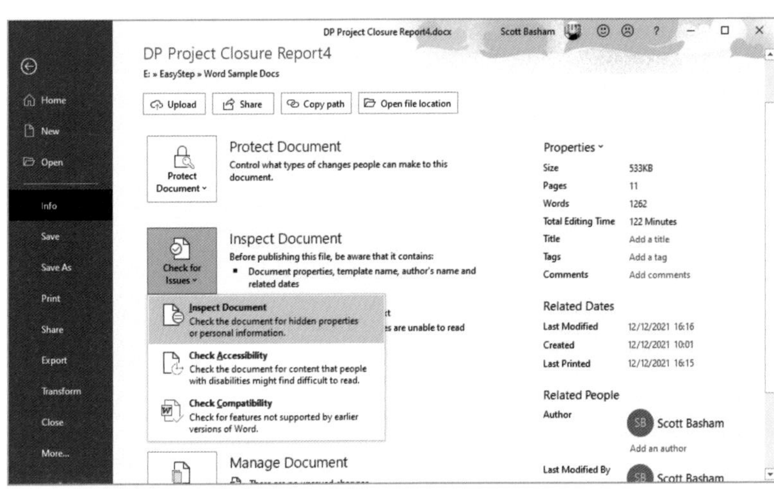

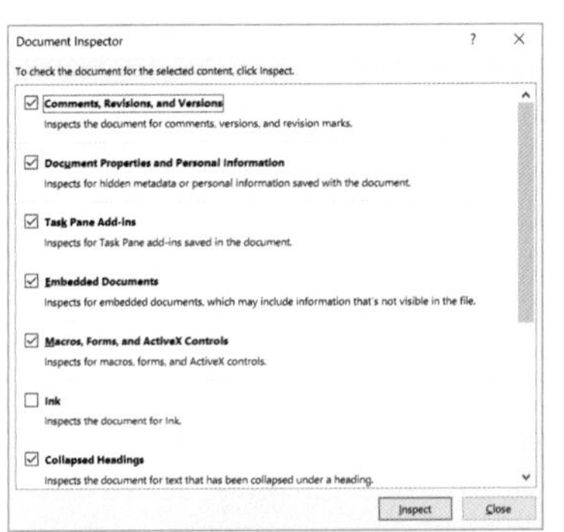

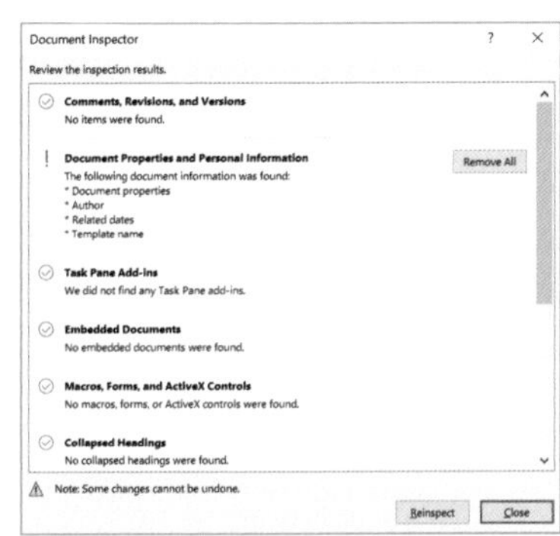

3. Click the **Inspect** button and **Yes** if prompted to save

4. The results will appear. You can get rid of any found items by clicking on the **Remove All** button. Click on **Reinspect** to verify the current state of play, then **Close** when done

The **Document Inspector** dialog lists different categories of content worth checking, some of which may be hidden but would be readable to someone with good technical knowledge.

Focus Mode

Focus Mode provides another way to view your document, with the bare minimum of distractions. You can still edit and change formatting, but the display will be just your document with no Taskbar, Status bar, or Ribbon.

1. Click the **Focus** button to the left of the View icons in the Status bar

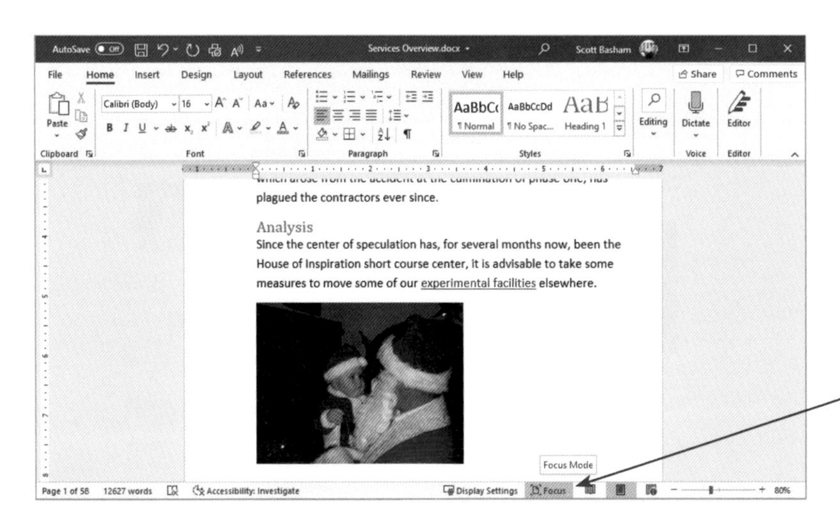

You can also invoke Focus Mode by clicking on the word "Focus" in the Status bar at the bottom.

2. You are now in Focus Mode, where it is easier to concentrate on your document's look and content. You can leave Focus Mode by clicking the **Restore Down** icon ◘ in the top-right corner

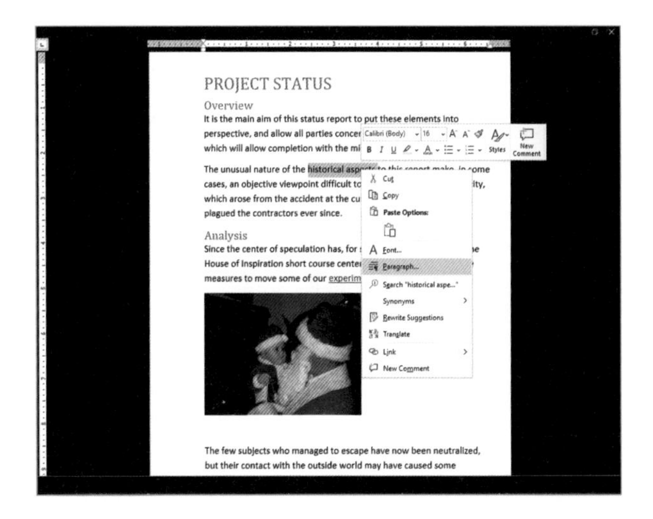

Although there are no visible controls you can still select text and then right-click to summon a pop-up menu of options plus the Mini Toolbar.

You'll need a current Office 365 subscription in order to generate Sway web pages.

Sway web pages

Sway is a free online Microsoft app that can display web pages, reports, newsletters and presentations in a way that looks good on most devices. It's easy to convert your documents to this format.

1. With your Word document open, click on **File**, then choose **Transform**

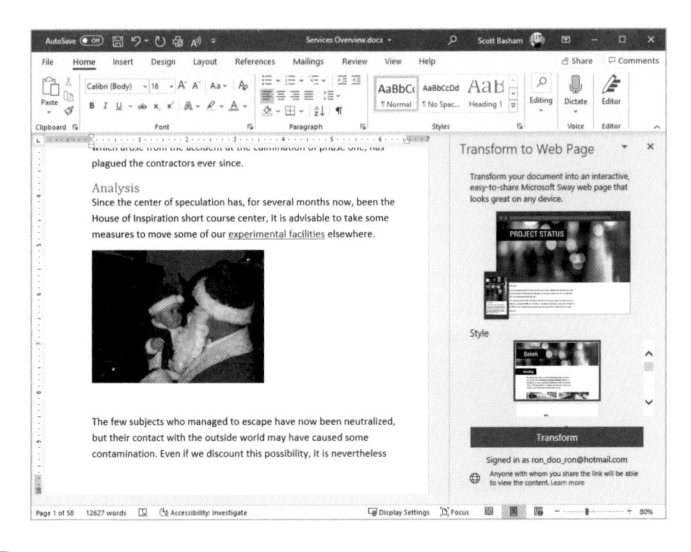

2. Check that the correct account is active and click the **Transform** button. After a few moments, the Sway web page is generated, uploaded and displayed in your browser. To make this available to others, click the **Share** button in the top-right corner

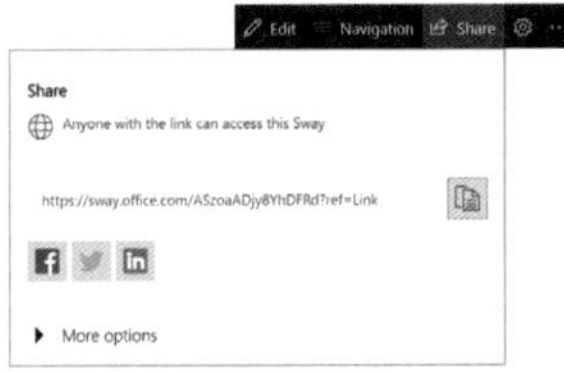

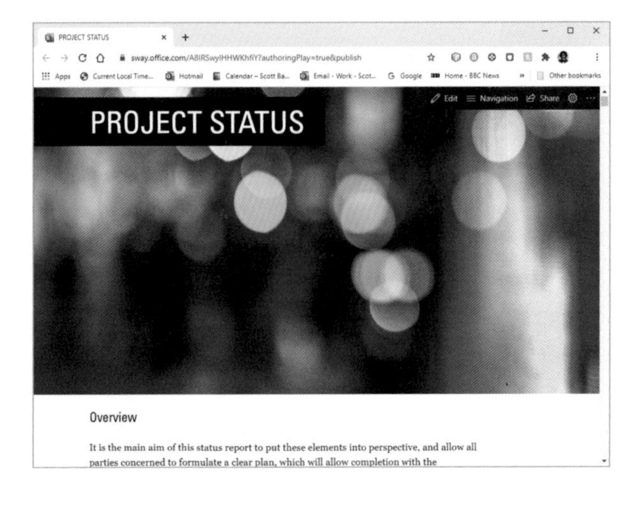

7 Files and settings

In this chapter we'll see that the File tab looks very different from the others. It lets you take a step back and consider work at the file level as opposed to working inside your document.

Info

1. With a document open, click on the **File** tab

2. By default, you'll see the Home screen, so click on **Info**. This gives you a useful summary of your current document's properties – listed along the right-hand side

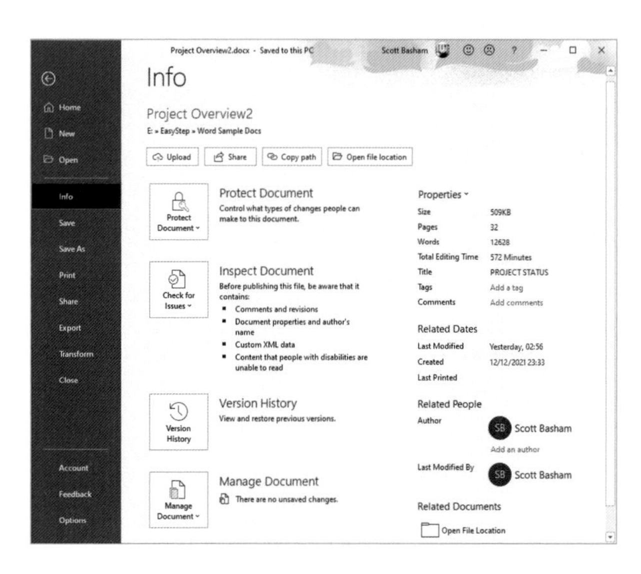

3. In the central part of the screen there are controls for changing the permissions, checking for issues before sharing or distributing, looking at version history and clearing up any draft versions of your document that may have been created automatically

4. If your current document is in a format for an older version of Word, you'll be missing out on some of the new features. If you want to upgrade it to the latest format, click the **Convert** button

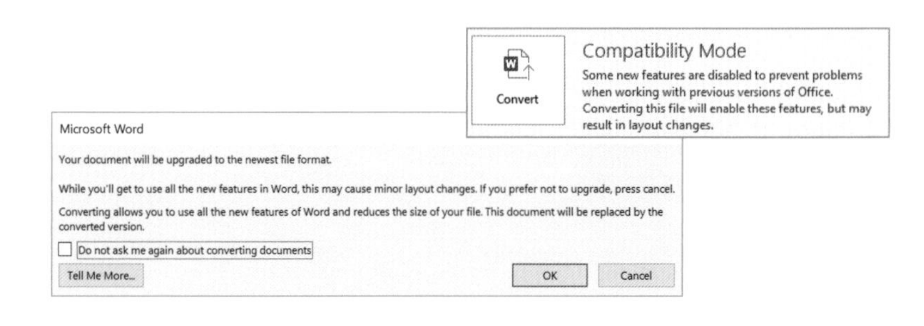

If you do convert your document to the current Word format, others using earlier versions prior to Word 2010 may not be able to open it. If you need them to work on your document then use **Save As** and select **Word 97-2003 Document** as the file type (see next page).

Save to local file

1. Choose **File**, **Save As**, then **This PC** to see this screen

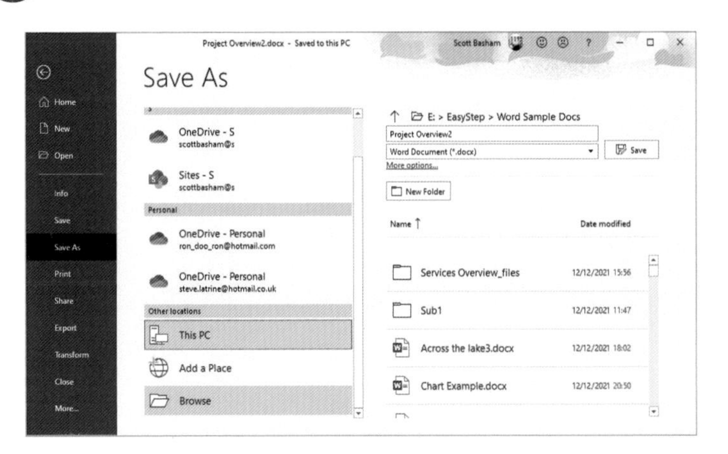

2. To select a location, choose the current folder, an item from the recently-used list, or click the **Browse** button

3. Open the **Save as type:** pop-up to see a list of file types. Useful types are PDF, Web Page, Plain Text and Rich Text Format

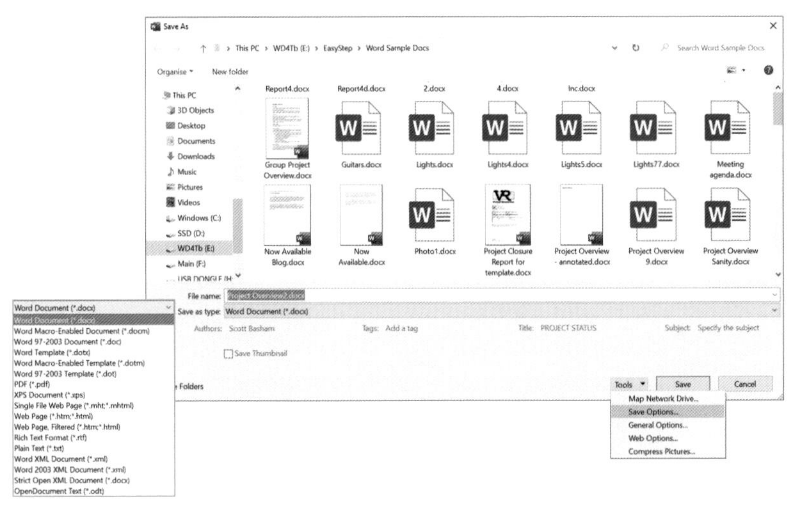

4. Click on **Tools** and choose **Save Options...** to control default settings such as file format and locations

5. Click **OK** and then **Save** to save your document

You have the option to save to the Cloud, using a service such as OneDrive. This means you'll be able to access documents wherever there's an internet connection. See Chapter 8 for more details on sharing features.

Plain Text is the simplest type – there's no formatting but your file will be readable on virtually any system.

Recently-used files

1. Exit Word (if it's running) then start it up again

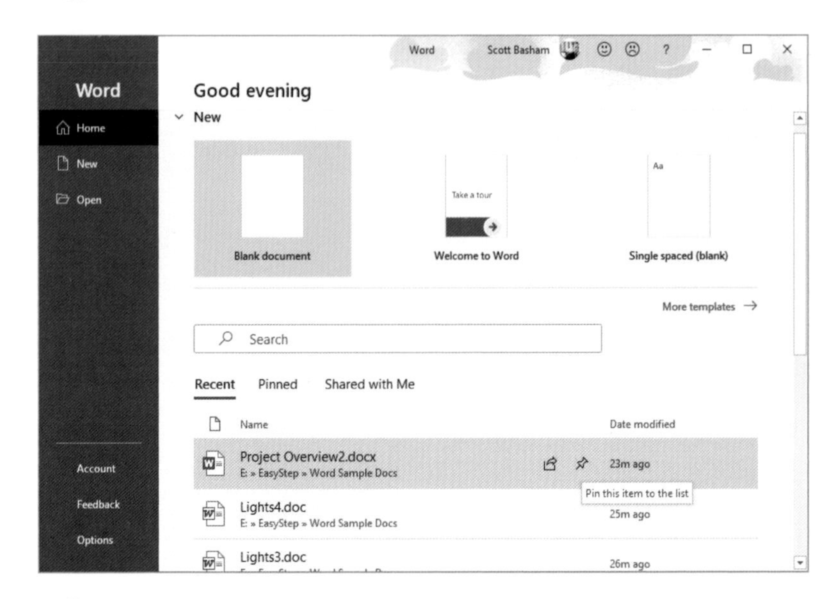

2. The lower part of the screen will list your recently-used documents, so in most cases you'll just click one of these to resume work

3. If you hover over one of these, a small **Pin** icon appears. If you click this then the document will be "pinned"; i.e. permanently added to the Pinned list

4. The item will now have a **Pin** icon next to it. Hover over it with the mouse and it will change to an **Unpin** icon . Click this to remove the pin from the item

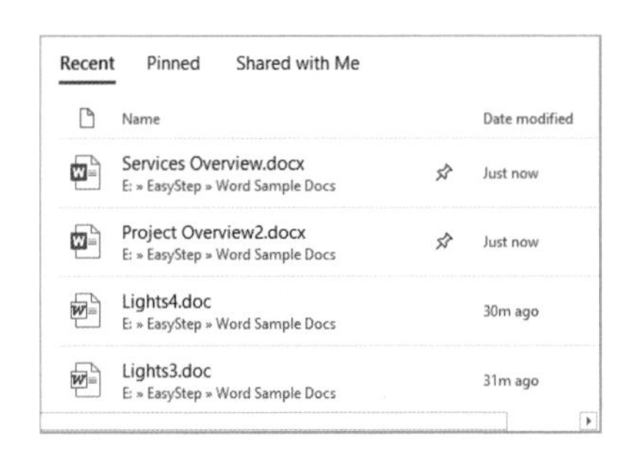

5. If the document you want to open is not in the available lists then choose **More Documents** at the bottom of the screen

Click on the **Pinned** heading in this dialog to see a list of just pinned items. The **Recent** list will show documents sorted by modified date/time with the most recent at the top. Clicking on the third heading allows you to see documents that have been shared with you. See Chapter 8 for more on this.

Opening local files

Within the **File** tab, **Open** gives you more options for opening files compared with the Home screen.

1. Go to the **File** tab and choose **Open**

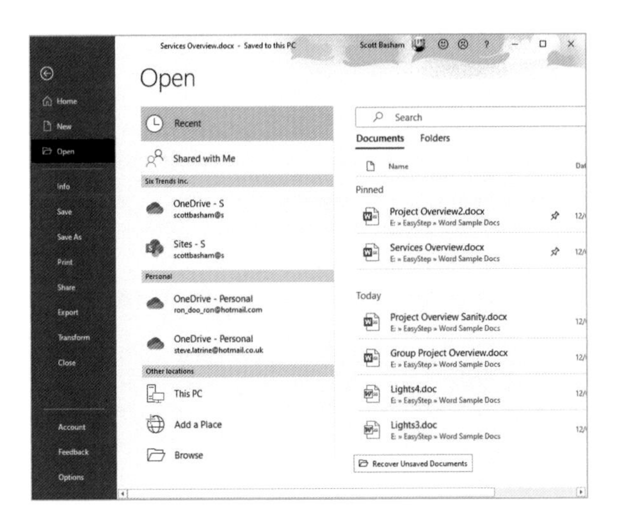

Recent files can include both online and locally-saved documents. Online shared documents are covered in detail in Chapter 8.

2. There are six main options for locating your file. By default, **Recent** is selected. On the right-hand side you'll see a similar list to the previous example, with any pinned items at the top. If the document you want isn't there then click on **This PC**

3. You'll now see a list of folders, so select one of these to navigate manually to your file's location. Alternatively, choose **Browse** to access more browse-and-search facilities

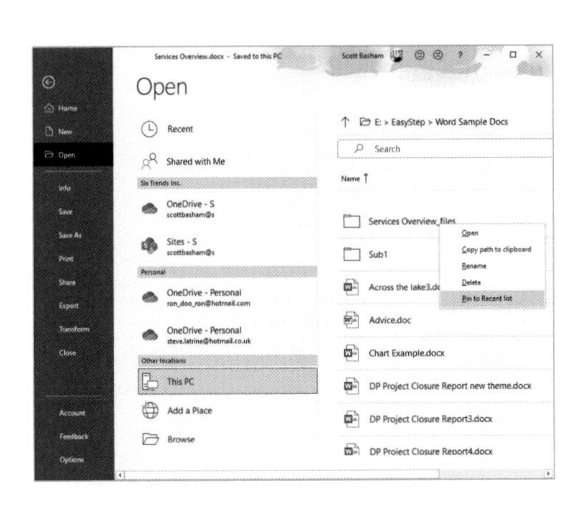

The list of recent folders also has a **Pin/Unpin** facility, so you can make sure that your favorite locations are always easily accessible.

Opening other file formats

Word can open a range of file types, including **.doc** (the native type for older versions of Word) and **.rtf** (Rich Text Format). Rich Text is a cross-platform standard for text, and has a reasonably extensive set of formatting features.

1. Click on the **File** tab and choose **Open**

2. Here, we opened an old document that was stored in **.doc** format as read-only. If you look in the title bar you'll see both **Read Only** and **Compatibility Mode** noted next to the document name

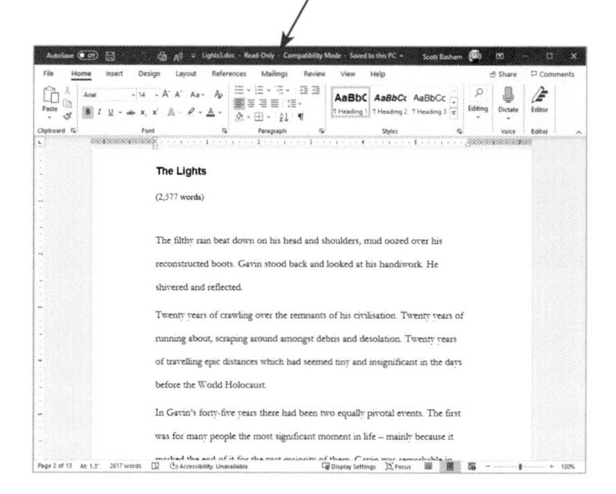

3. Go to the **File** tab and examine the **Info** screen

Note the indication that this is a read-only document. Also, Word's Compatibility Mode restricts available features to those from earlier versions of Word, so you can save and send to someone using an older software version.

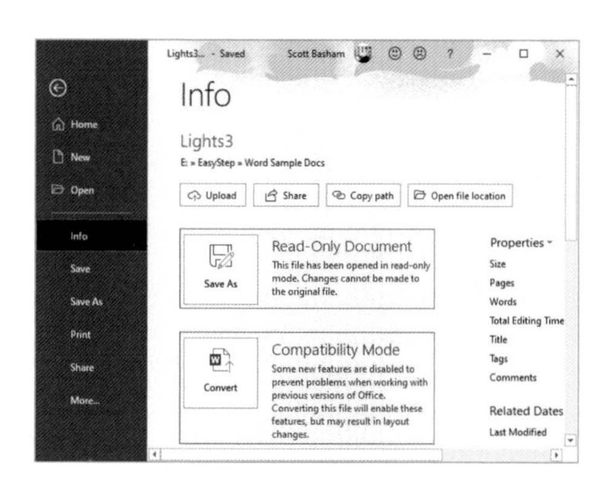

4. Click **Save As** to create an editable copy. The **.doc** file type is used by default, but you can change this easily

If you don't need your document to be edited in older versions of Word, then you should use the Convert feature to upgrade it to **.docx** format. You will then have access to the full range of Word's latest features.

Opening PDF files

Adobe Systems' Portable Document Format (PDF) is a very popular file standard for read-only documentation. A useful Word feature is the ability to open these and convert them into an editable format. You can then save in Word's own format, or re-export to PDF.

1. Click on the **File** tab and choose **Open**

2. Using any of the techniques covered in the previous examples, locate a PDF document

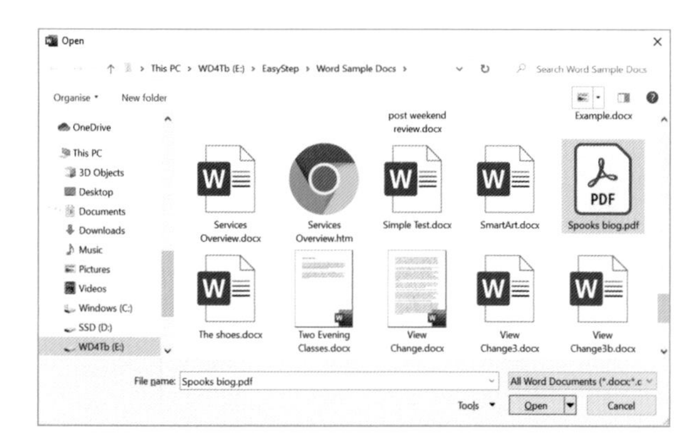

3. When you click **Open**, the following message will appear, reminding you of some of the limitations of PDF file conversion

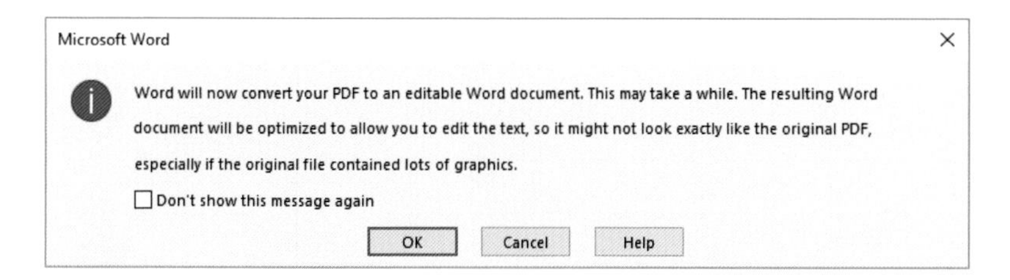

4. Click **OK**. A progress bar will appear at the bottom of the main window while Word is performing the conversion

5. If the conversion is successful, the document will display in **Print Layout** view

In this example, we've clicked on the Open dialog's **View** button and chosen **Large icons**. This is useful as some files can show up with a small preview of their contents.

PDF conversion is not always successful. For longer or more complex PDF documents, Word may run into difficulties and display message explaining the error(s).

LinkedIn

LinkedIn (owned by Microsoft) is a popular business social network designed to help people connect and share information related to their jobs, experience and skills. Microsoft Office applications provide integration with LinkedIn.

Click on the **File** tab and choose **Options**. Scroll down within the **General** section to see **LinkedIn Features**

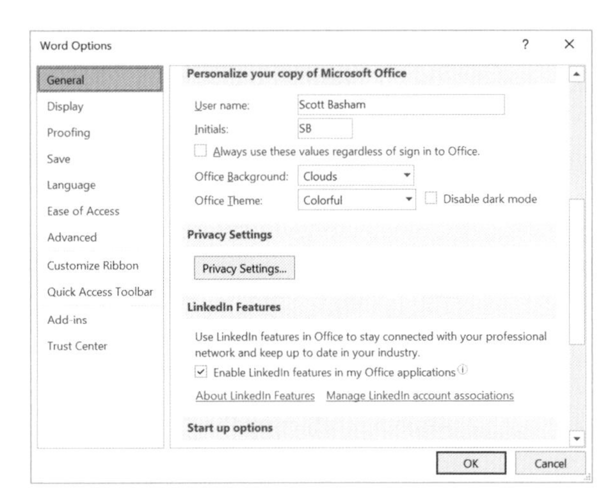

You can review your current login from the **File** tab, and also change this if necessary. For more details on online accounts, see pages 156-158.

2 If you have a LinkedIn account based on your current login then click on **Manage LinkedIn account associations**. This will take you to the LinkedIn website Account management page. If you have an appropriate account and Office installation then you'll have access to a **Resume Assistant** icon in Word's **Review** tab

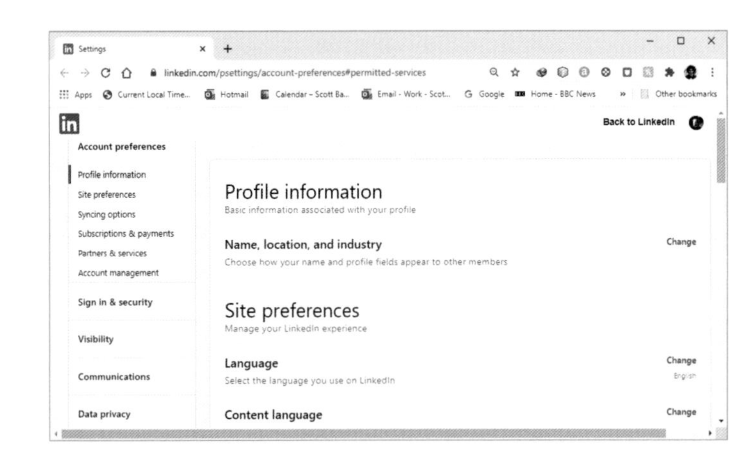

Printing

1. Make sure you have a document open. Choose **Print** from the **File** tab

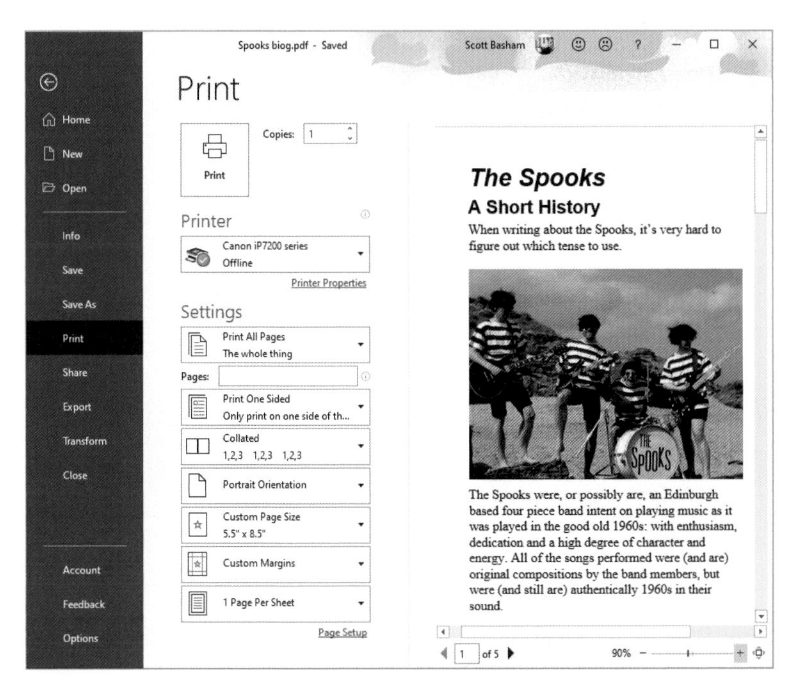

2. You'll see a preview of the current page, which is useful for checking margins and text flow. Click on the **Forward** and **Back** arrows at the bottom to move through the pages

3. Make sure the correct printer is selected, and that it is online. If your printer isn't listed, choose **Add Printer**

4. Review the other settings listed. If you don't want to print all pages then there are a number of other options available. For example, you could set a discontinuous range using "1-3, 5" (pages 1 to 3, followed by 5)

5. You can click on the **Printer Properties** link, or **Page Setup**, to access more detailed dialogs

6. Finally, go back to the top of the dialog, check the number of desired copies and then click **Print**

If you're printing on special paper then it's always worth clicking on the **Printer Properties** link. This will display the settings dialog for your particular make and model of printer, and will almost certainly contain controls for specifying paper type.

Using templates

Word has access to a wide range of templates, and has a useful screen for locating the best one for your needs.

To start off working with a single blank page, simply click the **Single spaced (blank)** item.

1. Click on **New**. On this screen you'll initially see a selection of the most commonly-used templates

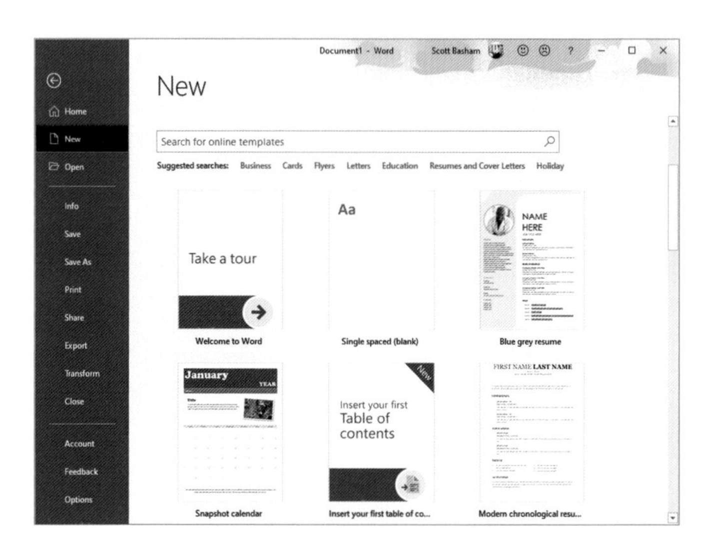

2. Click one of the suggested searches or enter your own search text. The example below searches for "agenda"

Click the **Back** button if you want to return to the initial screen with its suggested searches.

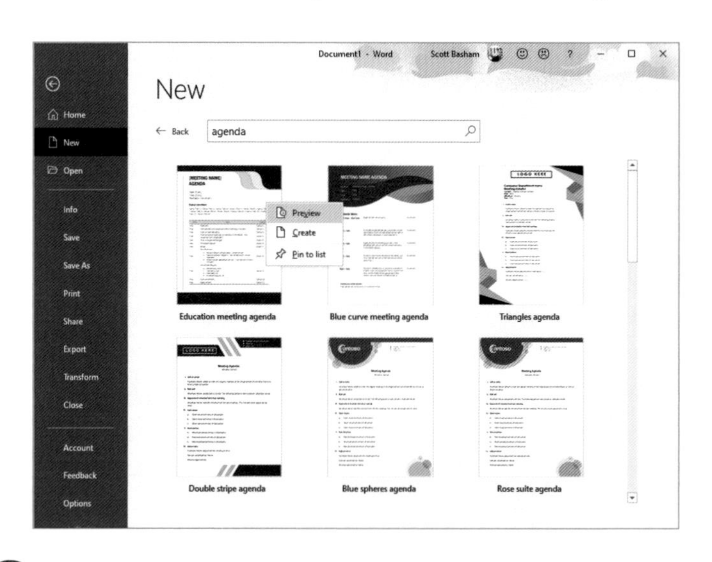

3. Scroll through the results and select a template

4. If you right-click on a template, a small pop-up menu appears. Choose **Preview** to learn more about the selected template

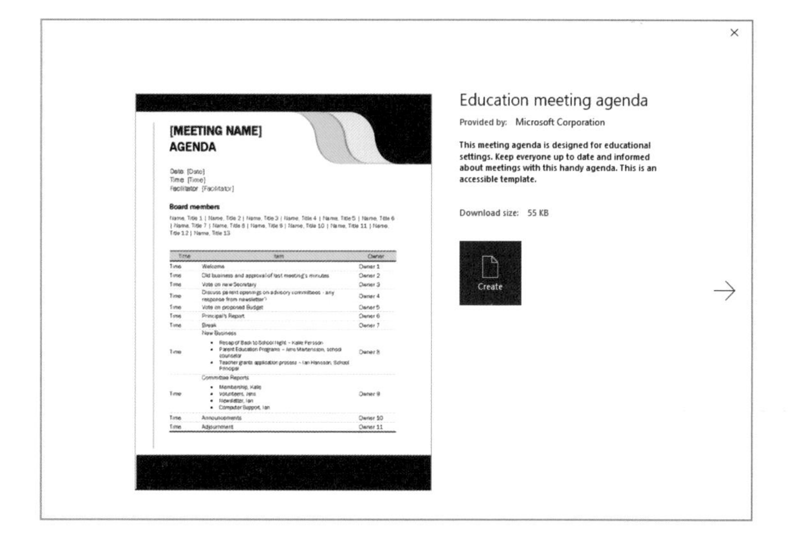

When previewing in this way you can use the **Left-** or **Right-arrow** icons to go to the previous or next template in the list.

5. If you're happy with your choice, click the **Create** button, or click on the **Close** icon to return to the main screen

6. Once you open a template, you can edit and add to the sample text, then save the document under a new name

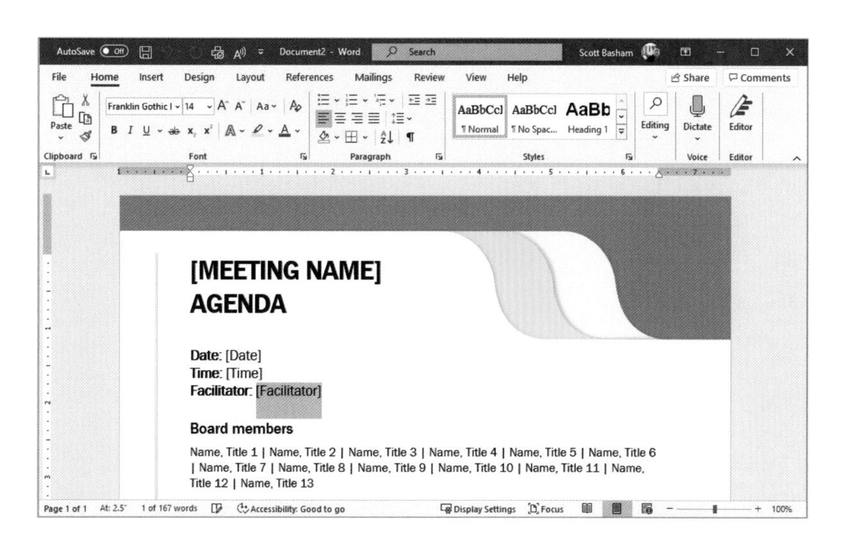

Although you're free to change settings such as font, size, spacing and color, it's usually best to stay with what was provided by the template. Most templates have their own particular design in order to allow you to concentrate just on the content.

...cont'd

Creating your own templates

A template is just an ordinary Word document saved as a special file type, and usually in a special location.

1. Create your document in the normal way. It may be worth using dummy placeholder text. When it's ready, choose **Save As** from the **File** tab and select a location

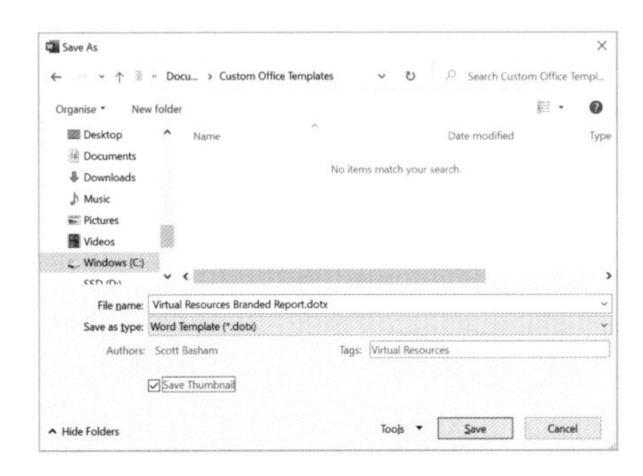

Tags make it easy for you to search for your templates later on. In this example, the company name "Virtual Resources" is being added as a tag so that any searches using those words will return this template (plus others with similar tags).

2. For **Save as type:** choose **Word Template (*.dotx)**. It's also good to check the Authors field, and add some tags

3. Note that Word will, by default, save the file in a special **Custom Office Templates** directory (it's best not to change this if you want to be able to access your template easily in future). Click **Save**

4. Go to the **File** tab and choose **Close**. Then, go back to the **File** tab and this time choose **New**, and click on the **Personal** heading to find your new template

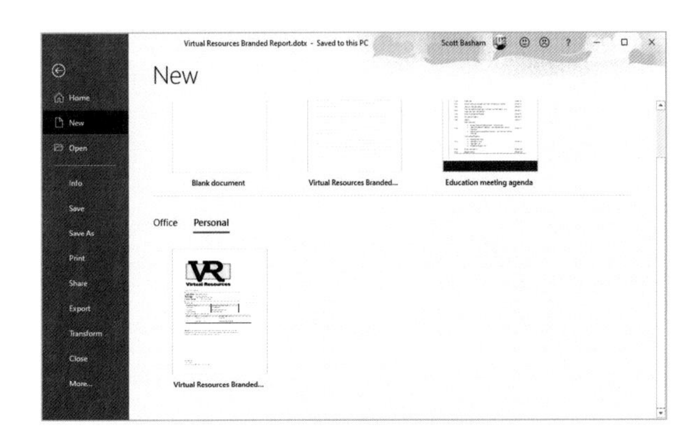

Options

We've already seen how to change certain options when we customized the Ribbon in Chapter 1. All these options and many more are available in one place via the **File** tab.

1. Make sure the **File** tab is active, then click **Options**. The dialog that opens is organized into 11 sections, with **General** options displayed first

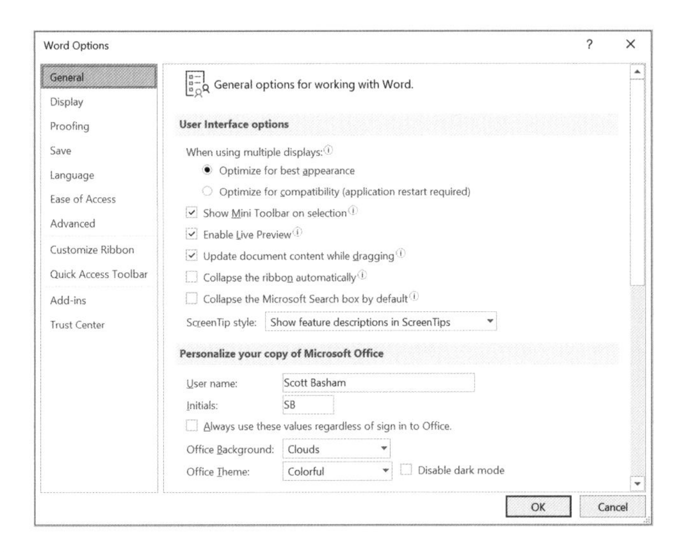

2. Unless your computer is very slow, keep on the **Show Mini Toolbar on selection** and **Enable Live Preview** options. The latter controls what happens when you hover over a formatting feature; e.g. hovering over a style in the Styles Gallery will temporarily show selected text in that format. **Update document content while dragging** enables the live preview when dragging objects

3. Click on the **Trust Center** section, then **Trust Center Settings...**. This gives an overview of security and privacy settings, and also links to Microsoft policies and guidance

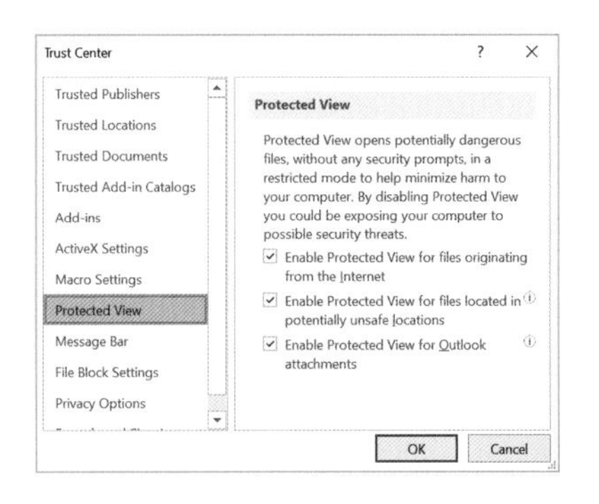

If you get an error message when attempting to open documents that were sent via email attachments or were downloaded from the web, then first check you're sure they came from a reputable source. If you are, then go to **Trust Center Settings...**, click on the **Protected View** section, then clear the three checkboxes shown in the illustration on the left.

...cont'd

4. Click on the **Display** section to control whether Word displays non-printing characters such as tabs and paragraph marks

5. This dialog also has printing options so you can, for example, elect to print without drawings created in Word. This will speed up printing and save on printer ink – simple blank boxes will be printed in place of the graphics

Many of the settings in the **Word Options** dialog have a small letter "**i**" in a circle next to them. If you hover over this you'll see a pop-up explaining what the setting does.

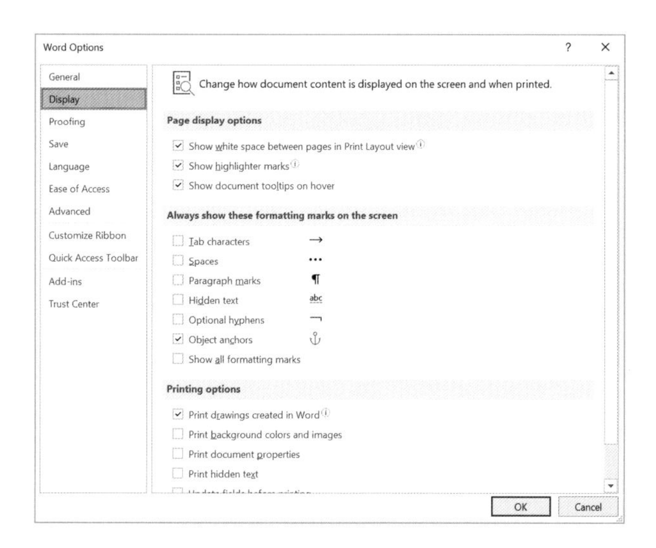

6. Have a look at the other sections. The largest of these is **Advanced**, which contains extra settings for editing, display, printing, and saving

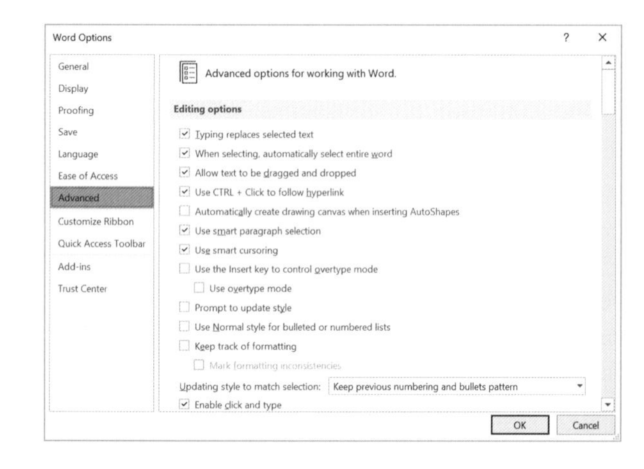

8 Sharing features

In this chapter we'll see how Word adds support for document portability and group working.

Roaming documents

In recent years Microsoft has added the ability to view and edit documents directly on the web, even if Word isn't installed on your computer. This means you're able to work on your files from any device with internet access, provided you've saved your document to a shared repository such as a Microsoft SharePoint server or a OneDrive storage area.

Using a shared area from Word

1. Let's assume you have a Word document you want to store in a shared area. First, it's a good idea to review the services associated with your online account. Go to the **File** tab and then click on **Account**

For sharing to work properly, Word needs to know who you are. Normally, the active account will be taken automatically from your Windows login. If this cannot be done then the first time you use Word you will be prompted for your username and password.

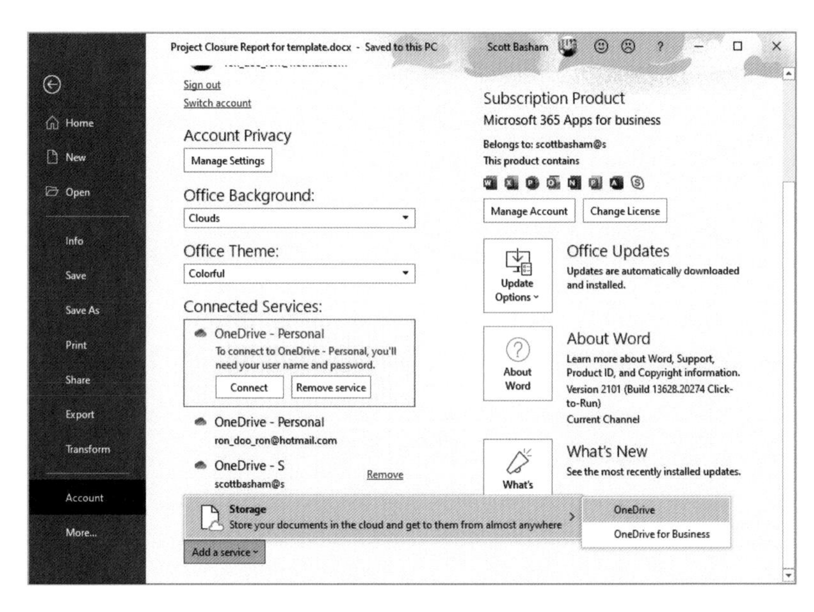

2. Check the account name and login listed under **User Information**. If this isn't you then click **Switch account** and select an option or choose **Sign in with a different account**

3. Now, look to see what is listed under **Connected Services**. Word may have already connected you to your personal or business space if linked to your login. It's possible to connect to multiple shared storage areas – this is very useful if you plan to work with a group of people on the same documents

4. If you want to make use of a new connected service, then provided you have an appropriate active account, you can add one in. Click the **Add a service** button

5. Once you have set a connected service for storage it will show up in the **Accounts** section. You will be able to select it next time you save a document

Anyone with a Hotmail or Outlook web account will have access to a OneDrive area for shared document storage. Log in to **outlook.live.com** or **outlook.office.com** to see this for yourself. If you do not have an account then it's free to set one up, or for an annual subscription fee you can sign up to an enhanced service with more storage space.

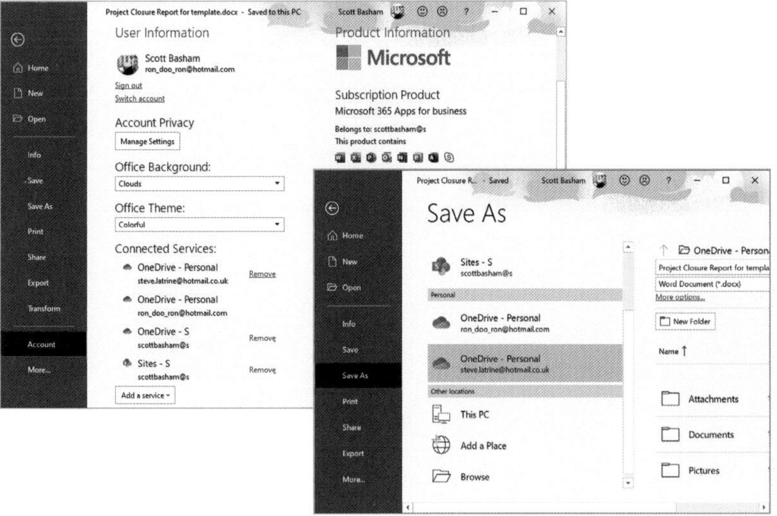

6. In this example, the current account has its own OneDrive connected service, and also access to others. Your account may be different from the above, so look for the cloud icon, which indicates an available online shared area. If you click on this, then the right-hand side of the dialog will display folders you have accessed recently. Here, you can click to specify a location for your document

...cont'd

This is the standard Windows **Save As** dialog. The file path shown will depend on how your connected service is set up – in some cases it will be a local directory on your hard disk, which your system will keep in sync with the online equivalent.

Make sure you save using the Word Document file type. Word's web-editing features will require you to use this standard native file format.

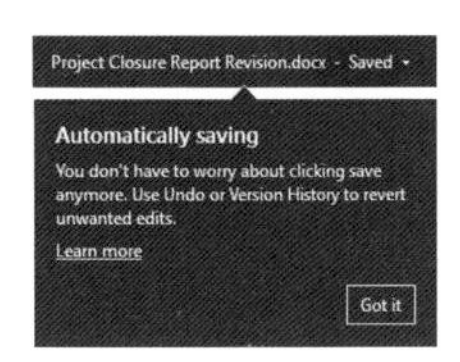

When you edit a document stored in a shared area, changes are automatically saved.

7. You will now see the directory structure of your online storage area. Double-click to move into a sub-directory

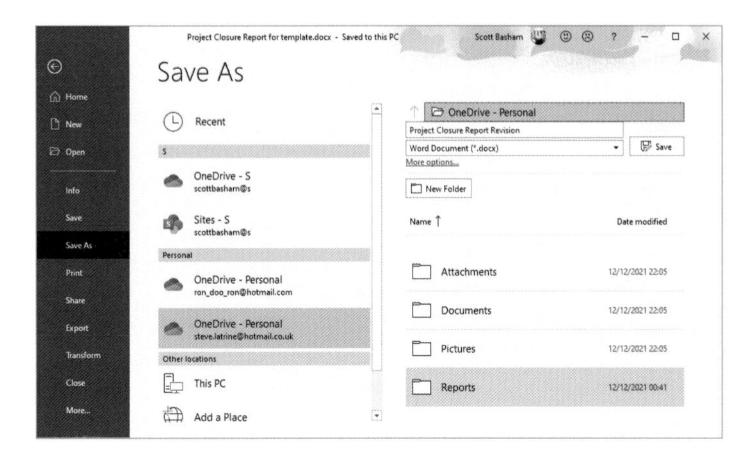

8. When you've found the right location, enter your file name and click **Save**

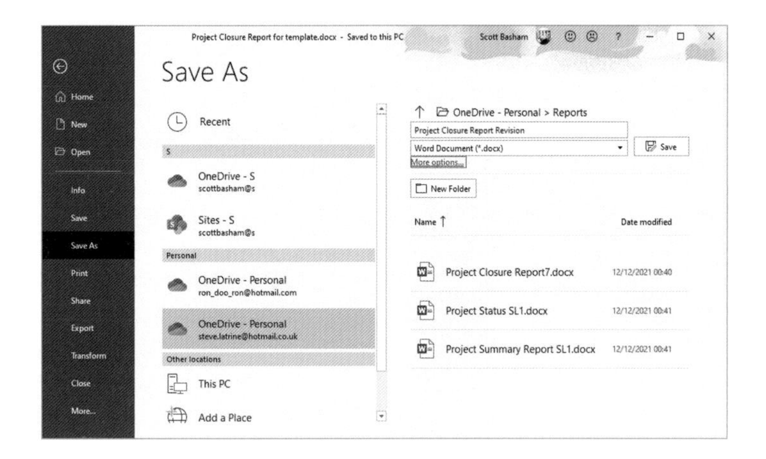

9. Now, you can close your document, or carry on editing. If you edit it and then click **Save**, the online location will be updated just the same as for a local file on your hard disk. As long as your computer is always online, you can use the Cloud storage as your main repository for documents and, as we shall see, this has quite a few advantages

Word Online

Imagine you're away from your main PC or tablet, and do not have access to an installed version of Microsoft Word. **Word Online** gives you the ability to read and edit documents directly within a web browser. In the following example, we'll access the Word document that was stored in OneDrive on the previous page.

Accessing documents from Word Online

1. Use a web browser to log in to your **outlook.live.com** or **outlook.office.com** account

2. At the top left of the screen, click on the icon to the left of the Outlook title to see the following application tiles. Your selection may vary from this – if the Word tile is not present, then click **All apps**

3. Click on the Word tile to see the screen below. Choose a document to edit from the Recent list, or click **Open from OneDrive** to browse for a file

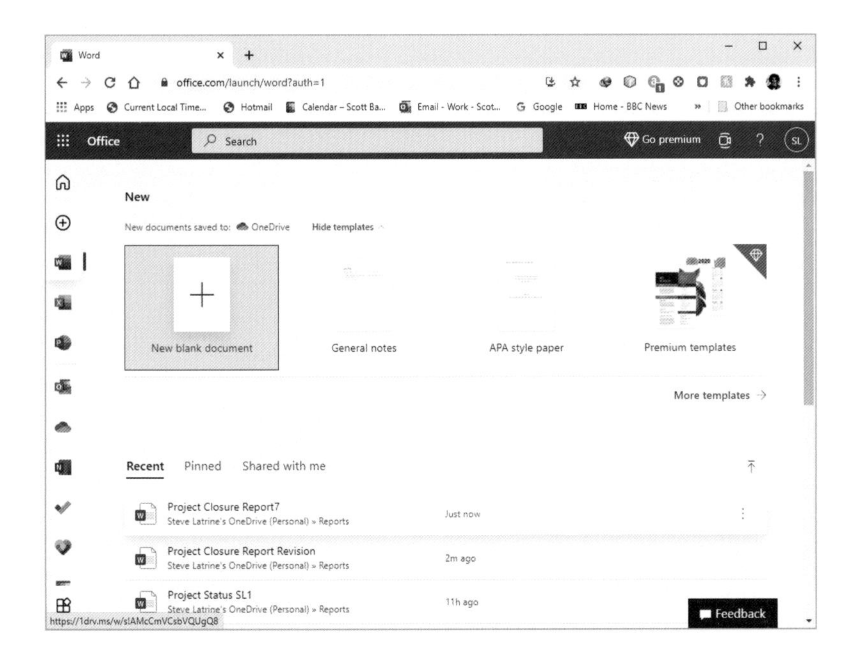

You can also invoke **Word Online** via OneDrive. Click on **OneDrive** and navigate to your saved file, then right-click and choose **Open in Word Online**.

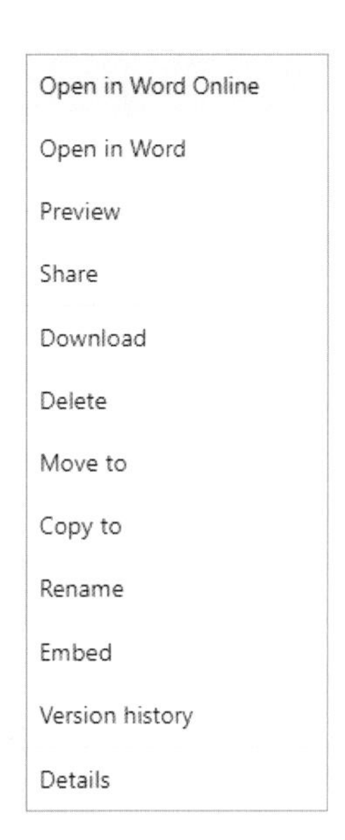

In the bottom-left corner of this illustration you can see a web URL for the selected item. Entering this URL into a browser will take you directly to the document.

...cont'd

4. The document opens in **Edit** mode. You can see its name and saved location in the blue title bar at the top

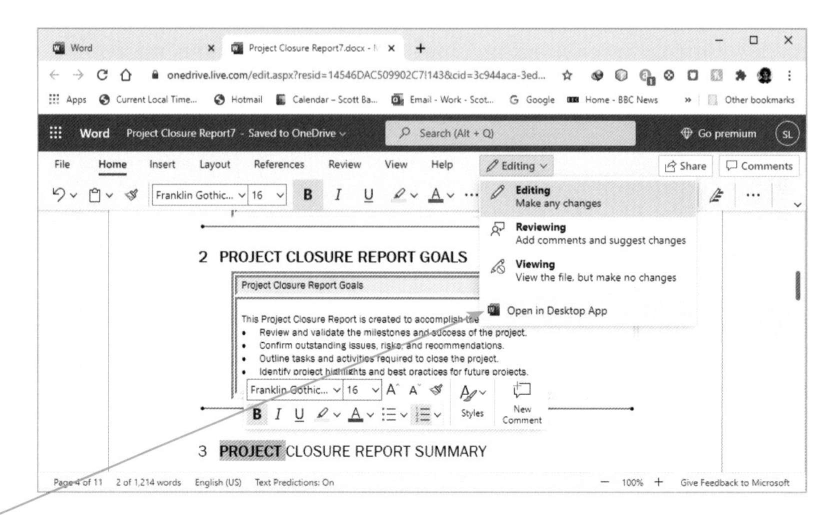

If you're using a device with Word installed, you might prefer to choose the **Open in Desktop App** option. You can see in this illustration it's in the final item in the pop-up menu that appears when you click the **Editing** button.

5. You'll see a web version of the familiar Word screen. Although there are fewer controls compared with the desktop version, it's still a very useful range of features

6. Experiment by reformatting some text or graphics. In this example we have changed the appearance of a table

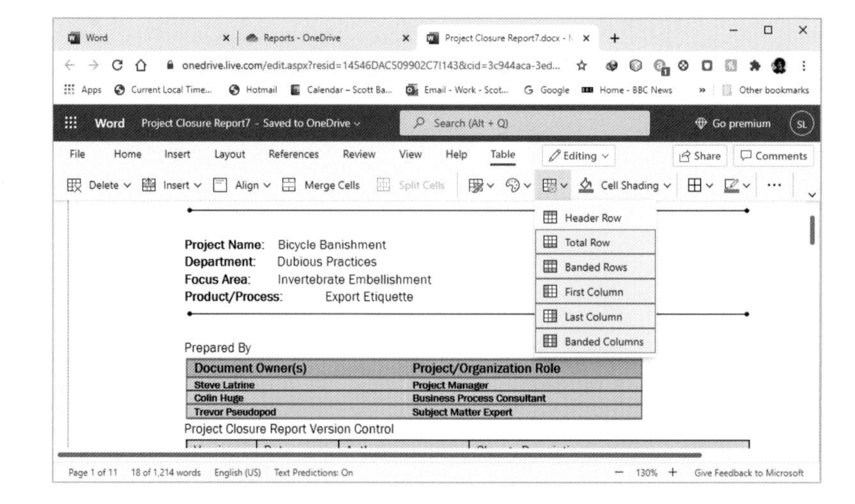

Now that you're working within the browser remember that clicking on an item in the Bookmarks bar will take you away from Word's Edit screen to another web page. If you do this accidentally then the browser's **Back** button will usually return you to where you were.

7. Click the **File** tab, choose **Info** and have a look at the options. The **Open in Desktop App** button is another way to invoke the desktop version of Word if available

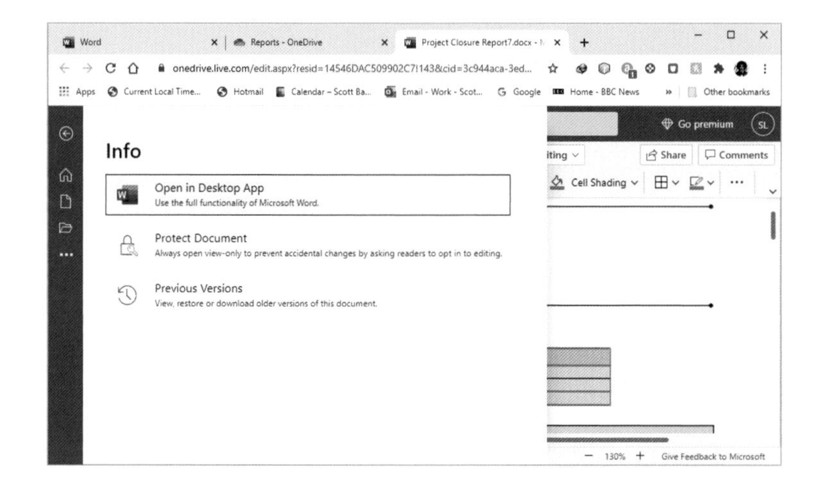

Note that the **File** tab contains **Save As** but there isn't a simple **Save**. This is because saving of the current file is handled automatically by Word Online.

8. Click on the **Left-arrow** icon to return to **Editing** view. In the blue bar near the top you'll see the file name, and a message that is normally **Saved to OneDrive**

9. Make an edit and you'll see the message in the blue title bar change briefly to **Saving...** (while Word Online updates the file stored in OneDrive), as in the example below. Once the word **Saving...** has disappeared the save has completed

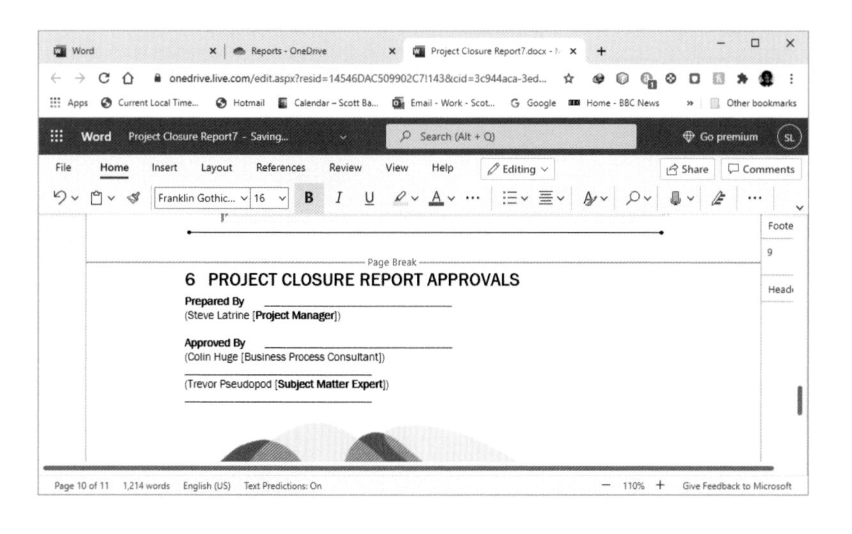

You can easily rename the current document. Simply click in the central blue area near the top where the document name is displayed and then edit or retype.

Working together

Once you have a document in a shared area such as OneDrive, you can collaborate with a number of co-authors. It's even possible for multiple users to work on the same document simultaneously, the key restriction being that only one person can edit a particular item at any time.

Preparing to share

1. In this example, we'll take a locally-stored document and go through the process of setting it up for online collaboration. Go to the **File** tab and choose **Share**

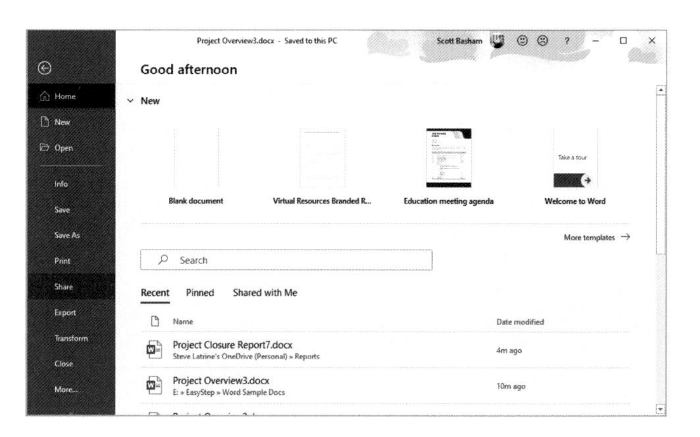

The sharing and collaboration processes you see in this chapter are similar across all Microsoft Office applications. Office 365 has been designed specifically to make team working on Cloud-based documents as easy and efficient as possible.

2. Select the area where you want the document to be stored

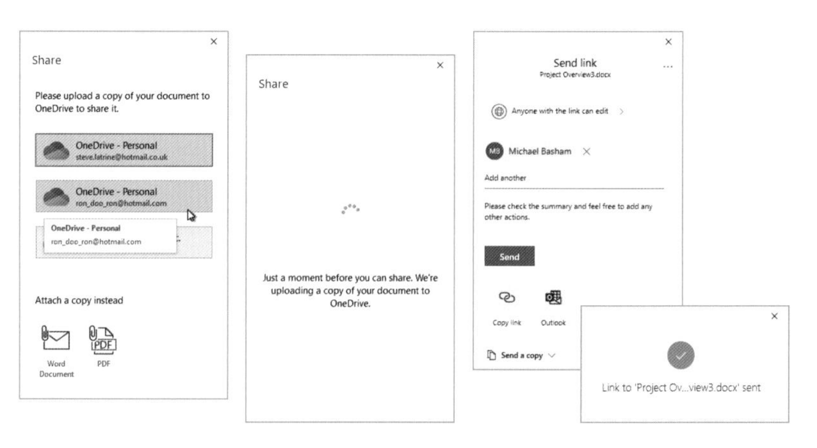

3. After uploading, the **Send link** screen appears. Enter the email address or account name of a person you want to share with, add an optional message, then click **Send**

4. The person you nominated will receive a message with a link that will allow access to the shared document

5. Now that you are back in normal **Editing** view, click **File** and **Share** Share once again to summon the **Send link** dialog

6. Enter the name or email address of another person who will access the document

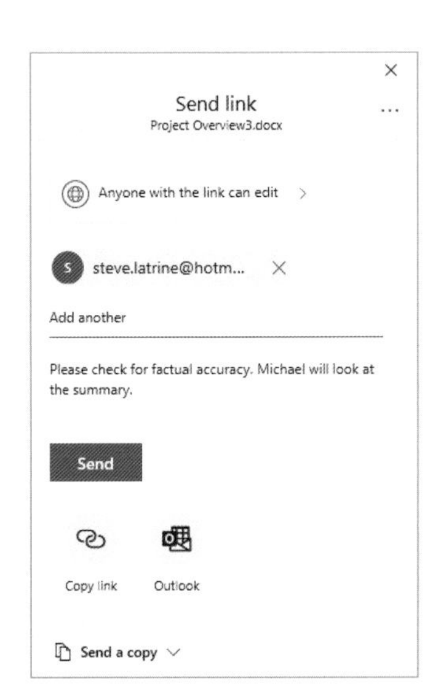

7. The person(s) you nominated will receive an email similar to the example below. Clicking on the **Open** button will allow viewing and, if allowed, editing of the shared document. It isn't necessary for those you nominated to have Word installed, as the online version can be used for viewing and editing

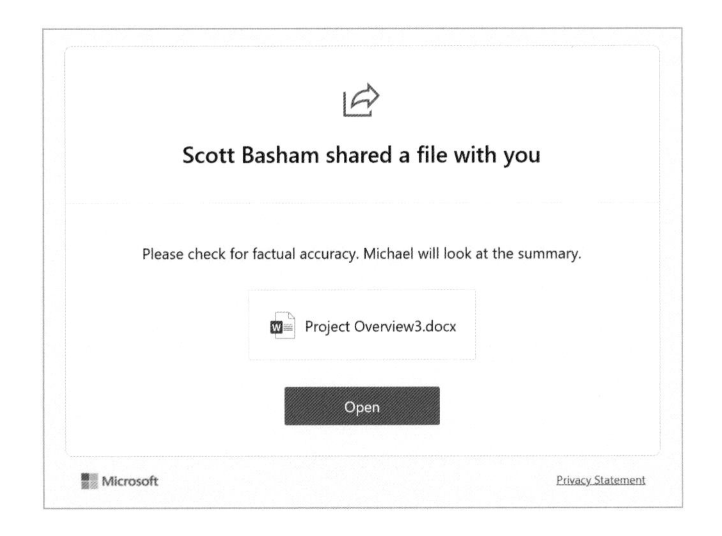

You can also use the **Share** button in the top-right corner of the main screen to invite more people to share the document at any time, rather than going via the **File** tab.

Another option is to use the **Send link** dialog to generate a link (URL) and send this to one or more recipients using either Outlook or via the **Copy link** button. This will allow you to paste a link into any email client or messaging application.

...cont'd

Be very careful about allowing multiple authors to work simultaneously on a document, particularly if you are not automatically sharing changes in real time. It's a good idea to allocate separate and distinct roles. For example, one person could make the main edits while another proofreads. The proofreader would not edit the text, but instead add comments. See pages 196-201 for more on comments and reviewing.

8. Also from the **Send link** dialog, click the three-dot icon ··· in the top right and choose **Manage access**

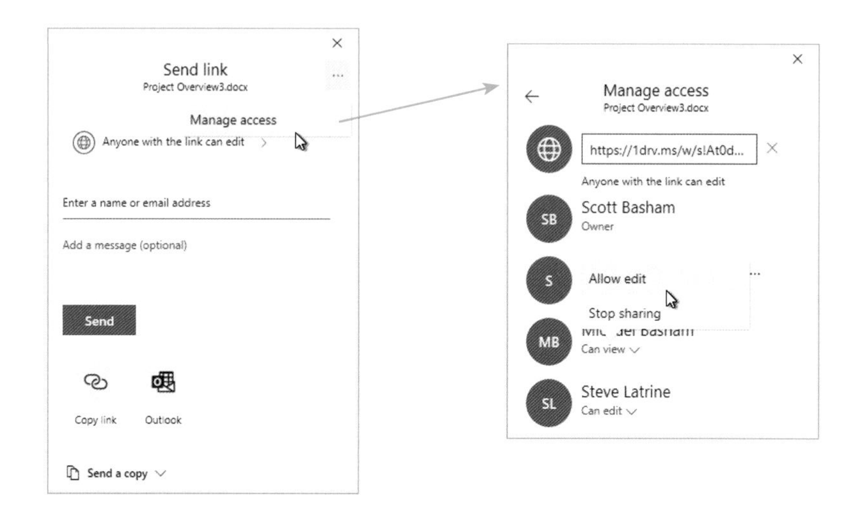

9. Click on the pop-up menu directly underneath any of the listed users. From here you'll be able to decide whether the person will be allowed to edit, or be restricted to read-only access. You can also click on **Stop sharing** to remove access altogether

We saw in on pages 74-75 that hyperlinks can be added into a Word document. These can point to the URL of a shared Word document, so if a user clicks on the hyperlink the document will open automatically. Whether it opens in the web app or the desktop app depends on this setting in Word's Options dialog.

Opening URLs directly from Word

From the **File** tab's **Advanced** options, anyone using URLs or hyperlinks that point to Word documents can elect to open them in their desktop app.

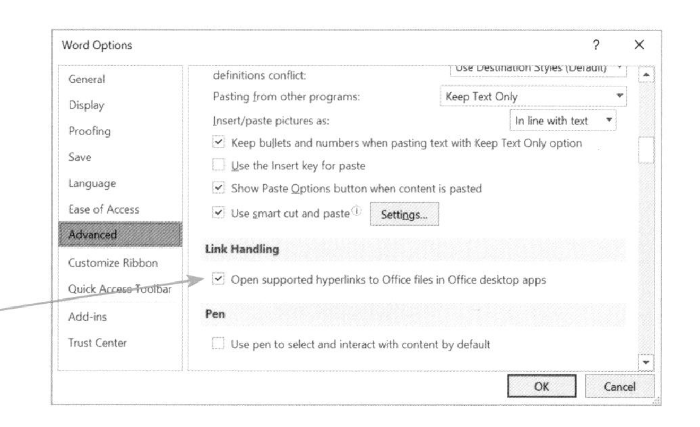

Multiple users working on one document

In the example on pages 162-164, Steve received an email advising him that he could work on our file. The email contained a hyperlink that would take him straight to that document. There, he would have the choice of using Word Online or the full version of Word (depending on what's available to him) to start editing. In this example, we'll start editing the document at exactly the same time as both Steve and a third user as well.

1. Open up your shared document in Word

Here, you can see the other people currently working on your document

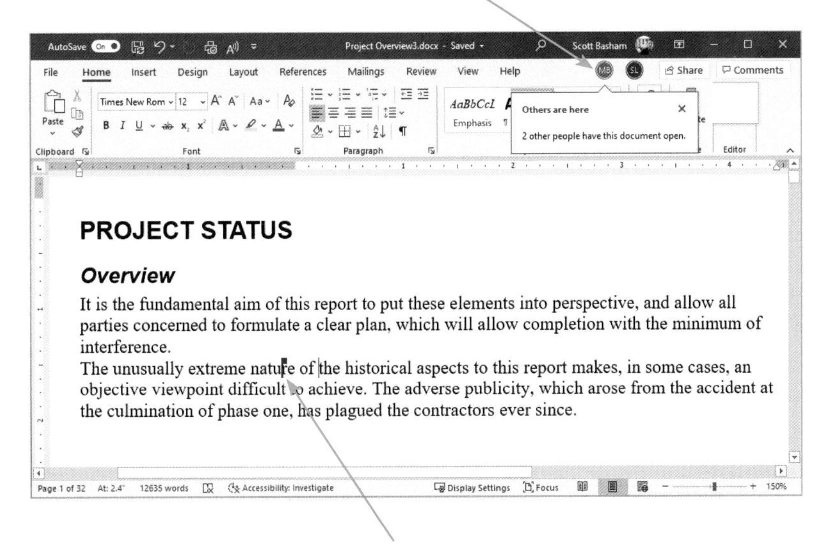

This purple icon indicates activity by Steve

2. As we're working we keep a look out for any sign of Michael's and Steve's activities. In the example above, Scott is the current user and a color-coded indicator has appeared, showing you that Steve is also currently editing the fourth word of the second paragraph

If you hover over one of the colored icons you'll see the full name of the person working on the document

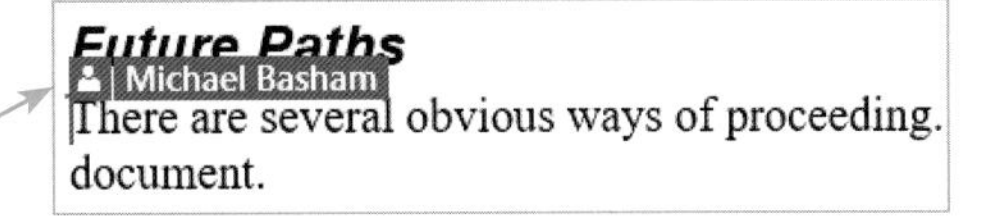

If you click on the icon for one of the other people who have your document open, you'll see their full name rather than their initials. You can also move directly to their current location, send them an email or open their contact card for further info.

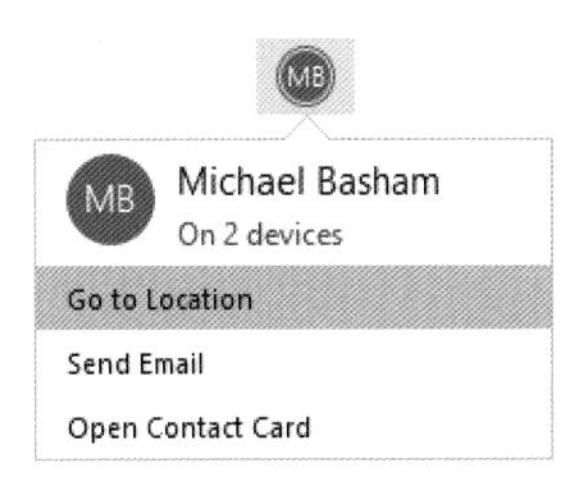

...cont'd

It is not always necessary for Word to lock an entire paragraph. If it assesses that it's safe to do so, it will let more than one person make changes. In this example, however, we can see that Word has decided to give Scott a lock over the whole paragraph until he completes his current edits.

3. In this example, Steve is the current user. You can see a blue indicator showing that Scott is working on the second paragraph. If Steve or Michael make an attempt to edit within that paragraph, Word will not allow this until Scott has completed his task

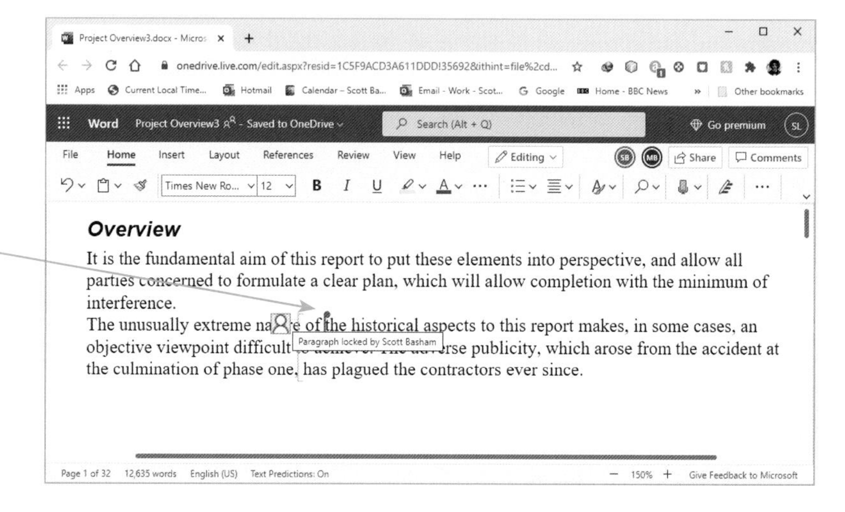

Text Predictions

In Word Online's Status bar you can switch **Text Predictions** On or Off. This allows Word to suggest the next word or group of words based on what you're typing. Press the **Tab** key to accept the suggestion.

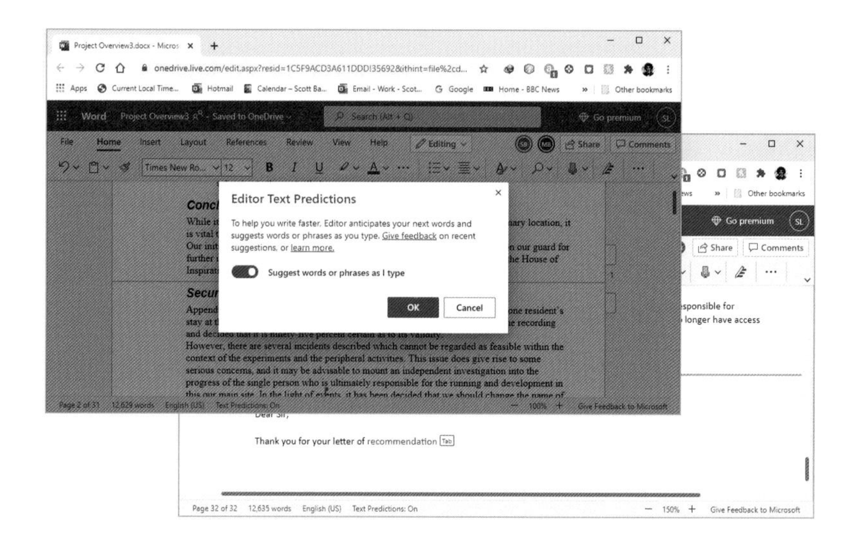

Text Predictions is available in other Microsoft apps such as Online Outlook.

Copies of documents

Sometimes you may want to work on your own copy of a document without any interference from others – even if the document is currently shared.

Save a Copy

1. When you're working on a shared document there is no **Save** button (as saving is automatic). If you click on **File** you'll see that there's a **Save a Copy** option in place of the usual **Save As**

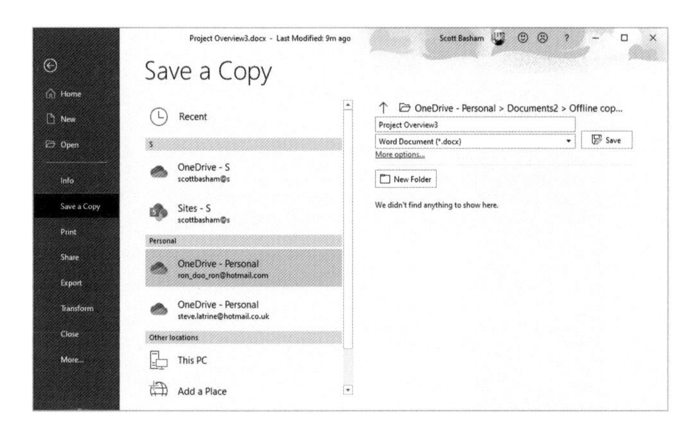

2. Choose a location and file name in the normal way. The new copy created will no longer be shared with the previous set of users

Sending a copy

When working with others, instead of online sharing you might decide simply to send out a copy as a Word document or a PDF file. PDF is a good option if you don't expect the recipient to perform any editing. Choose **File** and **Share**, then select one of the options at the bottom of the **Send link** dialog.

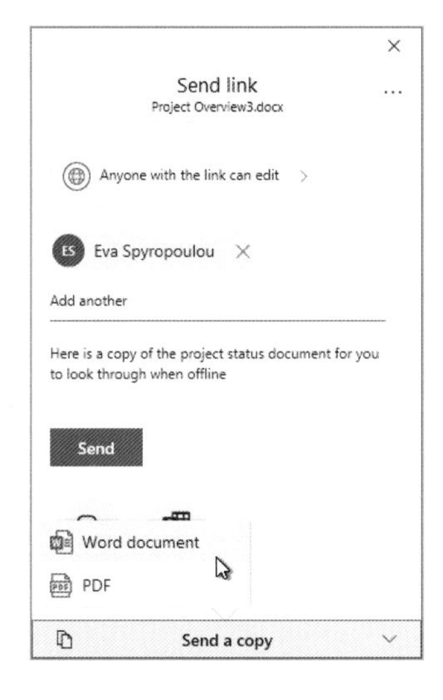

PDF (Portable Document Format) is a good option if you don't expect the recipient to perform any editing. Adobe's PDF Reader app is freely available on a wide variety of platforms.

Version History

Because online-shared documents save automatically, you may miss the ability to save manually at specific moments. However, the **Version History** feature gives you back this type of control.

Another effective way to control changes to your documents is via the **Tracking** feature – see pages 198-201 for more details on this.

Accessing Version History

1. Choose **File** and then **Info**. In this dialog click on **Version History**

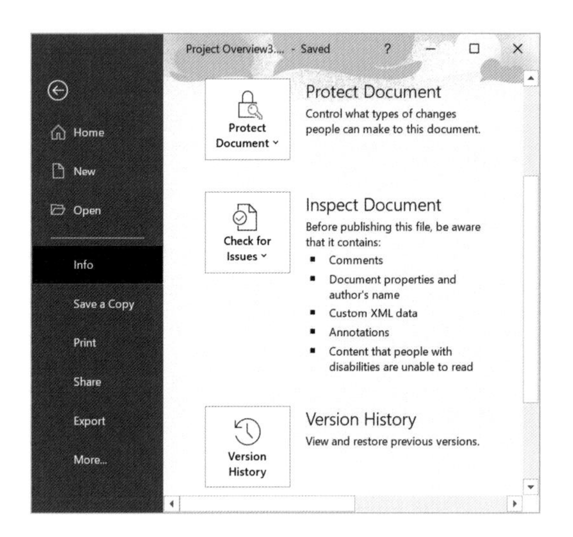

Click to select and open any of the listed versions. A new document window will appear, so you can decide what to do without disturbing the latest version. Just below the Ribbon you'll see controls to **Compare** this version with the current document, and to **Restore** the current document to the previous version.

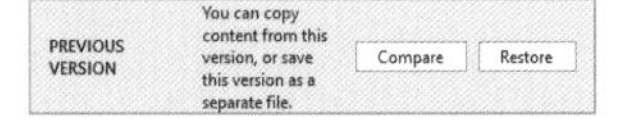

2. The **Version History** pane is now visible. You can scroll down through changes, starting from the most recent

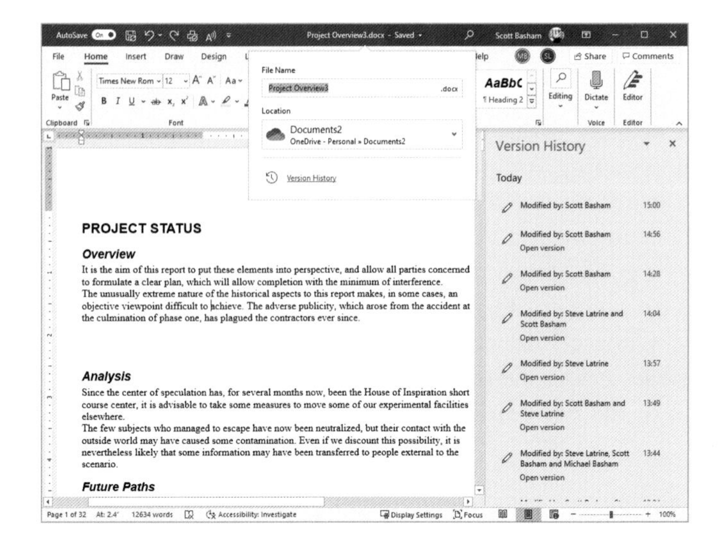

Adding annotations

If you have a touchscreen device then it's very easy to add annotations and highlights to your documents.

Accessing the Draw tab

1. If you're using a touchscreen device then you'll normally see an extra tab – **Draw** – in the Ribbon. If this isn't visible, choose **File** > **Options**, then click on **Customize Ribbon**. Make sure the **Draw** option under **Main Tabs** is checked

If your device does not have touchscreen capabilities you can still draw or annotate using the mouse or a drawing pad. Using the mouse makes freehand drawing difficult, but it is reasonably effective for highlighting.

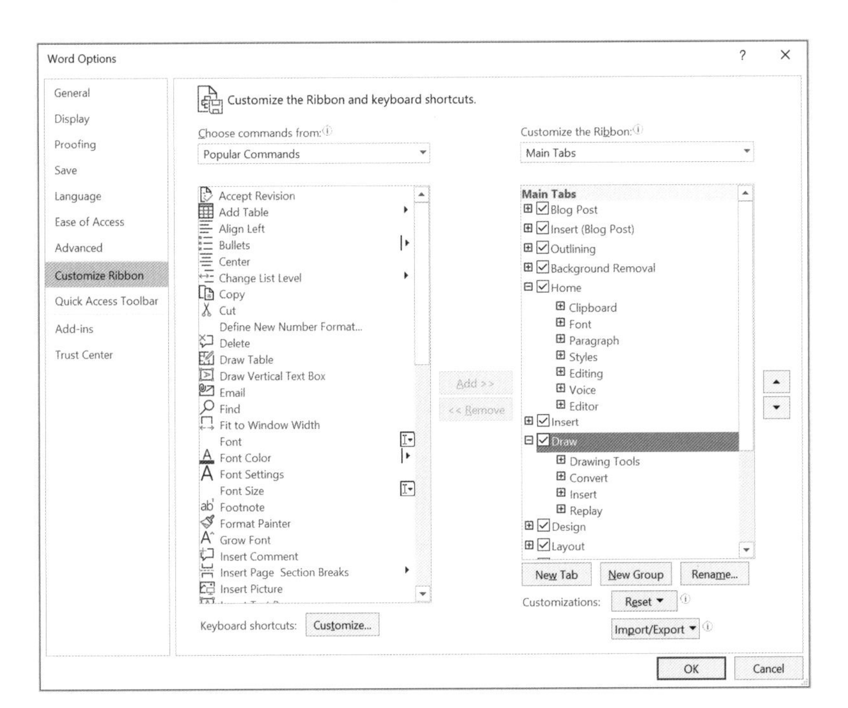

2. The **Draw** pane is now visible. On the left side is the **Drawing Tools** group

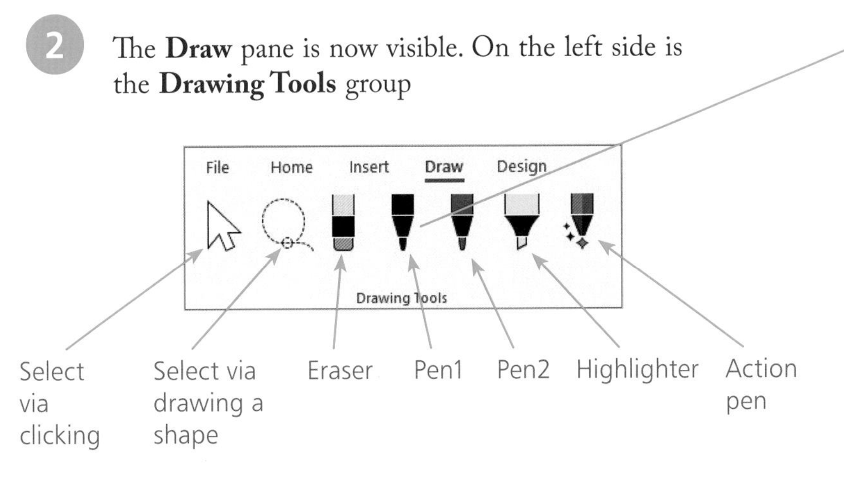

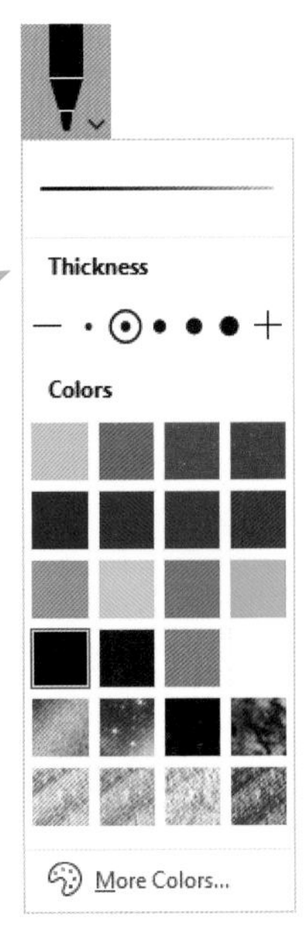

...cont'd

Using the highlighter

This tool is a good way to draw attention to areas of your document, just like a real highlighter pen (except it's much easier to erase or undo unintentional highlighting).

1. Make sure the **Draw** tab is visible and active. Click on the small downward-pointing arrow on the highlighter tool icon to see its options

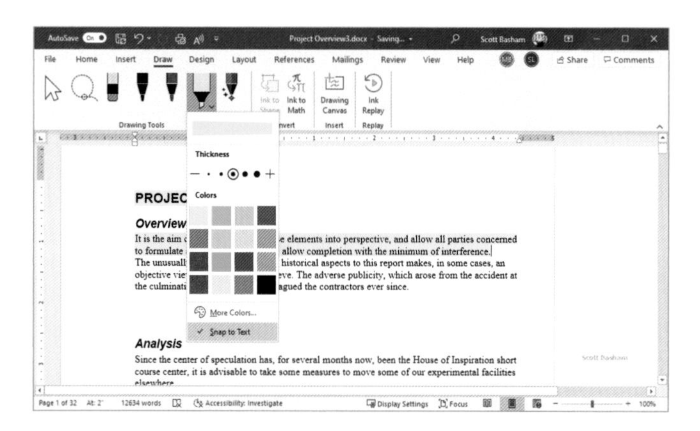

If you're working on a shared document, then the other users will be able to see the areas you've highlighted.

2. If you switch **Snap to Text** On then it will be much easier to apply the chosen highlight color to areas of text such as the paragraph shown above

Using the pen

The pen options are accessed in a similar way. You can adjust the thickness as well as the color. There are two pen tools – they both work in the same way, but it's convenient to have two styles available at the same time so that you can switch between them.

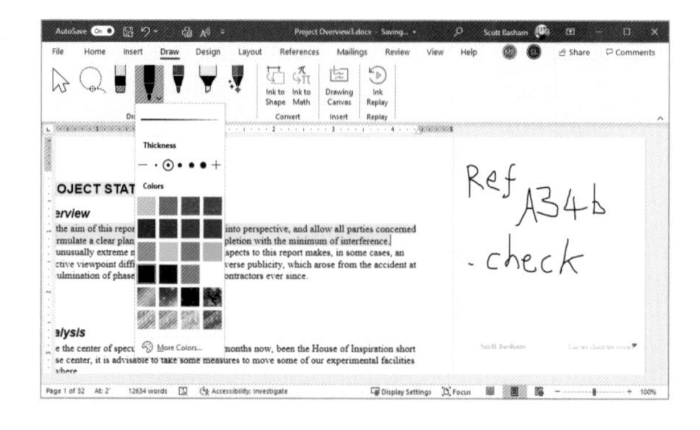

Freehand drawing

In the **Draw** tab there's a useful feature to convert your freehand drawings into regular shapes.

1. Make sure the **Ink to Shape** option in the Convert area of the **Draw** tab is active

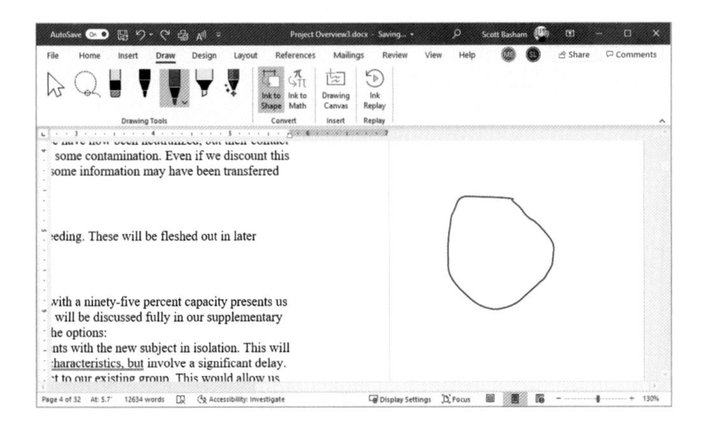

2. Try drawing an approximation of a recognizable shape such as the rough circle in the above example

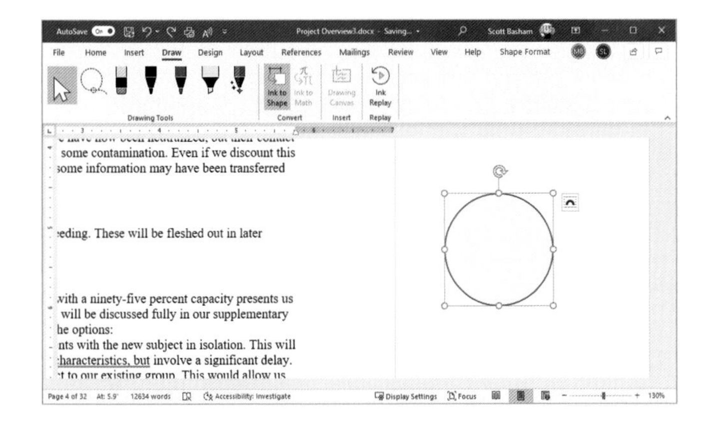

3. As long as you're fairly close to your intended shape Word will be able to substitute in a precise drawing object. This can be moved, sized and otherwise manipulated using the techniques we saw in Chapter 5

Remember you can use the **Undo** feature to try again if your initial attempts do not give you the desired results.

...cont'd

The action pen

If you have a pen for your device then the action pen can give you a very natural way of editing via **Ink Gestures**.

1. Click on the small downward arrow below the action pen icon in the Drawing Tools area

2. Select **Ink Gesture Help** from the pop-up menu

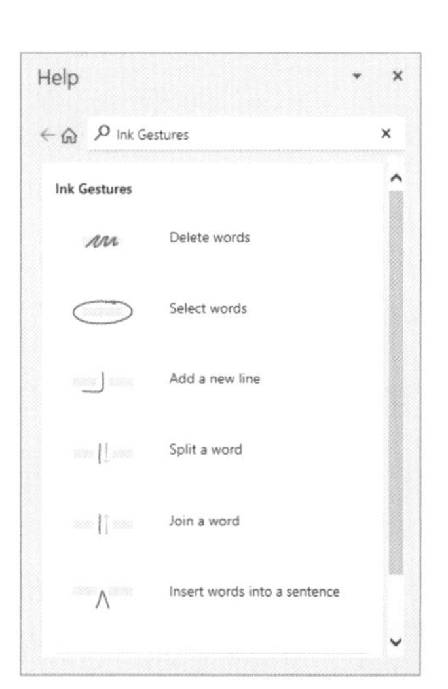

3. The **Help** pane shows you easy-to-learn gestures for deleting, selecting, splitting text, adding new lines or joining words together

4. Experiment with gestures such as scribbling to delete a paragraph

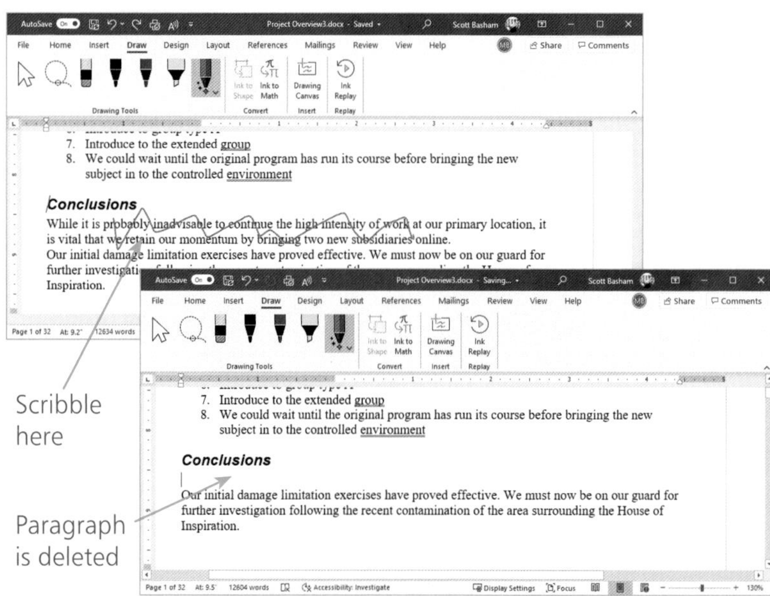

Have a good look to see if your gestures had the effect you intended, as it's very easy to delete or make other types of unwanted changes via a hasty swipe of a pen or finger. As long as you realize your mistake immediately, the **Undo** feature will be able to fix things.

9 References and mailings

In this chapter we'll look at more formal documents, covering indexing, Tables of Contents, and other types of references. We'll also look at creating automatic sequences of standardized documents.

Table of Contents

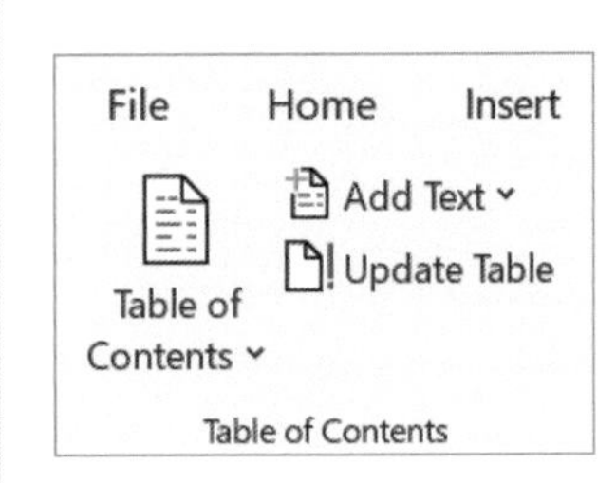

You can automatically create a **Table of Contents** by asking Word to look for instances of particular styles, or by using entries that you create manually.

Creating a Table of Contents

Open a suitably long document that uses a structure of style headings. Make sure the **References** tab is active so that you can see the **Table of Contents** controls on the left

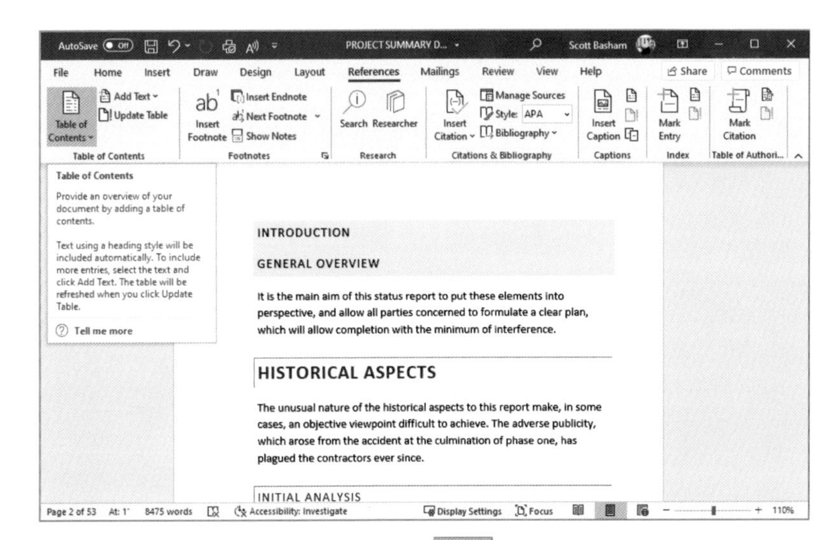

Each document can have a maximum of just one Table of Contents.

2. Click the **Table of Contents** button and choose one of the available preset styles

3. Word looks through your document and uses the headings to generate the Table of Contents. It calculates the correct page number reference and adds it to each entry

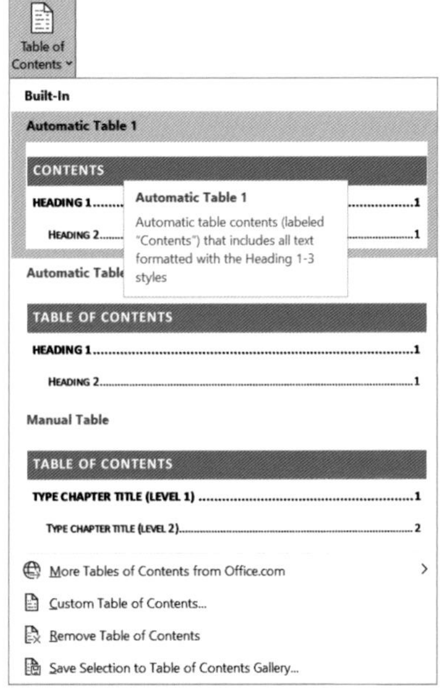

4 Note that the entries generated in the Table of Contents reflect the heading structure in the main document. They also behave like hyperlinks: **Ctrl** + **click** on any of these to jump straight to the relevant page

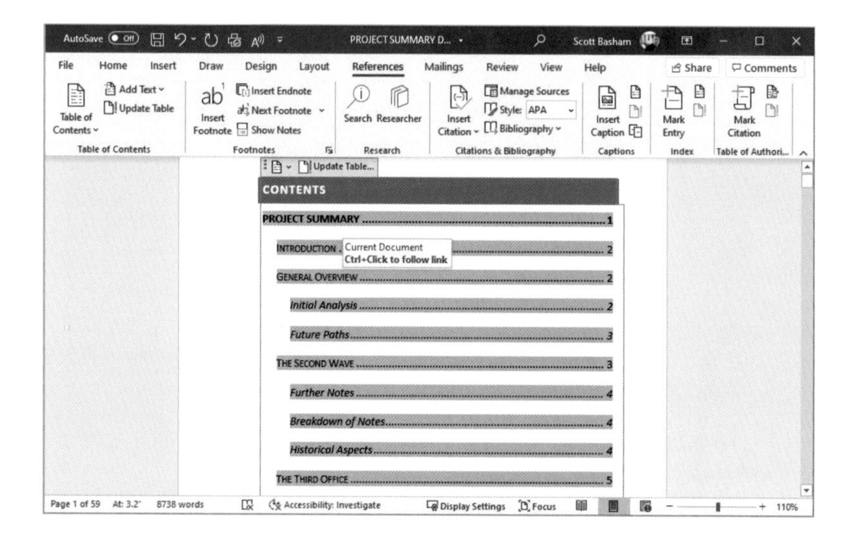

If you're using **Web Layout** view then the Table of Contents entries will be displayed with actual hyperlinks rather than page numbers, as you can see below.

Manually adding or removing items

1 Select some text that is not already in the Table of Contents, then click the **Add Text** button and choose a level number. The next time the Table of Contents is created or fully updated, the new entry will appear

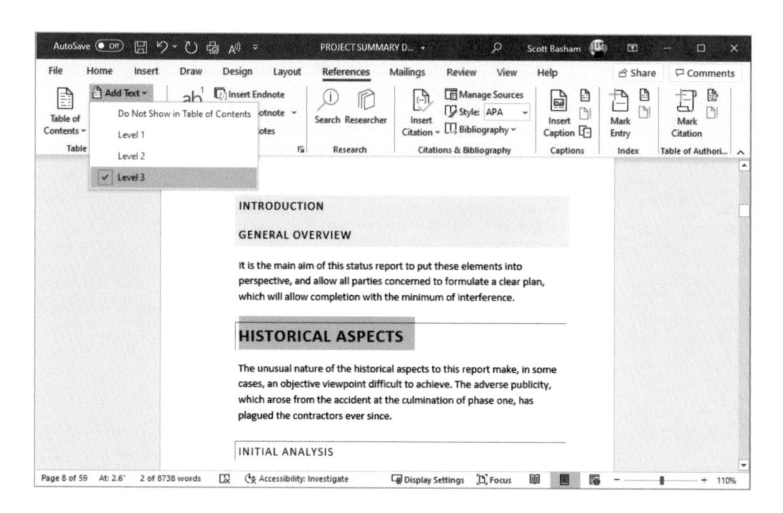

...cont'd

2. To remove an item, select some text that is already in the Table of Contents, then click the **Add Text** button and select **Do Not Show in Table of Contents**

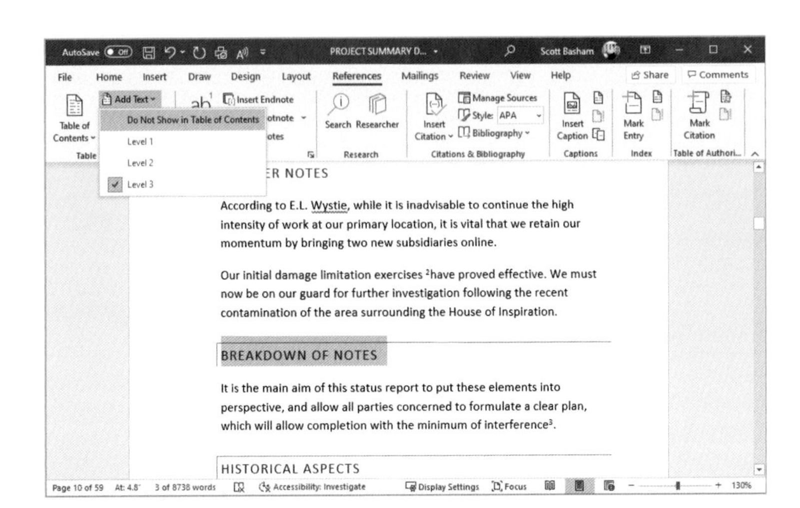

You can check at any time whether a piece of text is currently included in the Table of Contents. To do this, select the text then click the **Add Text** tool to see if it's currently assigned to any particular level.

Customizing your Table of Contents

1. Select a line in the Table of Contents and use the **Style Inspector** (see pages 50 and 54) to view its style

2. If you redefine this style then Word will automatically change all the entries of the same type. The new formatting will apply even if you recreate the table later

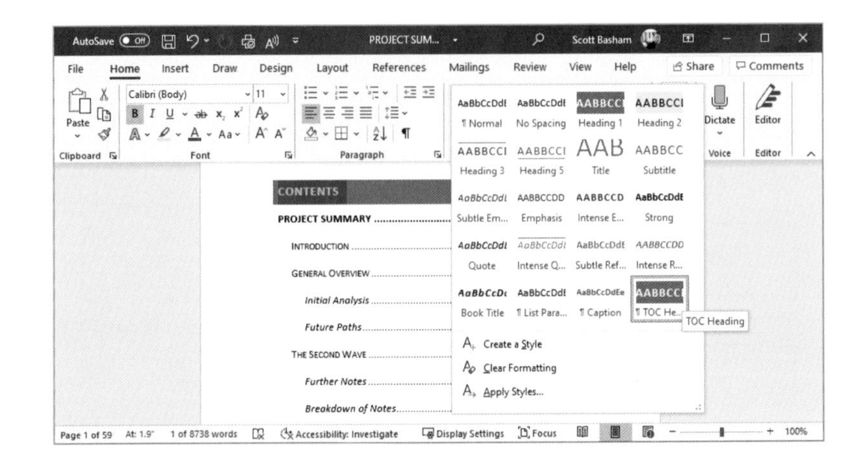

Updating your Table of Contents

1. As you continue to work with your document, text may move to different pages, pages may be inserted or deleted, and new headings may be added

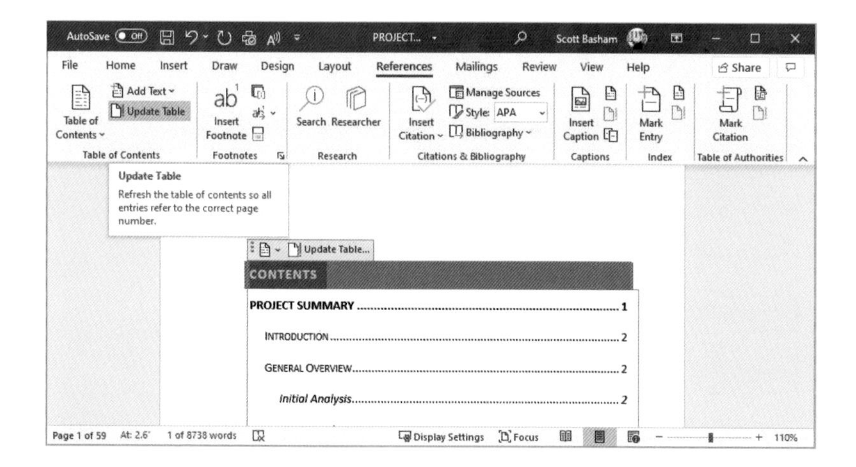

2. Click **Update Table** to rebuild the Table of Contents. You'll be given the choice of updating the entire table or just the page numbers of existing entries

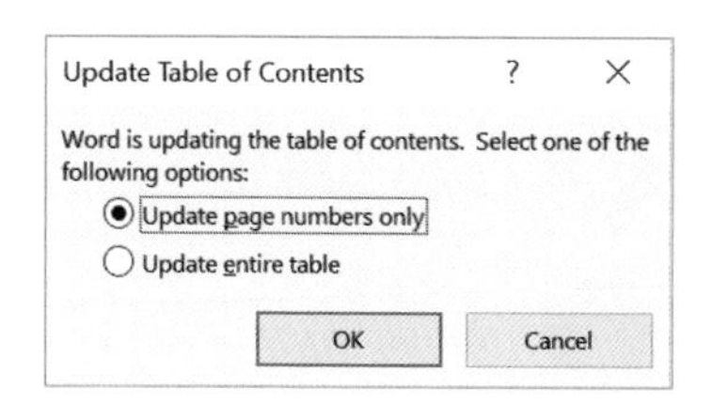

If you've added or removed items for your Table of Contents then make sure you select **Update entire table** rather than **Update page numbers only**.

Manually defining your Table of Contents

When you click the **Table of Contents** tool to create the Table of Contents, as well as the predefined styles there's a **Custom Table of Contents** option. In the dialog that appears, click **Options...** to choose which text styles to use.

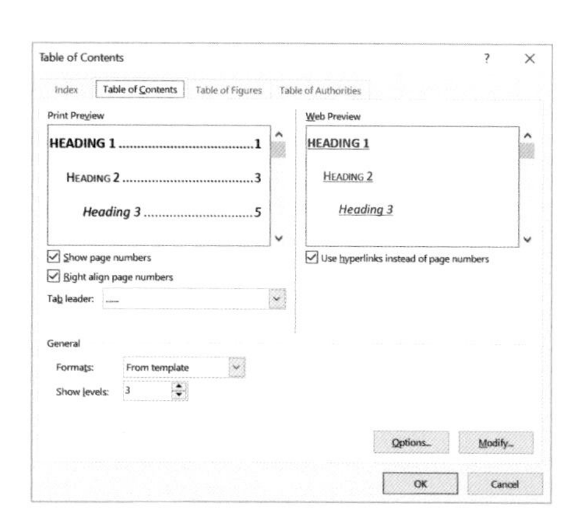

Footnotes and endnotes

These allow you to add a superscript number to a word or phrase that relates to explanatory text at the bottom of the page (for footnotes), or the end of the document or section (for endnotes).

Adding a footnote

1. Select the desired text and click **Insert Footnote** or press **Ctrl** + **Alt** + **F**

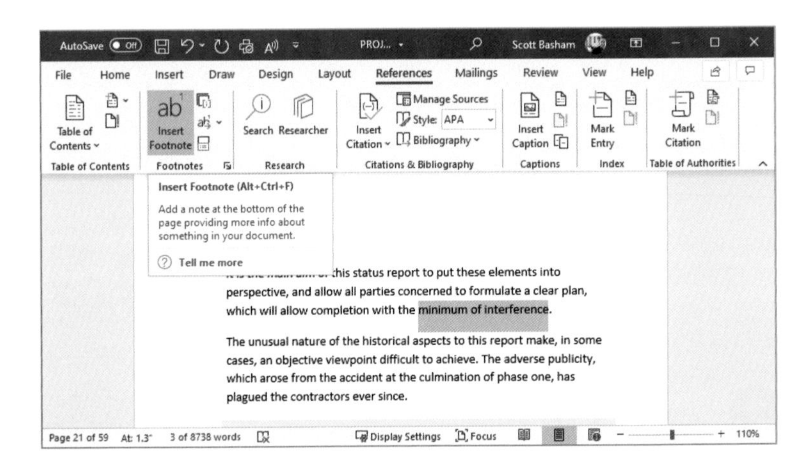

2. Next, add the footnote text at the bottom of the page

3. Note that the text you'd highlighted now includes a superscript footnote number. If you hover over this text, the footnote will temporarily appear as a pop-up

If you add new footnotes earlier on in your document, Word will automatically renumber the rest so that numbering is continuous.

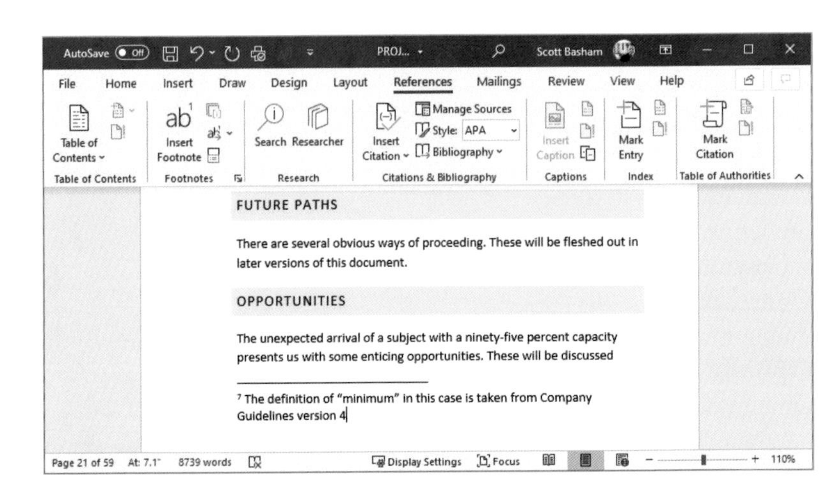

Adding an endnote

1. Select the desired text and click **Insert Endnote**

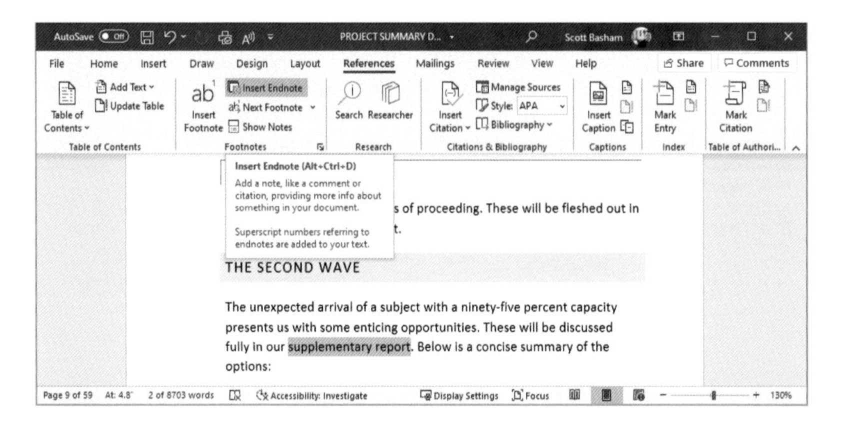

The keyboard shortcut for inserting an endnote is **Ctrl** + **Alt** + **D**.

2. Enter the text for your endnote in the space provided

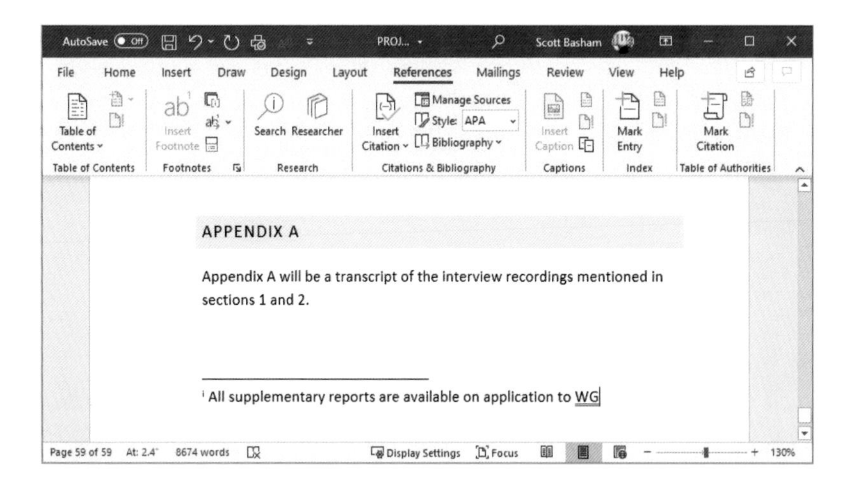

When you insert a footnote or endnote, the display automatically scrolls to the footnote or endnote area, ready for you to type in the text.

3. The **Show Notes** button will take you from the footnote back to the related text in the main part of the document

4. If you click the button a second time, you'll be taken to either the footnote or the endnote area

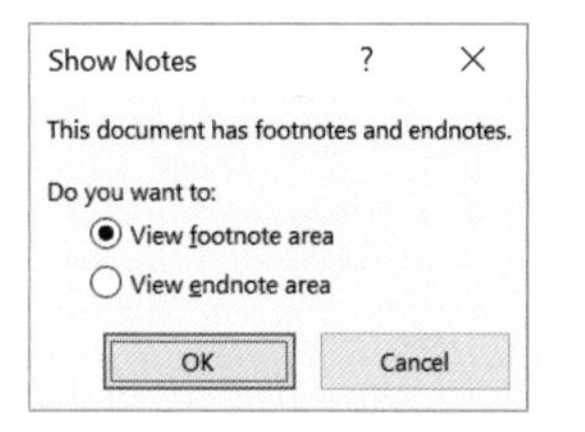

...cont'd

Navigating through footnotes and endnotes

1. Click the **Next Footnote** icon to see its pop-up menu
2. There are four options, allowing you to jump straight to the next or to the previous footnote or endnote

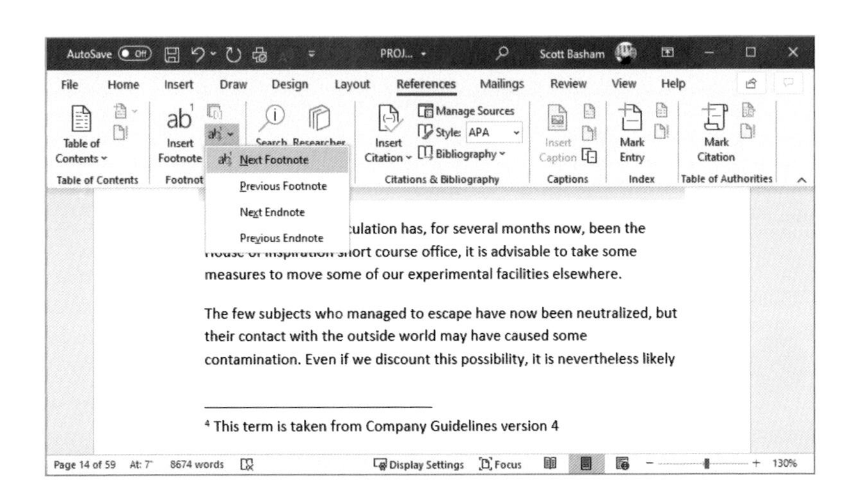

The Footnote and Endnote dialog

1. Click the icon in the lower-right corner of the Footnotes area to see the Footnote and Endnote dialog

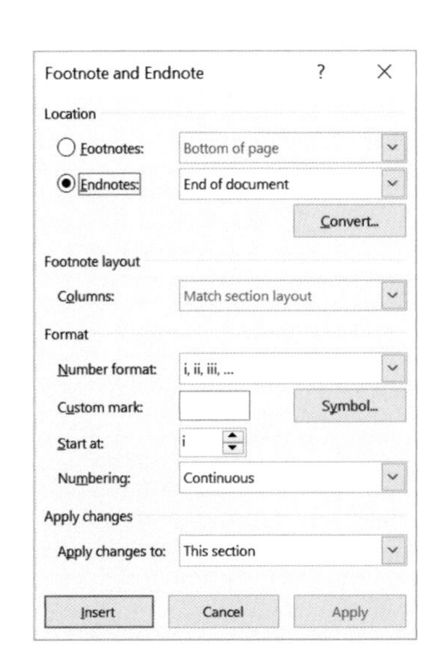

Here, you can specify where the notes are positioned – endnotes can go either at the end of the document or just at the end of the current section.

The number format defaults to Roman numerals for endnotes, but there are other options available.

You can also have different dialog settings for each section if you require that level of control.

Click the **Convert** button to switch around footnotes and endnotes, or to convert all notes to just one type.

Convert Notes

- Convert all footnotes to endnotes
- Convert all endnotes to footnotes
- Swap footnotes and endnotes

OK Cancel

Citations

Citations are useful if you need to add a reference to another author or publication within your text. Later on you can compile a standard bibliography that collects together all your citations.

Don't select the text, or the **Insert Citation** button will replace it with a citation. Instead, make sure you click after the main text, to indicate where you'd like the citation inserted.

Adding a citation

1. Click just after the reference in your main text. Click the **Insert Citation** button and choose **Add New Source...**

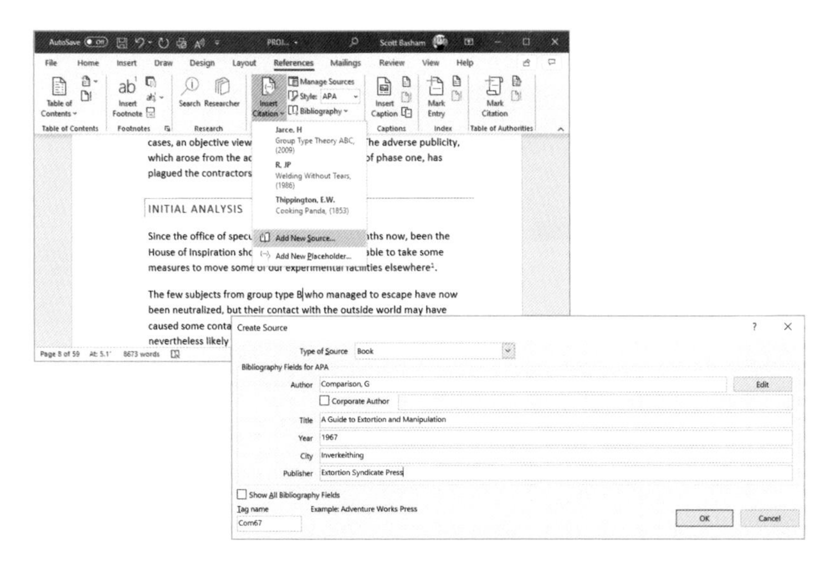

2. The **Create Source** dialog appears. Choose the source then enter the details and click **OK**

When you have all the citations you need, you are ready to create a bibliography. Move to the desired location, click the **Bibliography** button and choose one of the options.

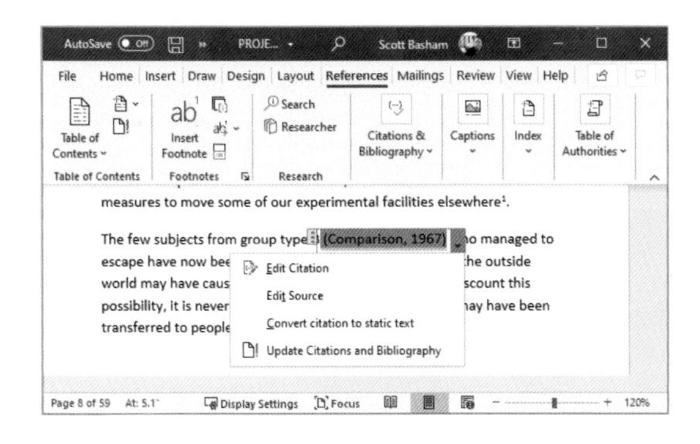

3. A short citation reference now appears next to your text. If you need to change any of the details you entered then click the **Manage Sources** button

Captions

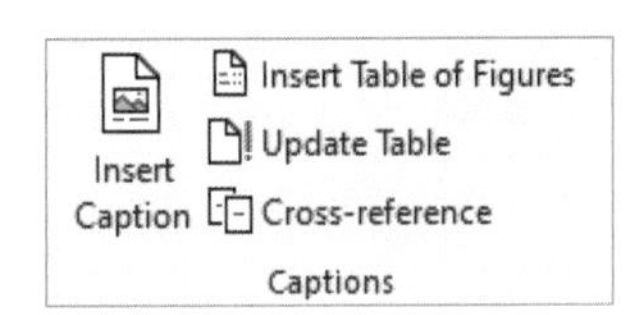

1. Select your element then click on the **Insert Caption** icon in the **References** tab

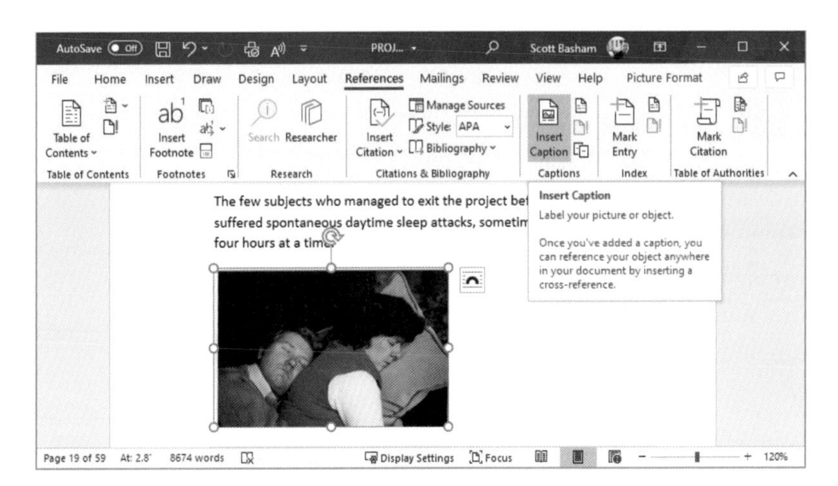

You can also add captions to equations and tables – follow exactly the same procedure.

2. Add the caption text to the dialog. There are three label options – **Equation**, **Figure** and **Table** (you can also use the **New Label...** button to add more options). Choose **Figure** for this example

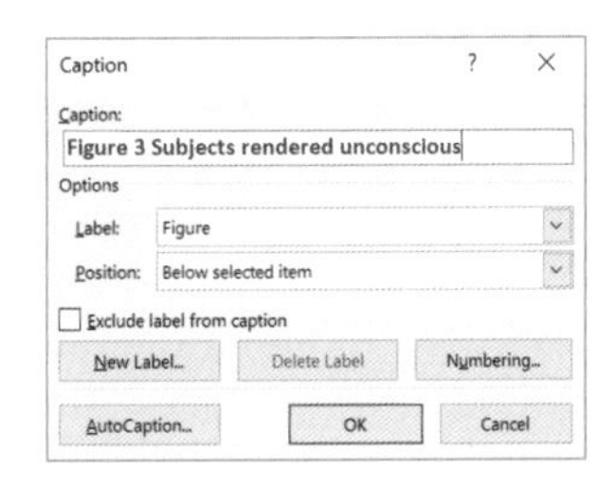

3. Captions will normally be numbered 1, 2, 3, and so on, but this can be changed by clicking on **Numbering...**. Repeat the process to add more captions (you don't need to add these in any particular order)

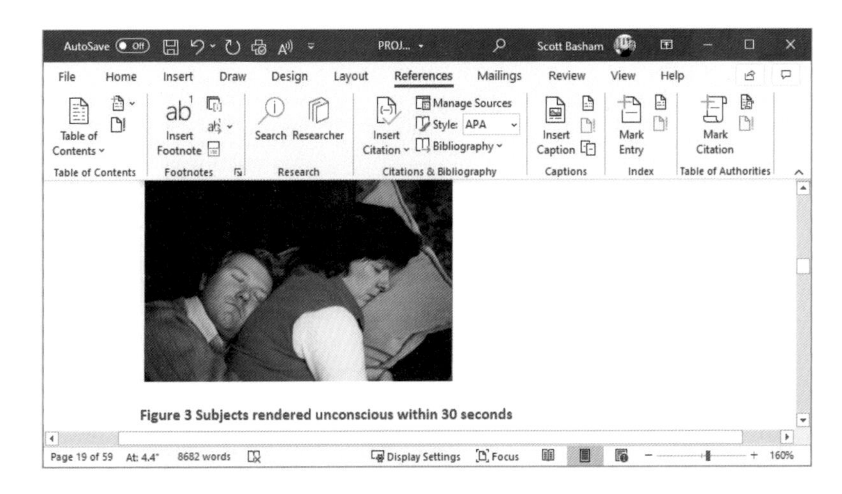

Tables of figures

Once you've created captions throughout your document, you can ask Word to build a **Table of Figures**.

1. Make sure your insertion point is placed where you want the Table of Figures

2. Click on **Insert Table of Figures**

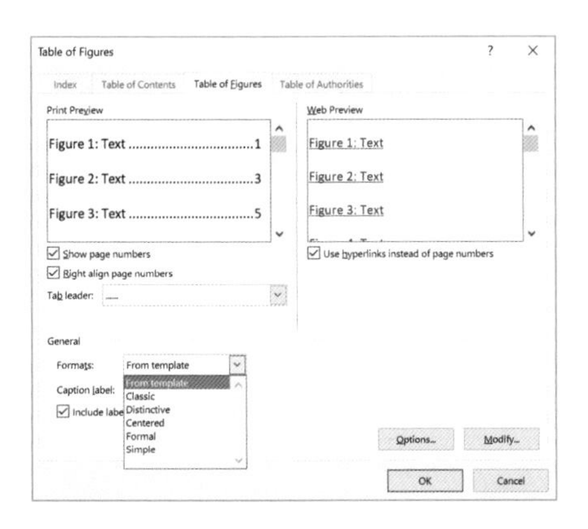

The **Table of Figures** dialog appears as shown.

3. Choose a format from the pop-up list. The **Print** and **Web Preview** areas will show you how this will look. Click **OK** to generate the table

4. If you make changes to your document, you should probably refresh the table. To do this, right-click somewhere within the table and choose **Update Field**

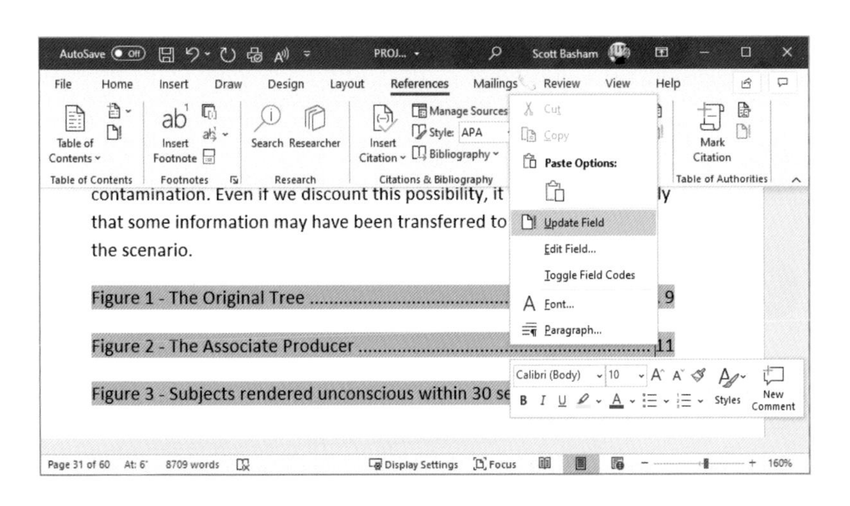

As with footnotes seen on page 178, Word automatically renumbers captions as you add them to or delete them from your document.

Indexing

Longer documents benefit greatly from a well-organized index. Word makes the process of creating an index fairly easy.

1. Select the text you want to add to the index, and click on **Mark Entry** (in the **References** tab) or press **Shift** + **Alt** + **X**

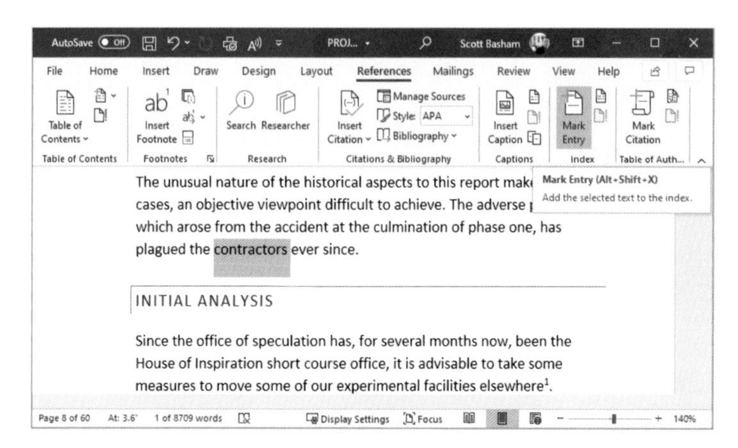

2. You can now edit the entry text, add a subentry, and choose whether the index will show the current page, a range of pages, or a cross-reference to another index entry

3. Use the **Bold** and **Italic** checkboxes if you want your index entry to be emphasized

4. When you have finished making your settings, click **Mark**, or **Mark All** if you want to mark all instances

5. This dialog is *non-modal*, which means that you can continue to work on the main page with the dialog still open. In this way, you can go right through your document, quickly and easily marking new entries, without having to continually reopen the dialog

You can create index entries with multiple levels. Add a second level by entering text in the **Subentry:** box. For a third level, add a colon and then more text after your current subentry.

6. As soon as you mark an entry, Word switches on the **Show/Hide ¶** feature so that you can see your index entries marked clearly as "tags" with curly brackets

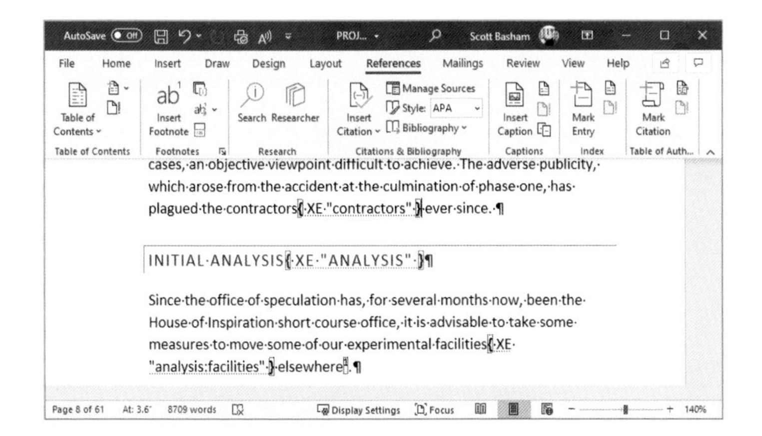

7. Place your insertion point where you'd like the index, then click **Insert Index** to see the finished result

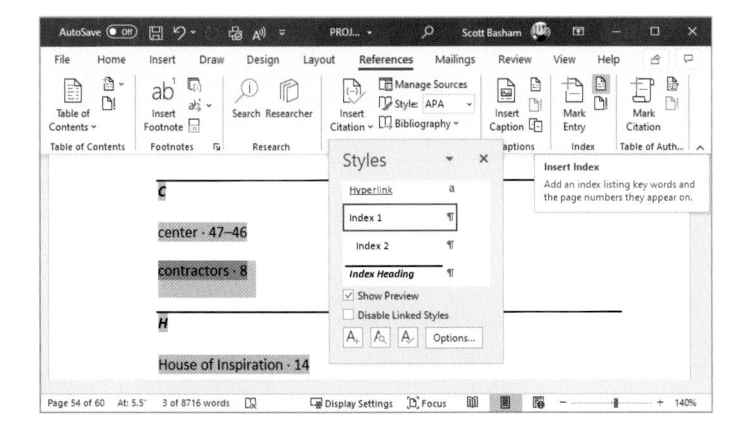

8. Click in one of the entries in the new index then use the **Style Inspector** to see how it is automatically formatted

9. Word uses special styles (**Index Heading, Index 1, Index 2**, and so on) to control the formatting. If you edit these styles, rather than the index text directly, then your formatting decisions will be preserved even if you rebuild the index later on

Using **Ctrl** + * you can toggle the **Show/Hide ¶** feature On and Off.

You can display the **Style Inspector** with the following: type **Alt** + **Ctrl** + **Shift** + **S** to summon the Styles panel, then click on the icon at the bottom.

If you edit your document so that the page numbers have changed, or if you have added more index entries, then you will need to rebuild the index. To do this, select the index and then click on **Update Index**.

Envelopes and labels

Creating envelopes

1. Activate the **Mailings** tab and, in the Create area, click **Envelopes**. The following dialog appears

2. Enter the delivery address and, optionally, the return address. Click the **Options...** button to select the envelope's design and dimensions from a list of standard sizes

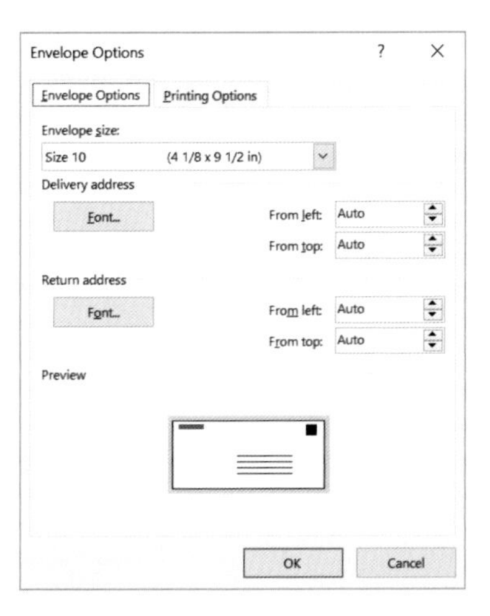

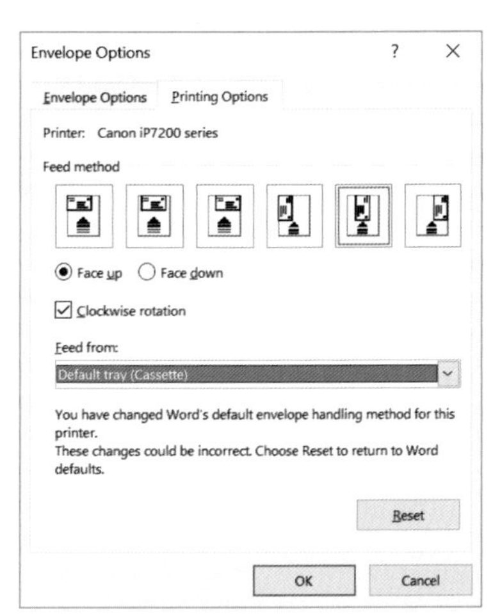

As well as the **Envelope Options** tab, this dialog has a tab for **Printing Options**. This lets you tailor the settings to match the way you load envelopes into your printer.

3. Click **Add to Document**

4. If you entered a return address, you'll be shown a dialog asking you whether you want to make this the default return address. If you click **Yes**, then you won't need to retype it the next time you create an envelope

5. Once you click **OK** in the dialog box, your envelope will be generated on a new page

Creating labels

1. Click the **Labels** tool. The following dialog box appears

2. Enter the text (usually an address) and choose between creating a single label or a full page of the same label

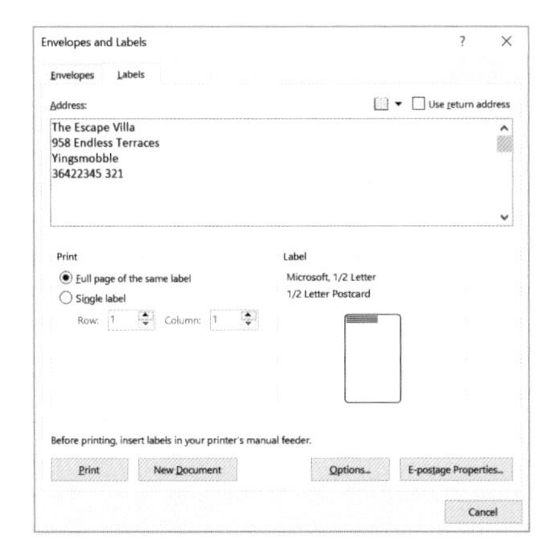

3. Click the **Options...** button, select the label vendor and then the label from the product numbers listed

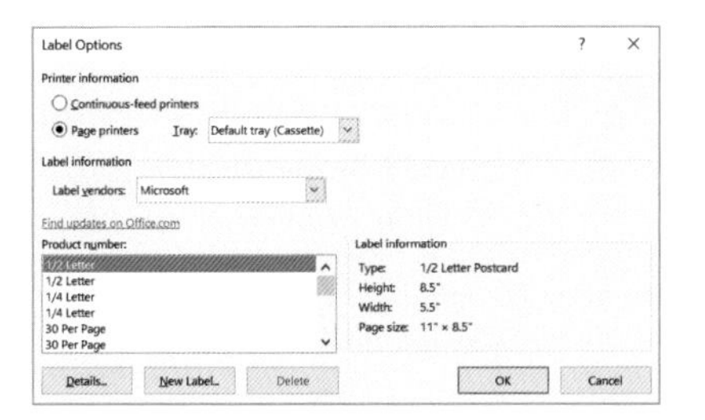

4. Click the **Details...** button to review the attributes of the currently-selected label

5. If you can't find the right label then click **Cancel** to return to the **Label Options** dialog, then click on **New Label...**

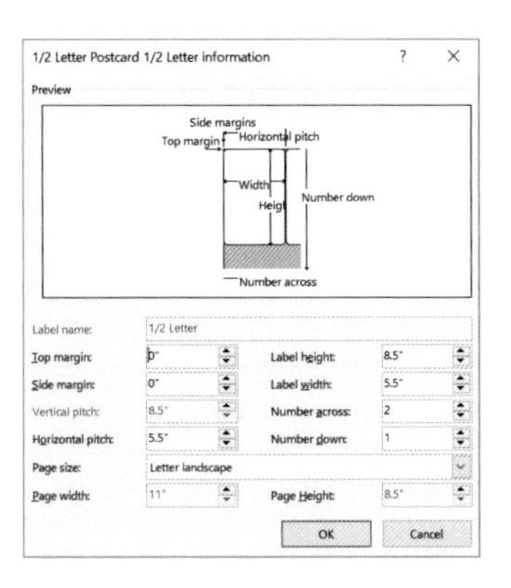

6. Click **OK** to return to the **Envelopes and Labels** dialog, then choose **New Document** to generate your labels

7. Your labels will be generated in their own document

Word will prompt you to save your new label document when you have finished working with it.

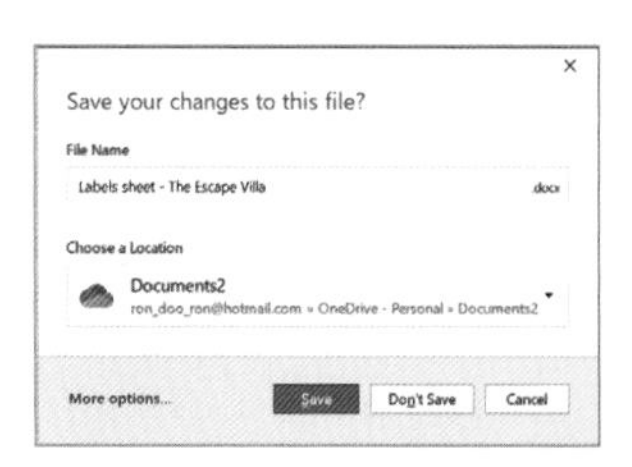

Mail Merge

There are several ways of setting up mail merging in Word, but the easiest is to use the Wizard, which guides you through the various stages of the process.

Mail Merge can be a real time-saver if you've a long list of recipients. However, if you've only one or two then it's probably easier to create your documents manually.

Using the Mail Merge Wizard

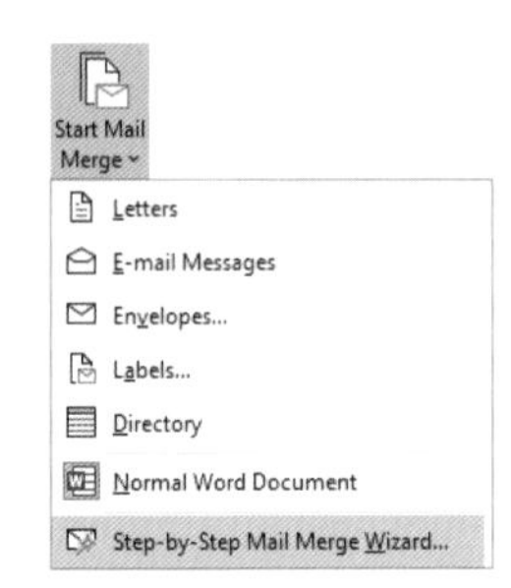

1. Click **Start Mail Merge** (in the **Mailings** tab) and select **Step-by-Step Mail Merge Wizard...**

2. The **Mail Merge** window appears at the right-hand side of the screen. If you drag on its title bar you can make it into a floating window. Select the document type then click **Next** to be guided through the steps

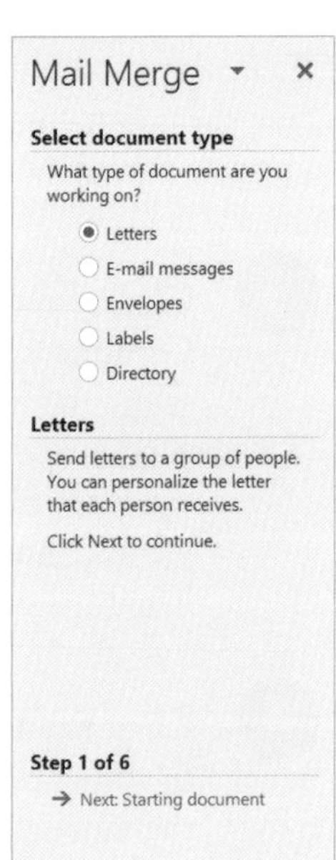

3. In Step 3 you'll be prompted to specify a list of addresses. This can be from a variety of data sources, such as your Outlook contacts, or can be entered manually

4. You can then write your document using special fields or placeholders, which are then substituted with values from each address before printing

Fields within Word appear as a name surrounded by angle brackets; for example: **<<AddressBlock>>**. Although you do not yet see the text that will be substituted for this placeholder, you can still control its positioning and formatting using the normal editing controls.

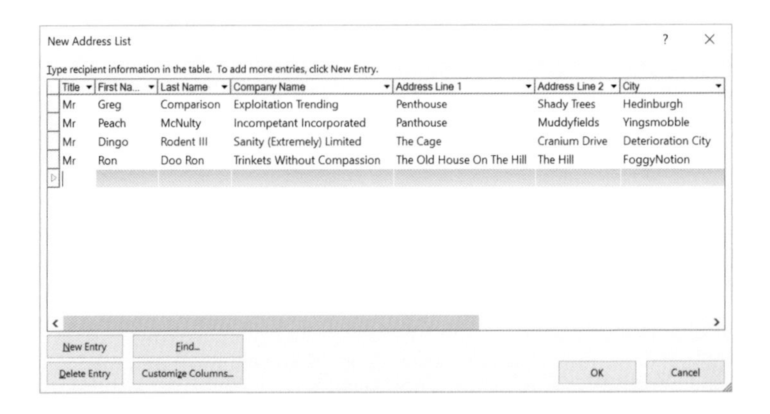

New Address List

Type recipient information in the table. To add more entries, click New Entry.

Title	First Na...	Last Name	Company Name	Address Line 1	Address Line 2	City
Mr	Greg	Comparison	Exploitation Trending	Penthouse	Shady Trees	Hedinburgh
Mr	Peach	McNulty	Incompetant Incorporated	Panthouse	Muddyfields	Yingsmobble
Mr	Dingo	Rodent III	Sanity (Extremely) Limited	The Cage	Cranium Drive	Deterioration City
Mr	Ron	Doo Ron	Trinkets Without Compassion	The Old House On The Hill	The Hill	FoggyNotion

New Entry | Find... | Delete Entry | Customize Columns... | OK | Cancel

10 Advanced topics

This chapter looks at various ways of checking your work. We'll see how to manage edits in collaboration with others. We'll also look at Add-ins, other ways to control your view, and then finish off by comparing versions of Word.

Proofing tools

Editor Thesaurus Word Count
Proofing

Word can access a number of English and non-English dictionaries, which it uses when running spelling or grammar checks.

1. As you type, Word will automatically check your spelling using its default dictionary. Any suspect words will be underlined in red with a wavy line. Right-click on each word to see your choices

You can also summon the Editor pane by selecting **See More** from the pop-up menu that appears when you right-click on text.

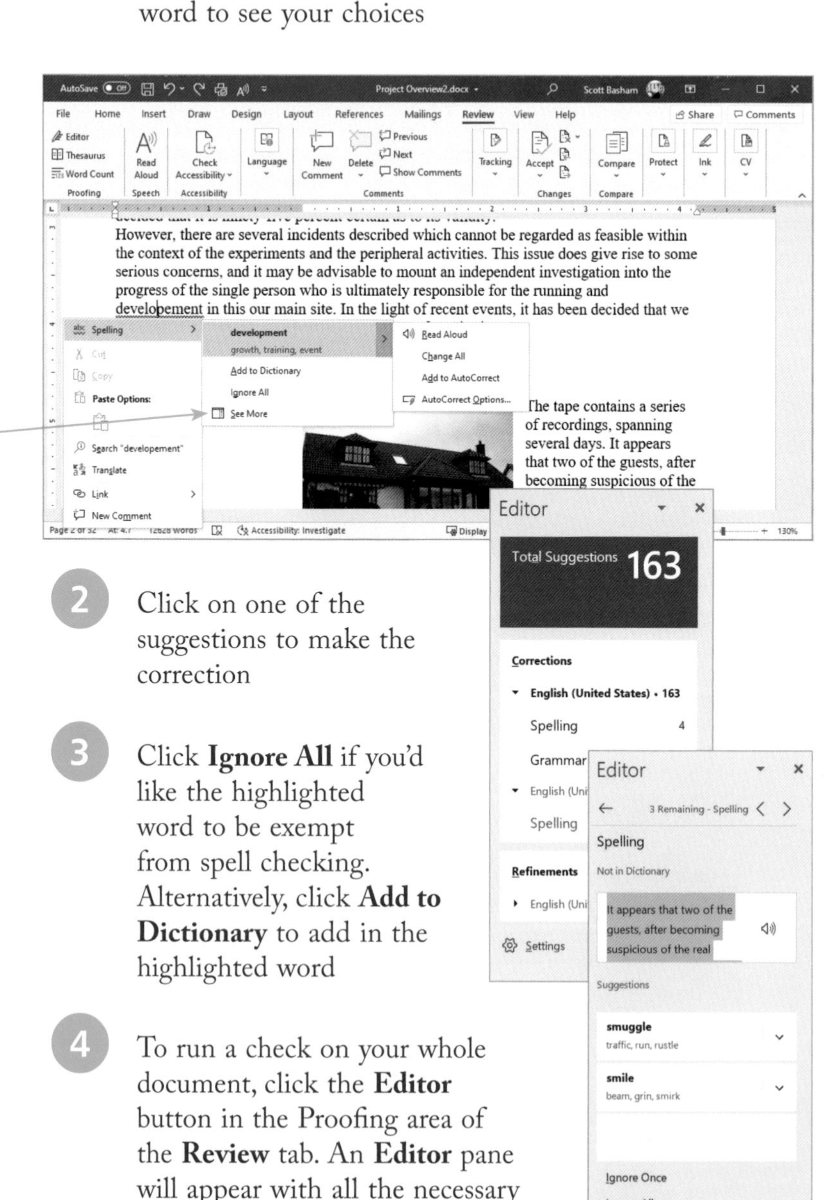

2. Click on one of the suggestions to make the correction

3. Click **Ignore All** if you'd like the highlighted word to be exempt from spell checking. Alternatively, click **Add to Dictionary** to add in the highlighted word

Rather than the whole document, you can also check just a section of text by selecting it in the normal way before clicking the **Editor** button in the Proofing area.

4. To run a check on your whole document, click the **Editor** button in the Proofing area of the **Review** tab. An **Editor** pane will appear with all the necessary controls and information

5. Once you've made a decision to change, ignore or add to the dictionary, Word will resume its search for mistakes. If it finds a problem with grammar then the Editor pane will switch from **Spelling** to show the **Grammar** controls

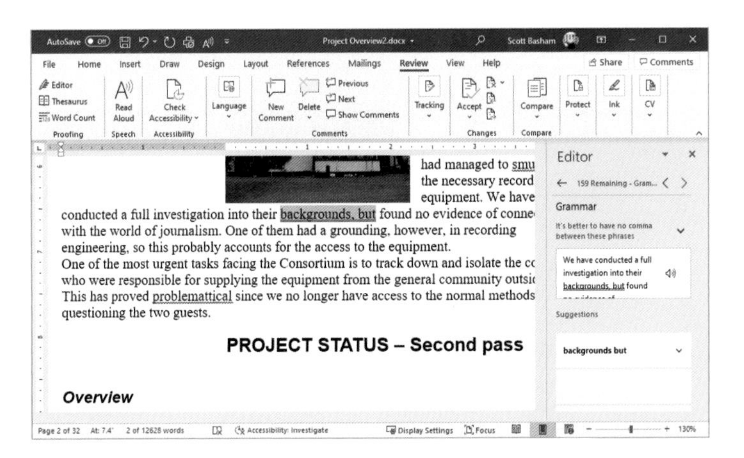

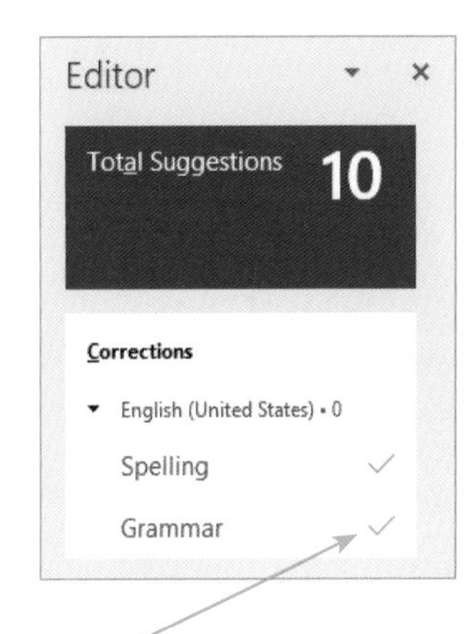

6. Review the suggestions and choose one if appropriate. You could also right-click on the word(s) in the document and choose **Ignore**, or simply edit the text manually

7. When Word has finished looking through the document, it will display a green checkmark ✓ next to Spelling or Grammar in the Editor pane

8. You can also right-click on any selected text and choose **Translate** to change to different languages

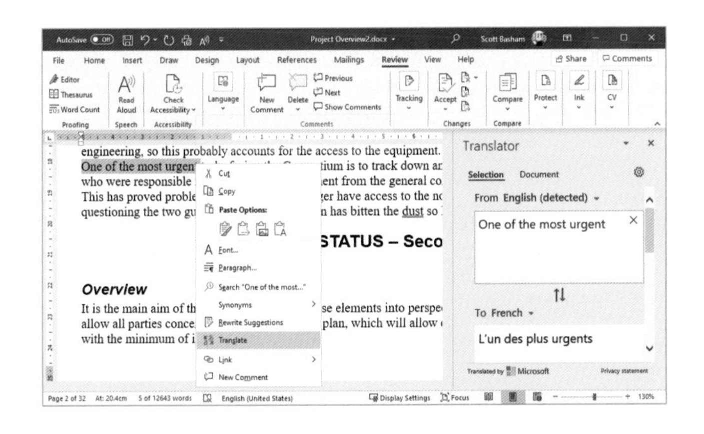

You can also access the **Translator** pane at any time by clicking the **Translate** tool in the Language area of the **Review** tab.

...cont'd

Customizing Grammar & Refinements

Don't forget

Whenever you invoke the **Editor** pane, Word will check your text according to the settings you made in the Proofing options screen.

1. Word gives you many options for checking your text. Choose **File** and **Options** then click on **Proofing**

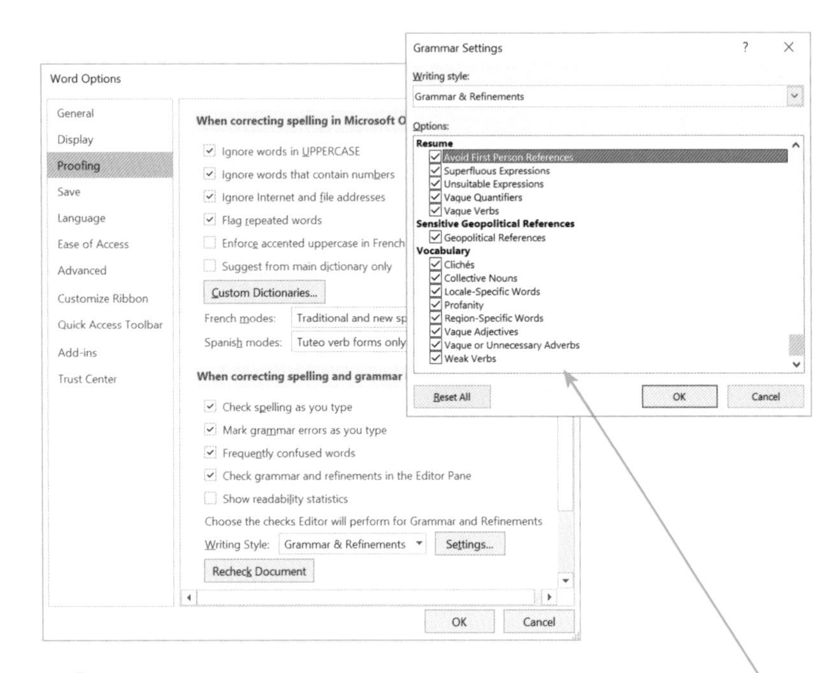

Hot tip

If you select a phrase you can right-click and choose **Rewrite Suggestions** to see if Word can come up with alternative ways of saying the same thing.

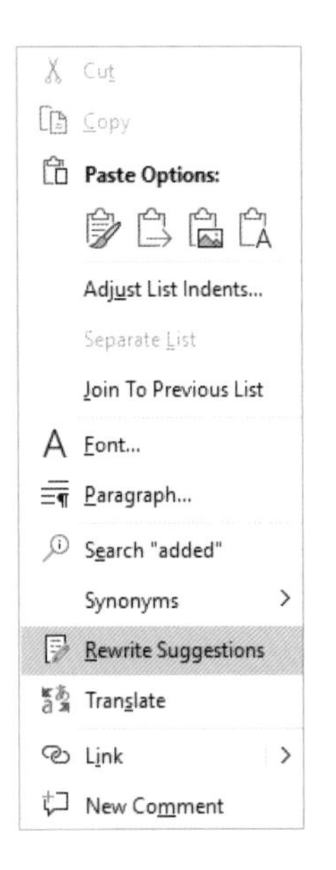

2. Scroll down to the **When correcting spelling and grammar in Word** section, then click on **Settings...** to see different categories of options. In this example we have activated all the options within the **Resume** category

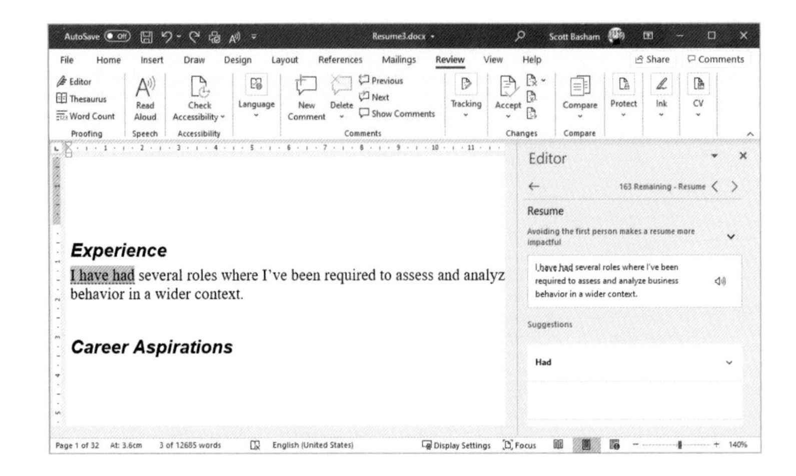

Accessibility

Word can check the accessibility of your document, highlighting things that may make it hard to read for different types of user.

1. Click on **Check Accessibility** in the **Review** tab

2. The **Accessibility** pane appears, displaying a list of potential issues with your document. In this example it is warning about text that is hard to see as its color does not contrast very well with the page color

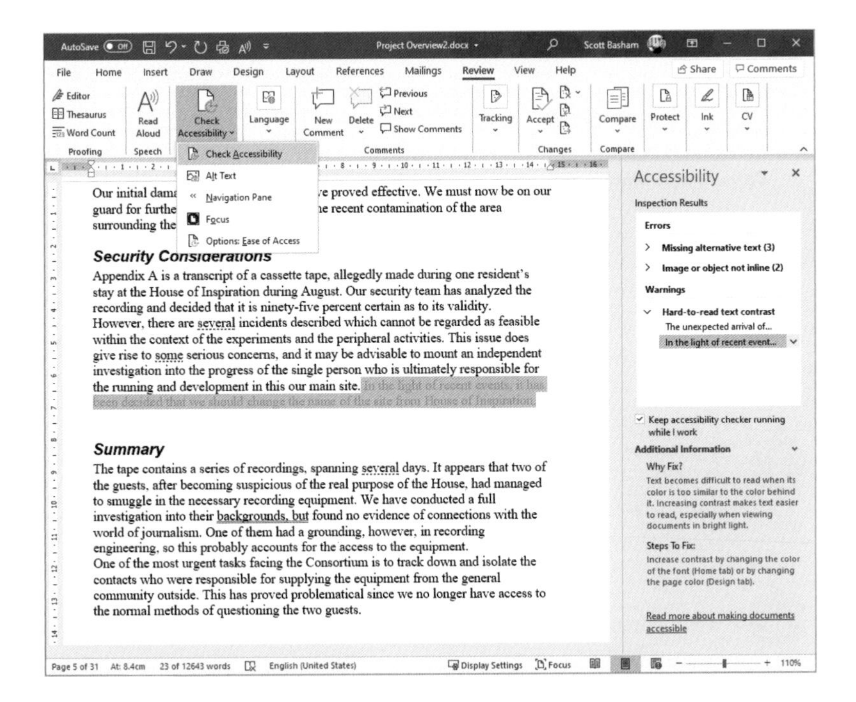

3. Here, Word suggests that some Alt Text should be added to a picture so that a blind person could benefit from a verbal description – perhaps using an audio reader utility

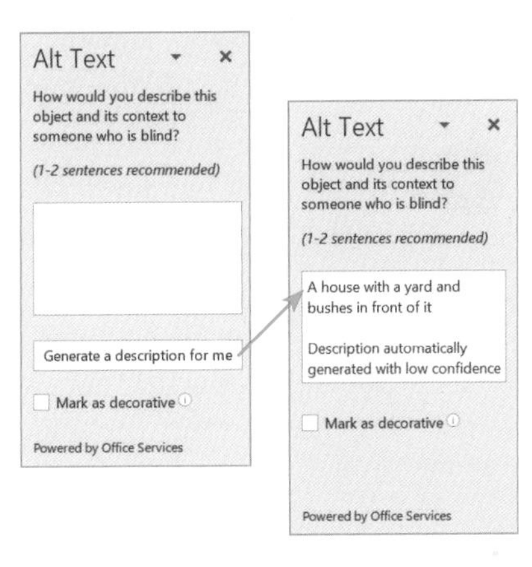

If you use the **File** tab and **Export** to create a PDF document, then Word will show an **Investigate Accessibility** button if it has any recommendations for making it easier to read for people with disabilities. This invokes the **Accessibility** pane.

Hot tip

Although Word can attempt to generate a text description for you, it's usually better to create your own Alt Text manually.

Thesaurus

1. A **Thesaurus** is a collection of synonyms (words with identical or similar meanings). Select a word then right-click and choose **Synonyms** from the pop-up menu

2. Choose one of the synonym options if you find something that you like

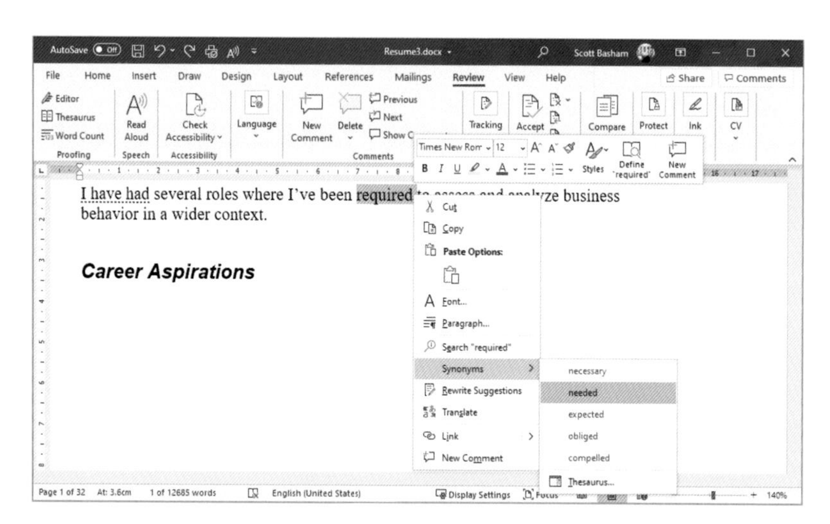

Another way to access the Thesaurus pane is to click on the **Thesaurus** tool in the Proofing area of the Ribbon.

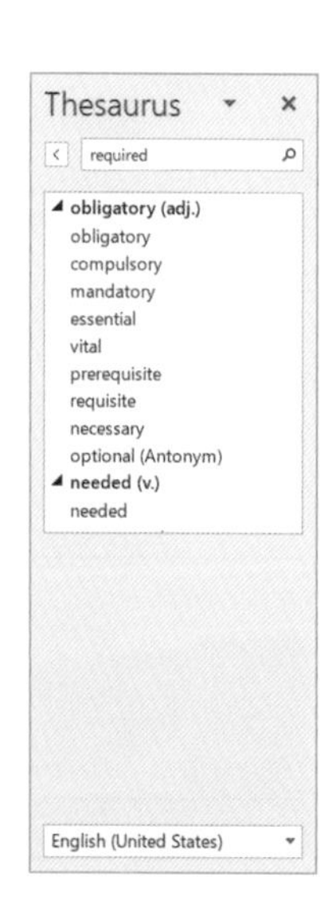

3. If you can't find a suitable word, then the **Thesaurus** pane can provide additional functionality. Choose **Thesaurus...** from the pop-up menu

4. The Thesaurus pane appears. Scroll through and select one of its options. The word will be moved to the main field at the top, and the list will now show you synonyms for that word

5. To go back one level, click on the **Left-arrow** icon

6. If you right-click in the list, from the pop-up menu that appears you can choose to insert the selected item, or copy it to the Clipboard

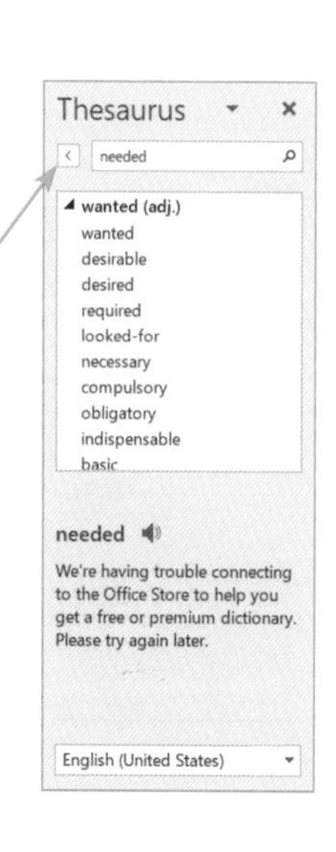

Search and Read Aloud

The Search pane

1. Select a word or phrase and then right-click to see a pop-up menu. This will include a Search option with your selected text next to it in double quotes

2. Click on this **Search** option. The Search pane appears, showing you results of web searches based on your text

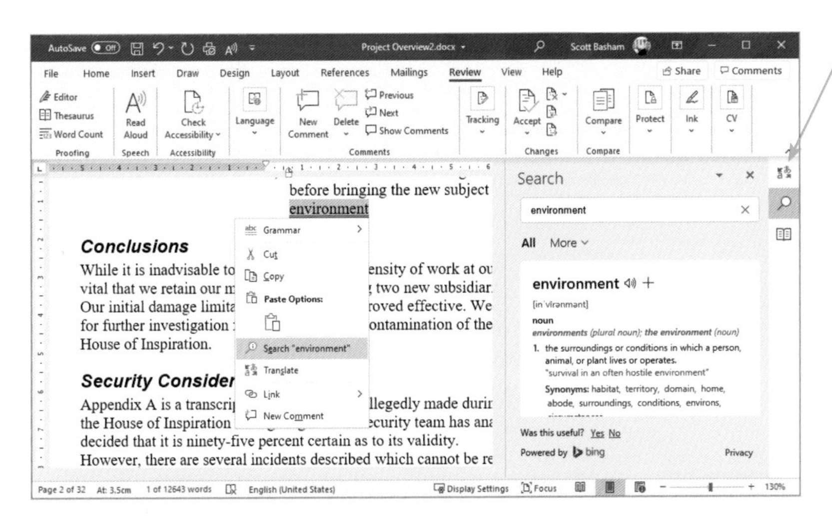

If there are multiple panes active you'll be able to switch easily between them by clicking on their icons. Here, the **Search** tab is visible, but the **Translate** and **Thesaurus** tabs are also present as icons.

Read Aloud

1. Either select some text or place an insertion point, where you want Word to start reading aloud

2. Click on **Read Aloud** in the Speech area of the **Review** tab to make sure the following controls are visible in the top right of the screen

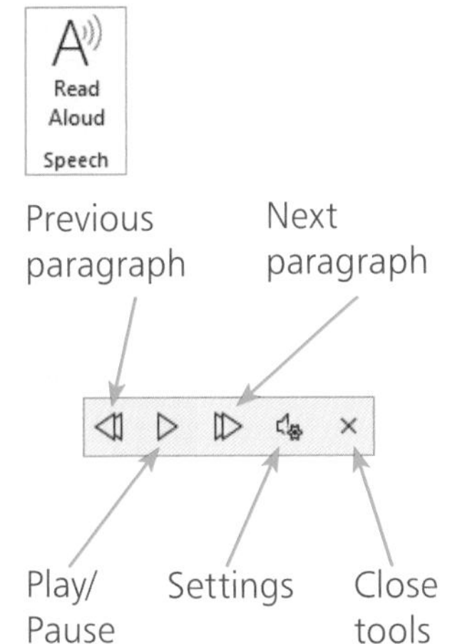

Conclusions

While it is inadvisable to continue the high intensity of work at our primary location, it is vital that we retain our momentum by bringing two new subsidiaries online.

If you click on **Immersive Reader** in the **View** tab you can invoke a view specially designed to help people with dyslexia and dysgraphia. It works by allowing you to focus on smaller sections of text at any one time, and can be useful for anyone who wants to make reading easier.

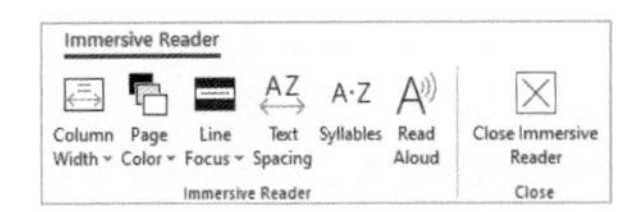

Comments

Adding a comment

1. Select the text to which you'd like to add a comment

2. Make sure the **Review** tab is active, then click the **New Comment** icon in the Comments area

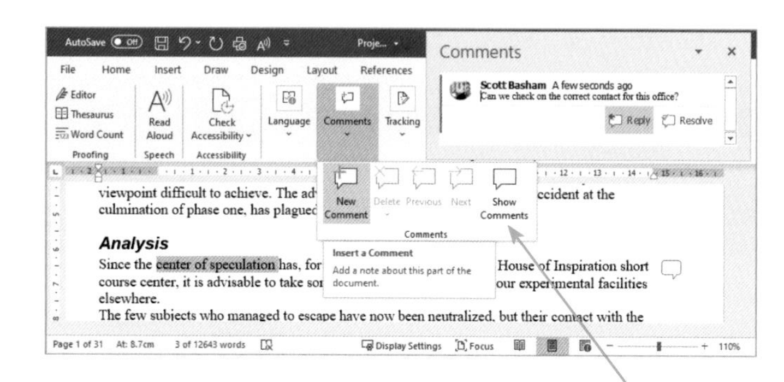

Comments are automatically logged with your username and the time they were made. This is useful if several people are reviewing a document.

3. Type in the area at the right (if **Show Comments** is active) or the **Comments** window that appears. Repeat this process to add more comments

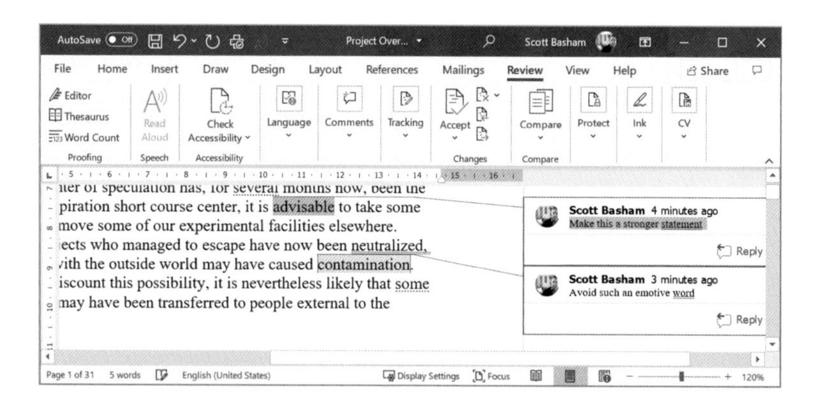

If you allow your mouse to rest over a commented piece of text, the comment will appear as a tooltip. This is useful if you cannot see the Markup area (if you are working in **Draft** mode, for example).

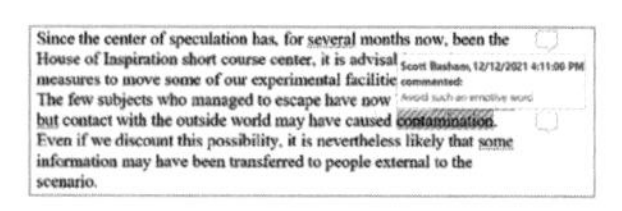

4. To delete a comment, right-click on it and then choose **Delete Comment** from the pop-up menu

5. You can move through the comments in your document using the **Previous** and **Next** buttons

6. You can also delete all comments from the **Delete** pop-up

Multiple users adding comments

We saw in Chapter 8 that many users can access the same document, sometimes even at the same time, if the file is in a shared area. The **Comments** feature takes account of this.

If you have a pen or touchscreen device you can add handwritten comments either directly into the document or in the Comments area.

1. In this example, Michael and Scott (each with their own assigned color) are using Word Online and are writing comments in the document we saw on the previous page

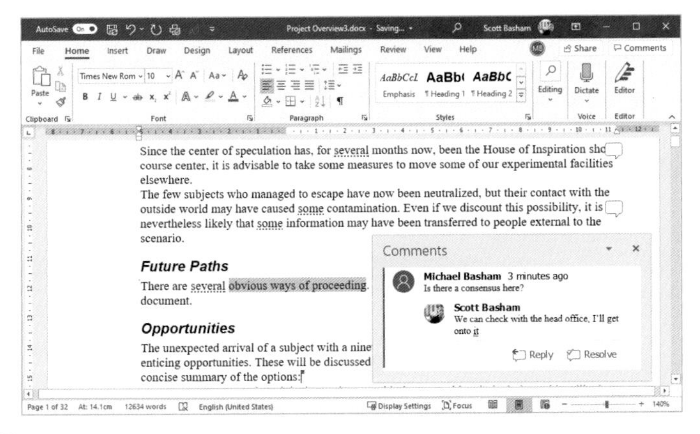

2. We can clearly see which comments are made by which person. Scott clicked on the **Reply** icon to respond to Michael's comment

3. This process can repeat, with the first user then commenting on the second user's comment

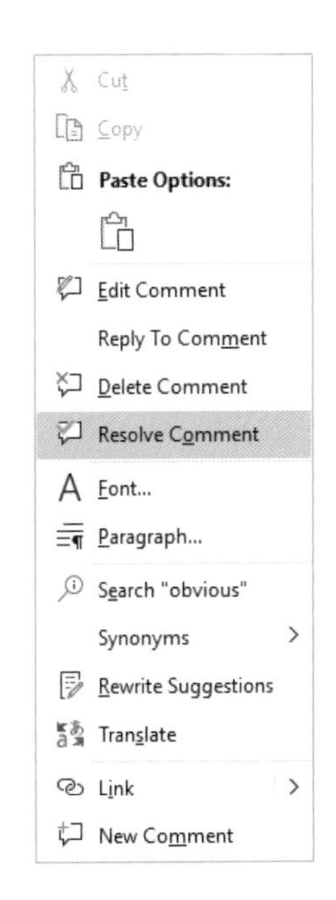

Marking a comment as done

Once an exchange of comments has ended with a satisfactory conclusion, you can mark this as **Resolved**. This will change the comments to a light-gray color so that they are less distracting, although you can still see them in case you need to change your mind later on.

1. Select a comment (right-click in the main page or click on an item in the Comments area) to see the icons for **Reply** and **Resolve**

2. Choose **Resolve** to complete the interaction

You can select a closed comment and choose **Reopen**. Right-click for further options, including **Delete Comment**.

Tracking

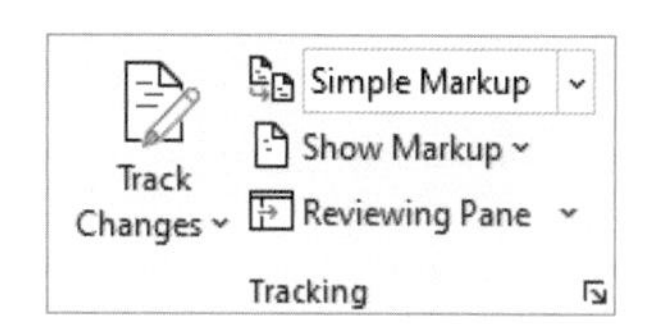

Sometimes it's useful to track changes you make to a document so that anyone can see exactly what's been done. It may even be necessary for someone to approve or reject those changes before they become permanently incorporated into the document.

1. To activate change tracking, click the **Track Changes** icon in the Tracking area of the **Review** tab

2. Now, your edits will be shown visually. Experiment by deleting text, adding in some new text, editing existing text or changing the format

When **All Markup** is selected from the **Tracking** tools, if you rest your mouse over any changed text then the name, type of change, and date/time appears as a tooltip.

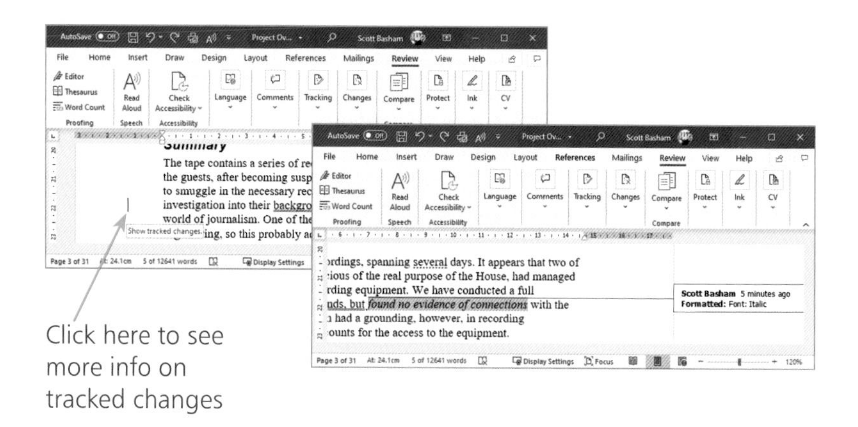

Click here to see more info on tracked changes

3. Use copy and paste to move a phrase, sentence or paragraph to a different part of your document

Deleted text can either be shown in a different color with a horizontal line running through it or noted in the right margin. A vertical line in the margin indicates that changes were made in this area.

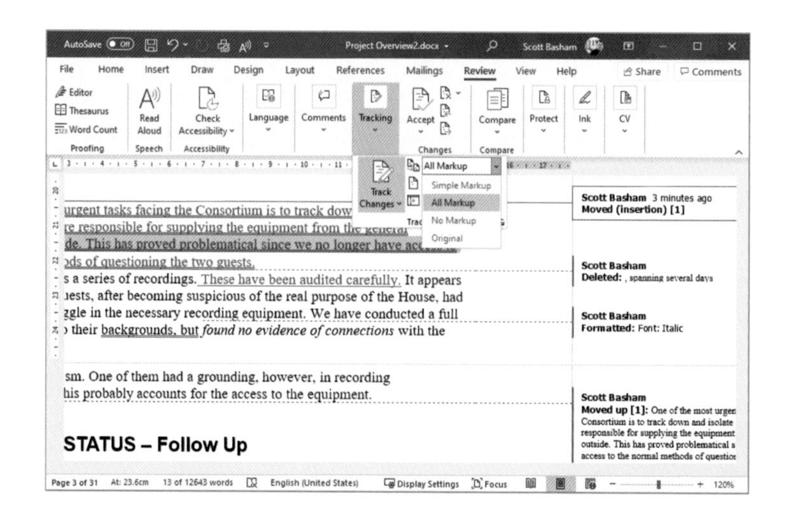

4. Click on the **Reviewing Pane** icon in the Tracking area, and choose one of the two options (**Vertical** or **Horizontal**) to make it visible

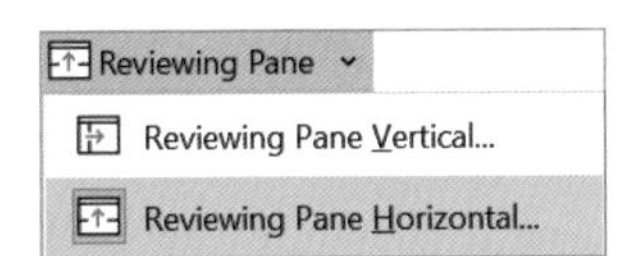

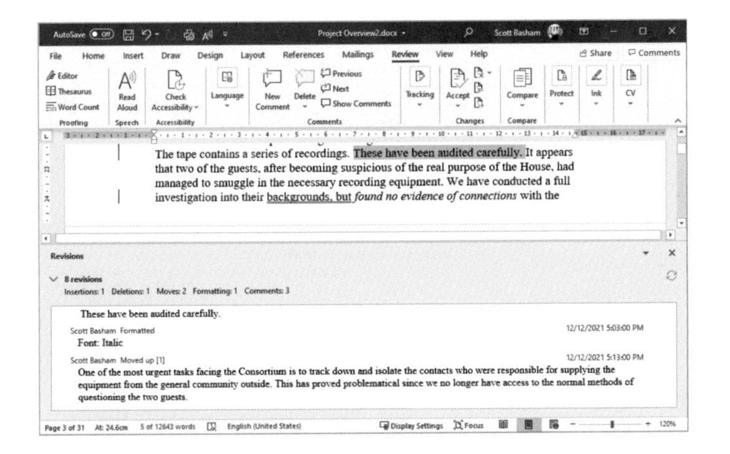

5. Make some more changes to your document and watch what happens in the Reviewing pane

6. The Reviewing pane contains a comprehensive summary of all the comments and revisions made. Clicking on an entry in the main list will take you to its location in the main document

7. Scroll through your document until you find a section with both comments and revisions (or make some new comments and revisions yourself)

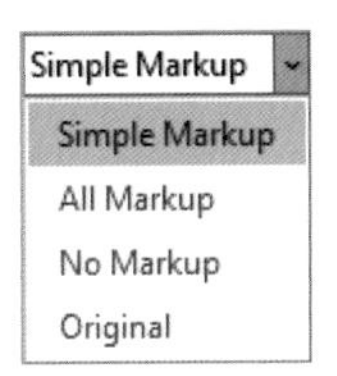

8. Now, switch between **Simple Markup** and **All Markup** so that you can appreciate the difference. Simple Markup is much easier to read – but you can still see changes by looking in the Comments area on the right-hand side

The Reviewing pane will list out all the tracked changes. Just below its title there is a summary that shows you the total number of revisions. Clicking the ⌄ icon beside it will toggle a breakdown summary On and Off of the various types of revisions.

...cont'd

9. The Reviewing pane still shows you what's changed. Also, a red vertical line to the left of the text indicates it has been altered. Click on this to see the tracked changes

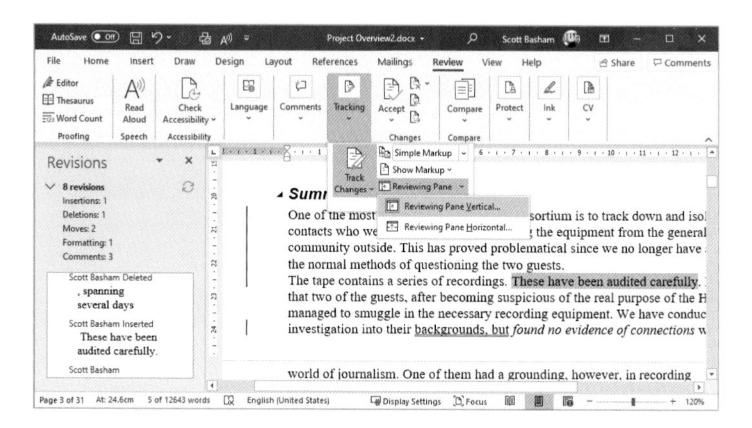

10. You can also choose **No Markup** to see how the document would look when finalized, or **Original** to see how it was before any of the tracked changes

11. When collaborating with other authors via a shared document, Tracking is useful regardless of whether the users are editing simultaneously or at different times. The example below is a continuation of what we saw in Chapter 8. Here, you can see the color-coded activity of two users working together

When the tracked changes are visible the vertical red line in the main text will change to a gray line. Click on this to hide the tracked changes again.

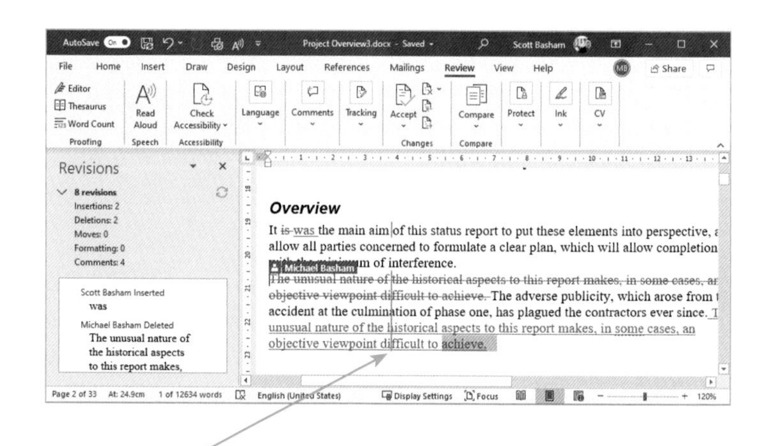

Click on the gray line to hide the tracked changes

Lock Tracking

If you'd like to insist that Tracking is switched on when you collaborate with others, then you can lock it On using a password.

1. Open the pop-up menu attached to the **Track Changes** icon in the Tracking area of the **Review** tab

2. Choose **Lock Tracking**

3. Enter a password, then once more to confirm, and click **OK**

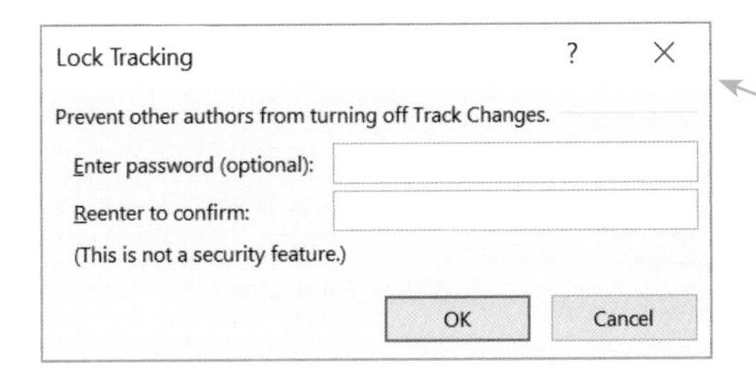

Beware

Lock Tracking is not a security feature as it does not password-protect the whole document. If you'd like to do this, have a look at the **Protect Document** feature detailed on pages 202-206.

Changes

Now, if there are changes in your document, you can take on the role of someone who reviews those changes. The tools in the Changes area let you work through your document looking at each change in turn – using the **Previous** and **Next** icons.

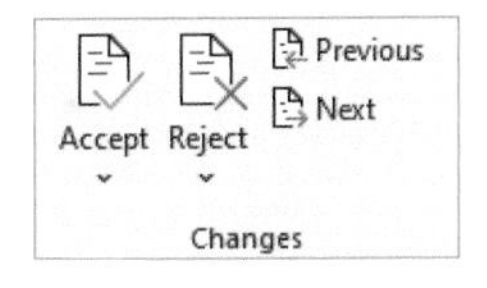

1. If you click the **Accept** button then the change is permanently applied to the document

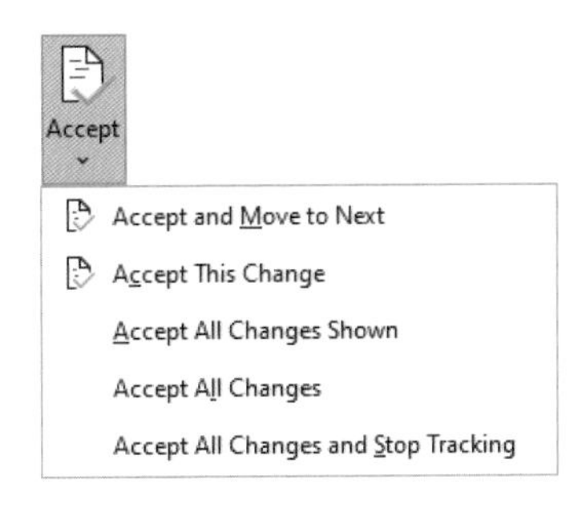

2. If you click **Reject**, the change is removed and the text reverts to its original state

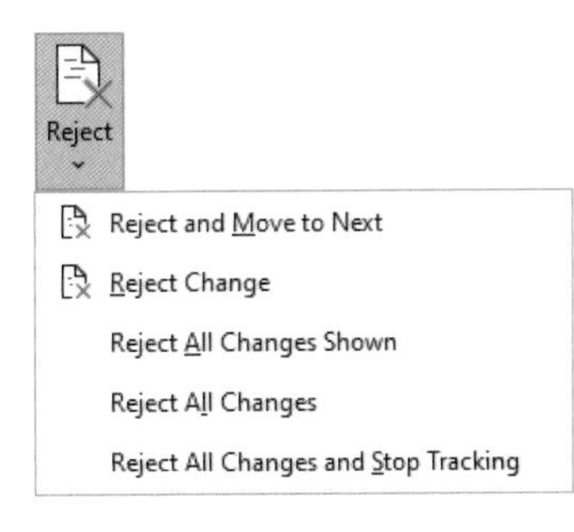

Protecting a document

Word allows you to protect your document in a number of ways. You can control which aspects may be edited: for example, you may allow a user to add comments but not to edit the text directly. If you are sharing your document you can also restrict permissions to certain users. Furthermore, you can set protection on the document as a whole.

Creating a document password

1. Make sure you have your document open. Go to the **File** tab and click on **Info**

2. Click **Protect Document** then **Encrypt with Password**

3. Enter a password, click **OK**, then enter it a second time to confirm

4. Save the document in the normal way. Make sure you remember the password you set

After you've set the password, the **Info** section of the **File** tab will remind you that a password is required to open the document.

Mark as Final

When you've finished editing your document you can **Mark as Final**, indicating to anyone who opens it that this is the definitive version and it should not be changed.

1. Go to the **File** tab and make sure the **Info** section is displayed

2. Click **Protect Document** and then **Mark as Final**

3. Save the document. The following message appears:

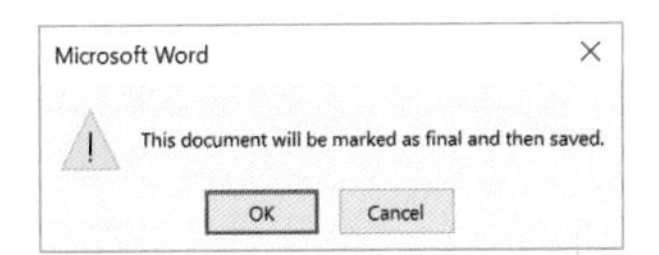

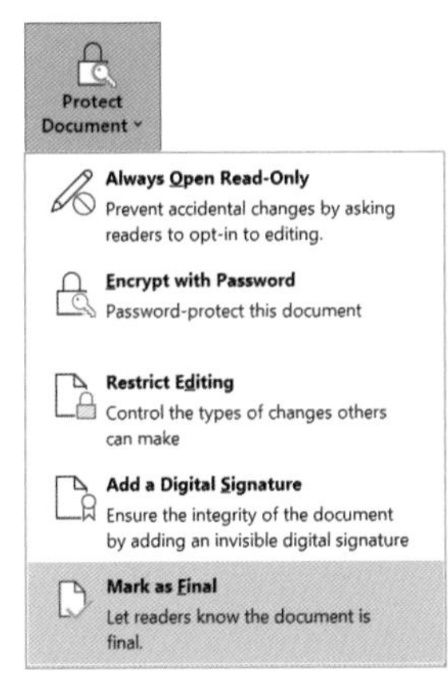

Although **Mark as Final** is a good way to let people know you are not expecting them to edit your document, it is not enforced. Anyone clicking the **Edit Anyway** button will be able to make changes. Using the **Restrict Editing** tool described on pages 205-206 is a better way to make sure it is read-only.

Digital signature

If you add a digital signature to a document, it can be used as a recognized form of authentication or approval that can be checked by others.

1. Go to the **File** tab and choose **Info**. Click on **Protect Document** and choose **Add a Digital Signature**. Choose a commitment type then click **Details...**

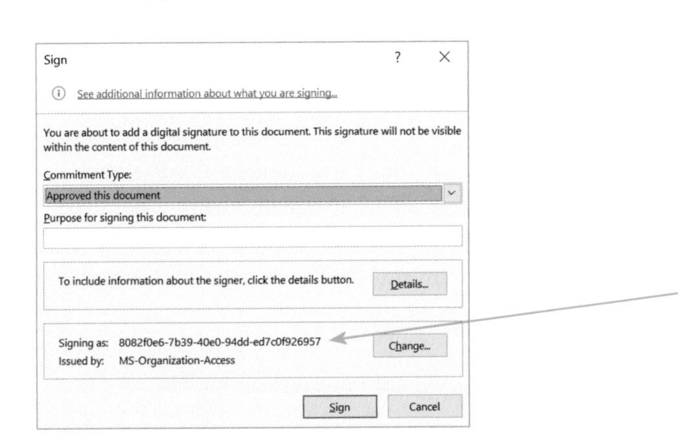

Check **support.microsoft.com** for guidance on how to obtain a digital certificate and create a digital signature. Word can automatically generate a certificate for you, but other people cannot verify the authenticity of this type of digital signature.

...cont'd

Don't forget

Once a document is signed it is not expected to change, as this will invalidate the digital signature. Word will present the dialog below, asking you to confirm that you want to go ahead – if you click **Yes** then any signatures are removed.

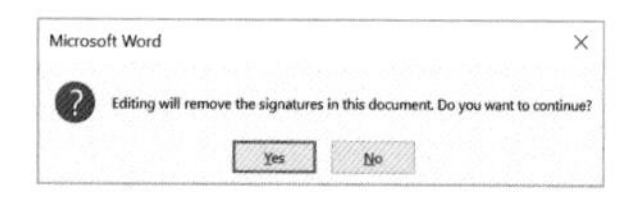

2. Fill in the **Purpose for signing this document:** field. Optionally, you can click **Details...** to enter more information about yourself

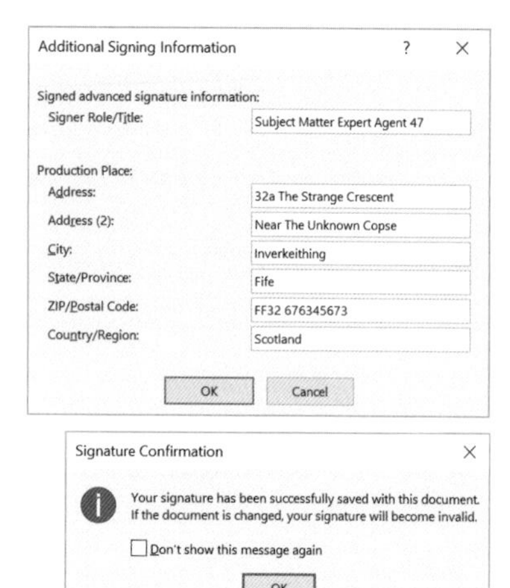

3. Click **OK**. The following message appears:

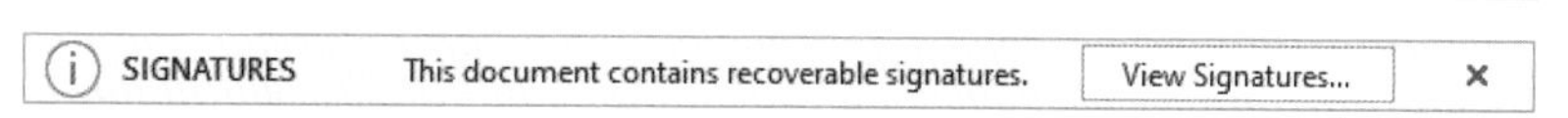

4. On opening the document a user will see a message indicating there is a digital signature. Any attempt to edit the document will automatically remove the signatures – if the document needs to change then it should be reviewed again and re-signed if appropriate

Opening a protected document

1. Go to the **File** tab and open the document you saved previously

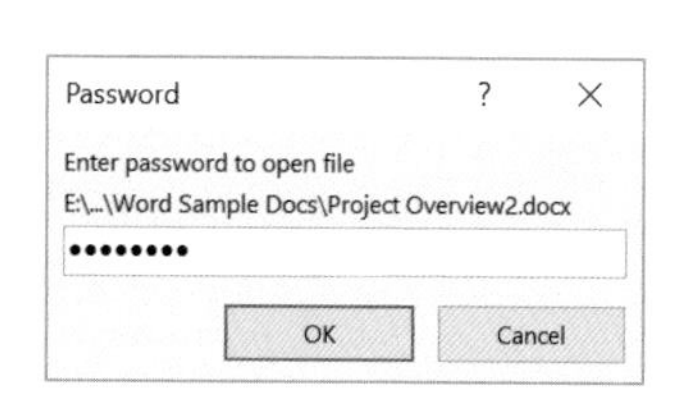

2. A dialog appears prompting you for the password. Enter the password then click **OK**

To remove the password from a document repeat the process described on page 202, but use a blank password.

3. If the document was marked as **Final** then Word will automatically select **Read Mode** when it is opened. If there were any inked annotations or comments then at the top of the window you'll see two messages, as shown in the following example:

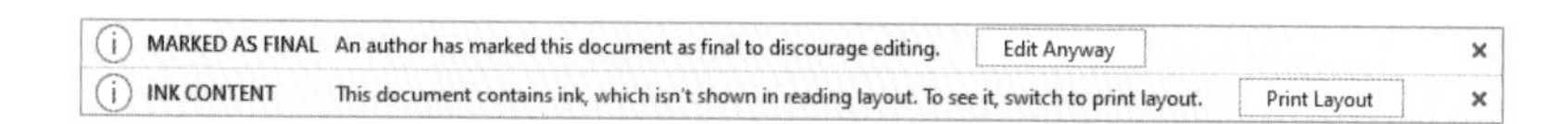

4. Go to **Layout Mode** and try to make some changes. You'll find you cannot change things – there will be a "locked" message in the Status bar at the bottom

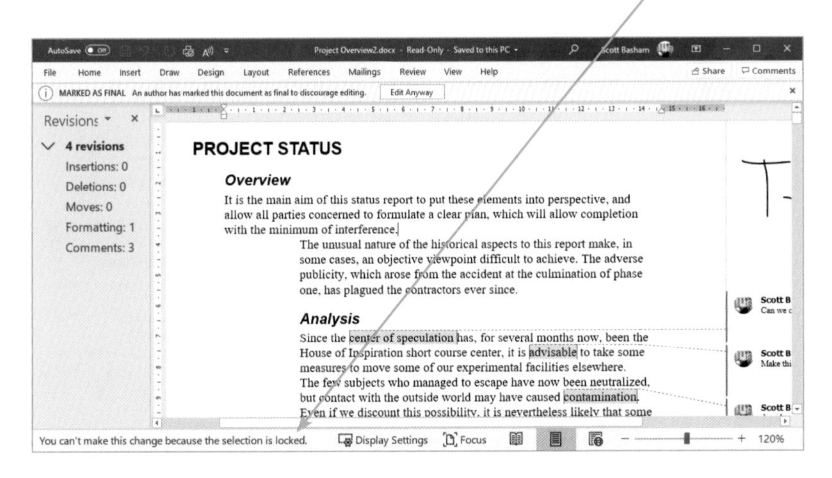

Restrict Editing

This offers better control over access to your document.

1. Click the **Restrict Editing** tool in the Protect area on the right-hand side of the **Review** tab. The **Restrict Editing** pane appears

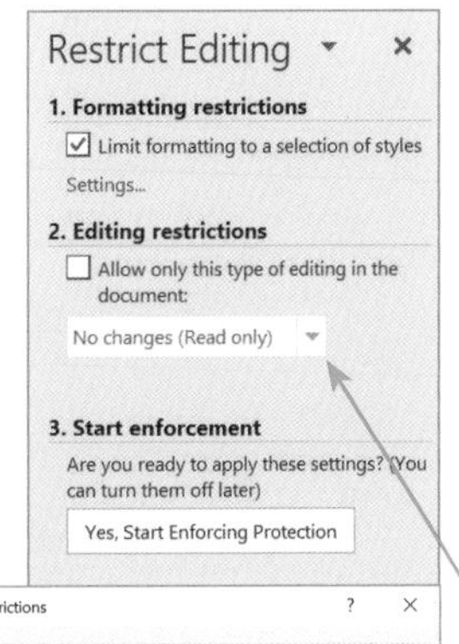

2. Switch on **Limit formatting to a selection of styles** then click on **Settings...**

3. From this dialog you can choose which styles are allowed – by default they're all enabled. Either review each one or, if you want to use just a few, click **None** then reselect the styles you wish to allow. Click **OK** when you've finished

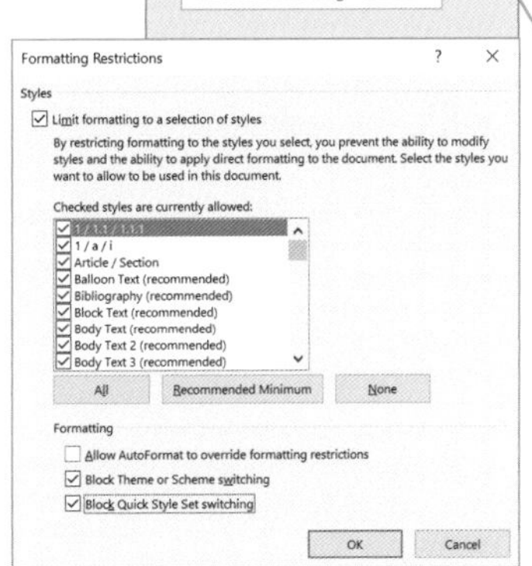

If you switch on editing restrictions and make sure the setting is **No changes (Read only)** then this prevents users from making any changes at all. This is more secure than the **Mark as Final** feature.

...cont'd

4 You may see the message below, asking you what you'd like to do with the styles you've forbidden

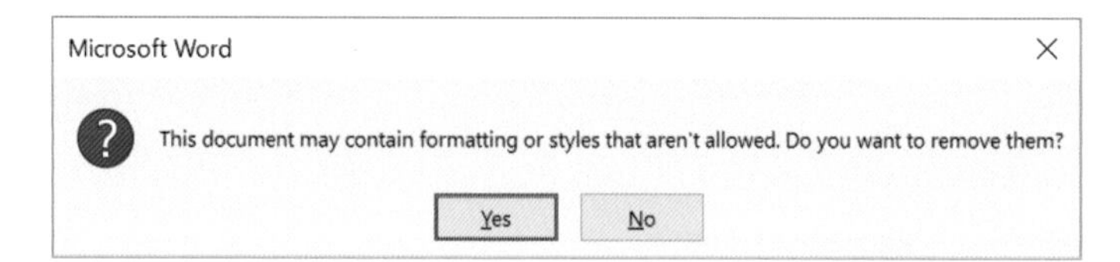

5 Alternatively, you can limit users' activities in several other ways by choosing an option for editing restrictions. **Tracked changes** means that tracking is compulsory and cannot be switched off. Choose **No changes (Read only)** to fully protect your document

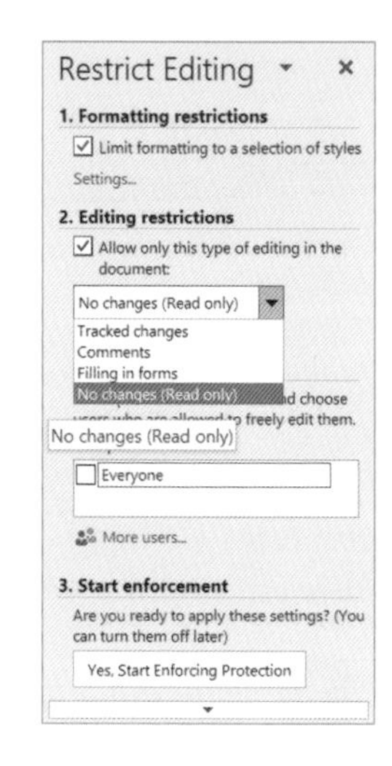

6 Make any last-minute changes to your document then, when you're ready, click **Yes, Start Enforcing Protection**

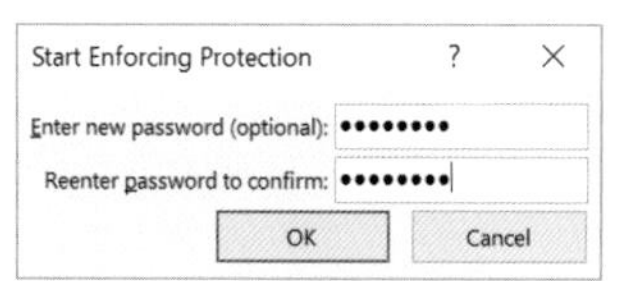

7 Enter a password, and then once again to confirm

8 Save and close the document

9 Now, reopen the document to check the level of protection

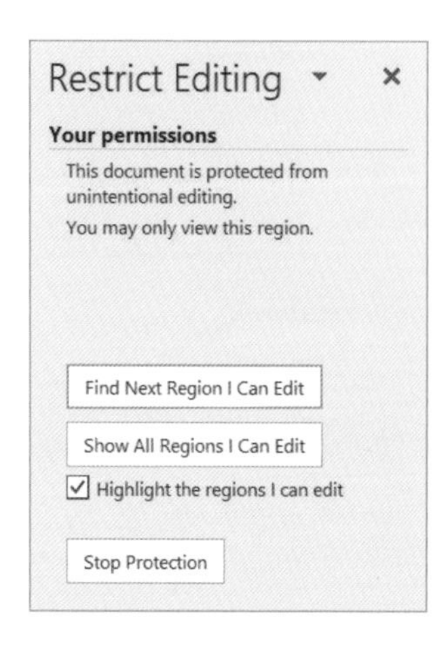

The **Restrict Editing** pane will remind you that the document is protected and you cannot make edits. If you change your mind you can click **Stop Protection** and enter the password to proceed.

The **Restrict Editing** pane has controls for finding and/or highlighting the regions you are currently allowed to edit.

Add-ins

Add-ins enhance Word by giving you access to external services such as online dictionaries or research sources. They can also provide new interactive objects for enhancing document content.

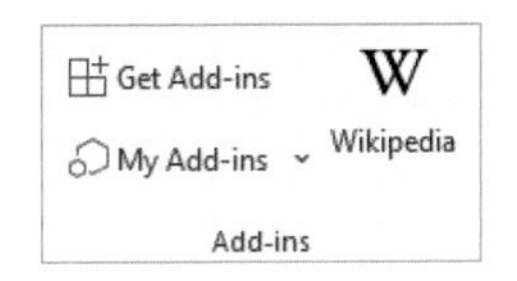

Reviewing available Add-ins

1. Go to the **Insert** tab and click on **My Add-ins**. You'll see the following dialog, listing the Add-ins currently installed in Word

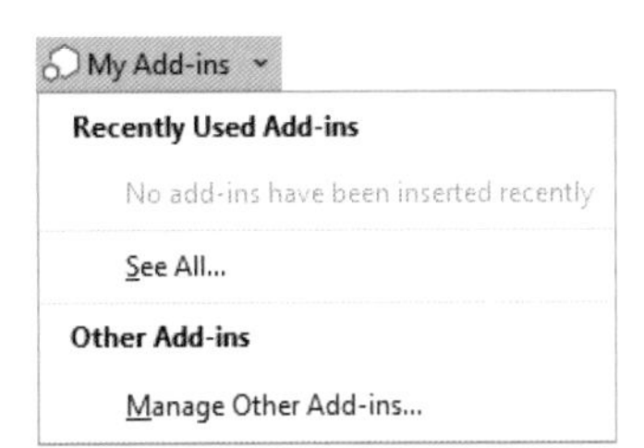

2. Click on **See All...** to see your currently-installed Add-ins in the **Office Add-ins** dialog

3. Click on the **Store** heading at the top of the dialog box

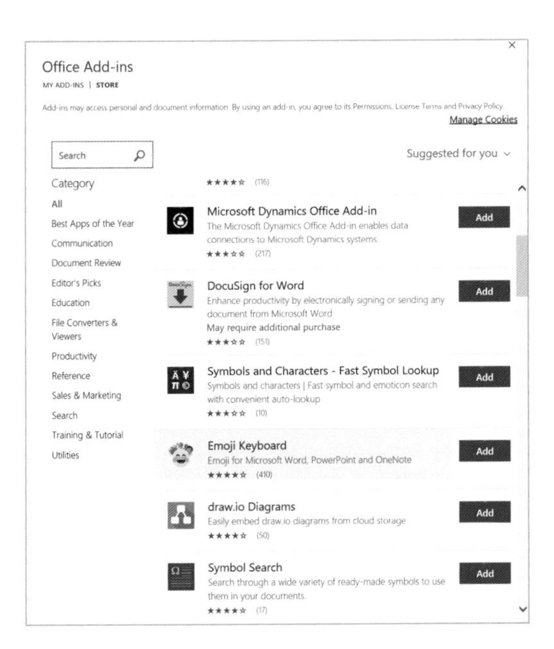

4. You'll see the range of Add-ins available, some of which are free and others requiring a purchase. You can search by name or browse by category. In this example we will locate the **Emoji Keyboard** and click the **Add** button

You can also click the **Get Add-ins** icon in the Add-ins area to go straight to the Store section of the Office Add-in dialog. Examples of Add-ins include utilities for adding QR codes to your document, sending faxes, and accessing Emojis.

Open the pop-up menu for the **My Add-ins** control and choose **Manage Other Add-ins...** to see technical information in Word's Options dialog.

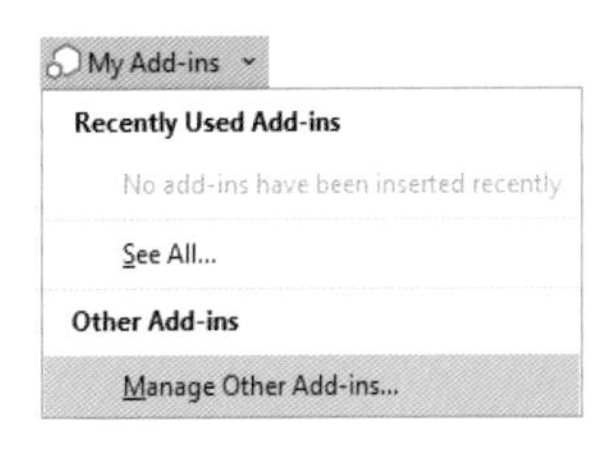

...cont'd

5. If all goes well, you'll then see a confirmation message **Add-ins loaded successfully** in the Status bar at the bottom of the main screen

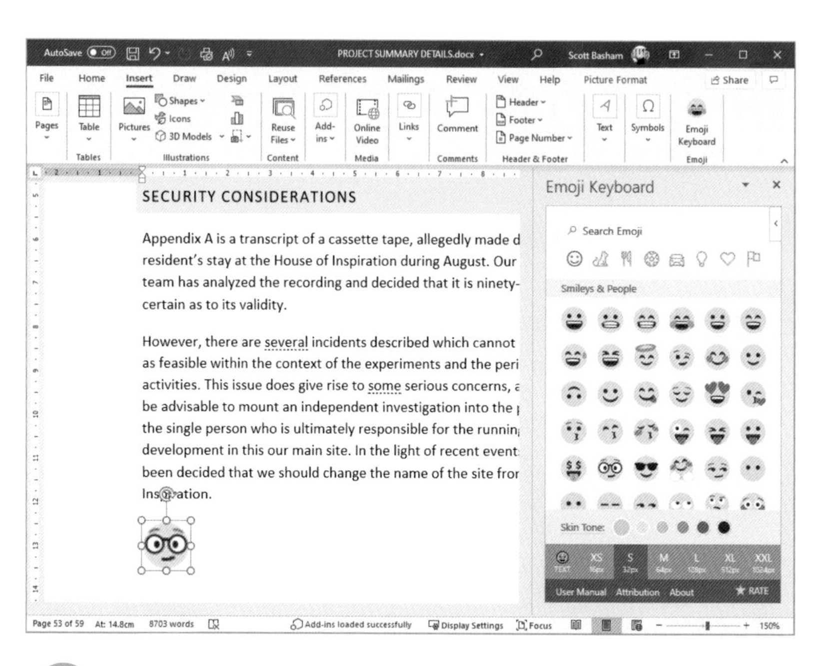

In this case a new tool is added to the Ribbon. This will show or hide a new Emoji Keyboard pane.

6. With this example Add-in, a new **Emoji Keyboard** pane appears. We can use this to search and browse for a wide variety of Emojis. Once we choose a size, we simply click on the Emoji to add it as a graphic at the insertion point

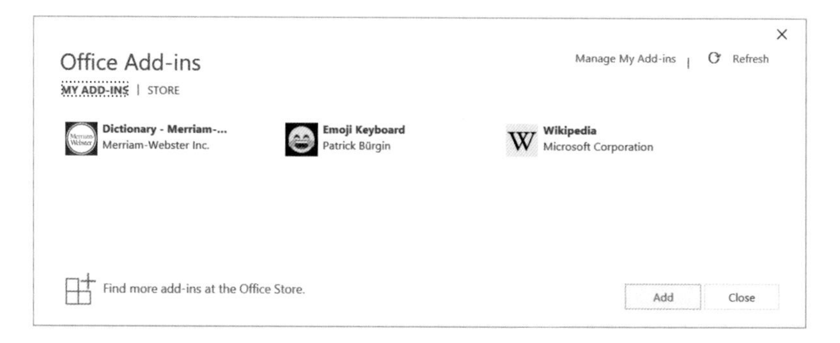

From this screen you can uninstall any Add-ins by clicking on their icon and selecting **Remove** from the pop-up menu. You can also view more details about an item or choose to **Rate and Review** once you've been using it for a while.

7. Now, go back to the **Insert** tab, click the **Add-ins** tool and select **My Add-ins** from the pop-up menu. You'll see your new Add-in listed along with any others

Other viewing features

Split window

Sometimes you can find yourself constantly scrolling back and forth between two locations in your document. Split is a feature that lets you divide your window into two regions, each with its own scroll bar.

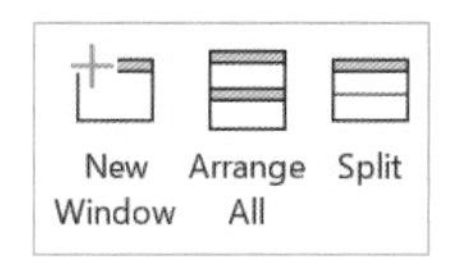

1. Go to the **View** tab and click **Split** within the Window area

2. You now have two windows that can be scrolled individually

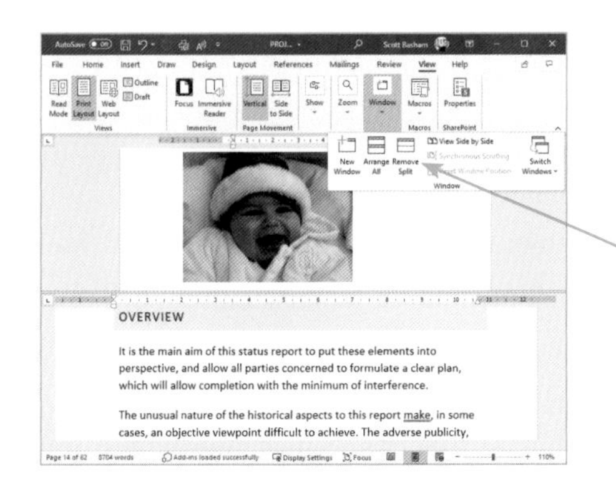

Click on **Remove Split** if you want to return to a normal single window.

Page Movement

Word normally uses vertical scrolling to move you through your document, but you can decide to scroll horizontally instead.

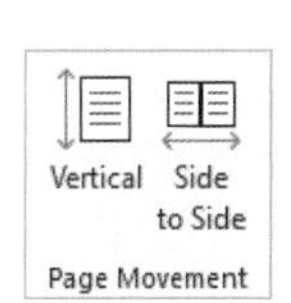

1. Go to the **View** tab and click **Side to Side** within the Page Movement area. You can now scroll from left to right, more like with a traditional book

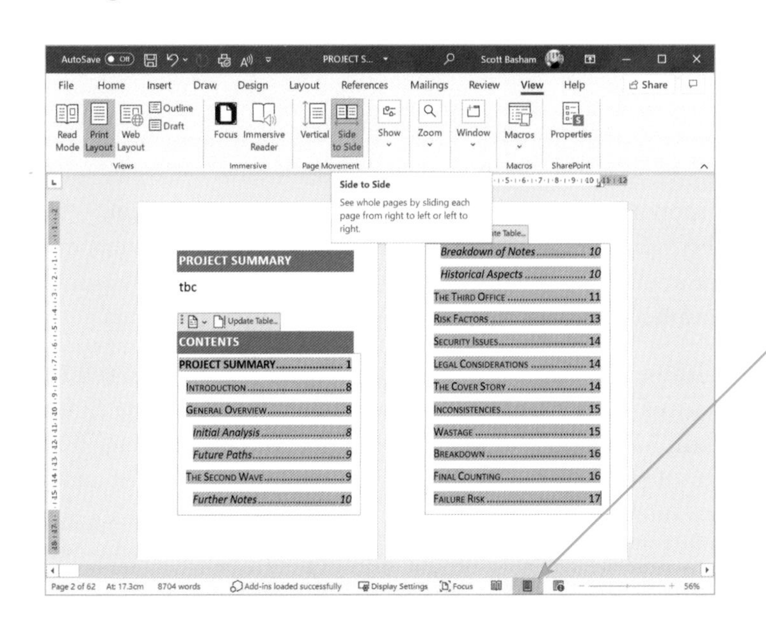

In this example we are working in the **Print Layout** view mode (check the icon at the bottom to verify which mode you are in). In **Read Mode**, scrolling between pages is always done from left to right, so the **Page Movement** setting would be irrelevant in that case.

Office 365 vs standalone

If you go to the **File** tab and choose **Account** you'll see which version of Word you're using. You can also control how often updates are downloaded and installed.

Office 365 and the standalone version of Word are closely related. Most of the features and techniques you'll see explained in this book will work equally well with both versions. So, what exactly is the difference between them?

Office 365 has for some time been Microsoft's Cloud-based subscription service, giving businesses and individuals access to the entire range of Office products. Cloud-based services provide easy synchronization of files and remote access. Another key difference is how the user pays for the software. For a subscription service such as Office 365, payments are made monthly or yearly. The user is effectively renting rather than buying software outright. This means a smaller initial outlay, but the cost is ongoing.

Standalone Word as a product comes with a perpetual license, so this is a one-off purchase. Microsoft recognizes that some people prefer this concept of ownership, and also that some are not yet interested in the features and benefits of Cloud-based services.

Examples of features that are present in Office 365 but not standalone Word are the large library of stock images; Dictation; the Editor pane described on page 190; and the Application Guard (this makes it safer to use files that may have been infected with viruses, worms, or other kinds of malware).

There is another important difference when it comes to support and updates for Word. If you're using Office 365 then its software is in support as long as you keep paying the subscription. Furthermore, when Microsoft is ready to add new features to the Office applications then these updates are automatically installed and available to the user.

Standalone Word, on the other hand, has its feature set (which is a subset of what is available in Office 365) frozen at the time it's released. Microsoft will offer support for security and bug fixes over a set period of years. However, new features are not added continuously as with Office 365. To get extra functionality you'll need to either purchase a newer version of Word (if and when it's released) or switch to an Office 365 subscription.

Symbols

A

B

C

D

E

F

G

M

N

O

P

Q

R

S